CORPSE

SUSAN PARRY

Viridian Publishing

Published in the United Kingdom in 2005 by
Viridian Publishing

Viridian Publishing
PO Box 746
Woking
Surrey
GU24 0AZ

www.viridian-publishing.co.uk
Email: viridian.tc@virgin.net

ISBN 0-9544891-4-4

*For my sister Pat
and my parents Ann and Ron*

Chapter 1

An old man in dark brown corduroys, with a tanned face and wispy white hair, was coming up the station steps.

'Mr Bartholomew?' asked Millie.

'Oh, ay, you must be Miss Madeline.'

'Yes, but everyone calls me Millie. I hope I haven't put you to any trouble?' But he was already behind the van untying the string and making room for her case between the pairs of shears, sacks of dog food and the other paraphernalia in the back.

'Get in, young lady,' he said and Millie obediently climbed into the passenger seat, removing some old gloves and balancing them neatly on the top of a pair of Wellington boots at her feet.

When Bartholomew started the van, they shot forward leaving a cloud of blue smoke in their wake. Millie could hardly make herself heard above the noise of the engine.

'It's a nice day,' she shouted.

'Ay,' Bartholomew replied. A silence followed and then he said, 'Sorry about yer Mum'.

Millie hated talking about her mother's death and pretended she hadn't heard.

'How's Gran?' she asked.

'She's 'ad a nasty accident, terrible it was.' Bartholomew was fighting with the gear lever as they struggled uphill.

'Oh dear, is she alright?' Millie asked, wondering if she would have to go back home.

'Oh ay, she's a good 'un, your grandmother,' He replied, revving the engine.

Millie was surprised by this last remark, it seemed high praise for a man of few words.

'And 'ows yer Dad?' he asked.

'He's on holiday with his girlfriend.'

Millie settled back, rather uncomfortably, thinking about Dad and Fiona sunning themselves on a sandy beach, while she had to come up here. She wondered about Gran's accident but the noise of the engine prevented any further conversation. There was nothing to see but stone walls, fields and trees. There were sheep in some fields, and a few had wandered onto the road but Bartholomew ignored them completely, except to swerve when absolutely necessary.

More fields and walls. The end of civilisation for three whole weeks, thought Millie. They were soon stuck behind a coach and Millie felt certain that Bartholomew was usually more vocal about the obstruction than his restrained 'Damn' every time it slowed down. When a signpost announced that they had arrived in Reeth he slowed down to allow the coach to turn off onto the green. There were several pubs and teashops, and a large bus shelter where people sat watching the activities of the day trippers. Bartholomew put his foot down as they drew out of the village in a burst of smoke. They were following the road signposted to 'Gunnerside' and Millie wondered aloud how far they were from Mossy Bank.

'Bout quarter of an hour,' shouted Bartholomew.

They passed Low Row and in a few minutes reached Gunnerside, a small village with a pub but no sign of any shops. Millie was checking her mobile for text messages and realised that she had no signal.

This, she thought, was going to be a really bad holiday.

'Next one,' said Bartholomew as he slowed down and turned off up a steep hill.

Millie's stomach began to feel funny as the van slowed at the sign announcing Mossy Bank and then stopped outside a row of small stone cottages. Climbing out of the van awkwardly, she stood searching for Laurel Cottage. The house had a 'Bed and Breakfast' sign outside. That can't be right, thought Millie, but followed Bartholomew up the path, clutching her bag and sweater.   'Right then, I'm off,' he said, putting her case down on the step, and then he hobbled swiftly down the path before she could thank him.

Turning back to the open front door, Millie was uncertain whether she should go straight in. Knowing that she shouldn't need to knock, she pushed it open and stepped inside.

'Hello,' she shouted tentatively and a figure she recognised appeared from the door at the other end of the room.

'I'm afraid we don't have any vacancies at the moment.'

'Gran, it's me.'

'Oh, Madeline, I'm sorry, I thought you were a guest.'

Millie knew that her grandmother was flustered and simply said, 'I'll get my case from the step.'

Millie was impressed by the cottage - the furniture, pictures and flowers. It was quite different from Gran's home in Purley, as if she had undergone a personality change when she moved.   Her grandmother asked about her journey and fussed over her as she made tea and found home-made cake. Millie sat on a stool by the door and watched as she moved round the tiny kitchen. She remembered Gran being fatter and more bossy when she last saw her, three years ago.

'It suits you living here,' Millie said.

'I love it, Madeline,' Gran confided. 'You know the cottage belonged to a friend who moved up here from Purley. She often asked me to come and stay after your Grandad died but I never did. I came to her funeral and her sister told me it was for sale. I fell in love with it there and then and I decided to take it. That's why it all happened so quickly. I moved up as soon as I knew you and your Dad could manage on your own.'

'Was the furniture her's as well?' asked Millie quickly.

'No, I decided to start again. I sold everything and bought furniture at auctions and in second hand shops. I made the curtains myself and chose the crockery from here and there.'

'It looks very different to your old place, Gran.'

'Thank you,' she said, and Millie realised that it was probably Grandad who chose things, even though Gran seemed to be having the main say. Certainly the garden had been his domain and the cottage garden she had seen when she arrived was very different to the formal rose garden in Purley that Grandad had planted.

'Can we look outside?' Millie asked. Her grandmother took her proudly round the little plot at the front; she pointed out the lavender and the roses climbing on trellis by the front door.

'These were your Grandad's favourite, they're beautiful, smell them.'

Millie obediently put her nose into the blooms. She could almost believe that she did remember them from the garden in Purley.

'Is there a back garden?'

'Oh no, not really, go and have a look.'

They walked back inside, through the kitchen and into a small area with a washing line and a vegetable plot. Beyond this was a small dry stone wall and then fields that fell down into a wooded area at the bottom.

'Down there is the river, the Swale,' she explained and went on to talk about the hills in the distance and the villages beyond, how their names came from Norse, like Muker meaning a small cultivated field.'

A black cat brushed past Millie's legs.

'This is Jasper,' said Gran.

'I didn't know you liked cats.'

'Oh yes. When I was a child we always had three or four cats around the house. Jasper really came and found me, we like each other, don't we Jasper? It was your grandfather, he was allergic to the fur, and anyway he didn't like them. He hated cats in the garden. I told him the best way to keep them out is to have your own, but he never agreed.' She looked a little embarrassed, as if she shouldn't really be talking about Grandad like that. Millie wondered what he would have thought of Gran taking guests.

'Do you have anyone staying at the moment?' asked Millie.

'Ah.' She paused, 'Yes. I've got a couple of university students from Lancaster who are working on Gunnerside Gill. There's no problem though, I can sleep on the sofa, it turns into a bed, and you can have my room. It's difficult you see because they're here quite a lot and I didn't want them to go somewhere else.'

Millie couldn't really argue but she wasn't happy about Gran giving up her bedroom for students.

'Are they married then?' Millie asked casually, knowing that Gran would hardly encourage any other relationships under her roof.

'Well, no, but they're very good friends,' she replied, turning away to hide her embarrassment.

Millie was quite surprised. Gran, who had always been so straight-laced about these things was changing in many ways it seemed.

'When will I meet them, then?' Millie asked, trying to make the question light and pleasant.

'Tonight. They'll be back for their meal at about six o'clock.'

Millie was disappointed; Gran was cooking, not particularly for her but for two students.

'Let me show you your room and you can have a wash, change into something more relaxed.'

Millie had worn a skirt and high heels because Dad had told her to look smart. He said that Gran was always going on at him for not making sure that Millie had smart clothes after Mum died. That was one of the reasons they fell out. She followed her grandmother up the small staircase between the sitting room and the kitchen. Standing in the doorway she surveyed the small bedroom. It had an old-fashioned double bed with a wooden headboard, a locker next to it, rugs on the floor and a pine chest of drawers. The window looked out of the back of the house and she could see sheep in the field next door. The sun was shining into the room, illuminating wild flowers in a pottery jug on the chest. Millie unpacked her clothes and arranged them in a deep wooden drawer, lined with lavender-scented paper. There was no room in the wardrobe so she put her skirts and dresses on coat hangers dangling from the back of the door and went to find the bathroom.

'Mr Bartholomew said you'd had an accident.' Millie was back downstairs in jeans and her favourite pink top.

'It's fine now, no problem Madeline.'

'Everyone calls me Millie now, actually.'

'Oh, yes dear, of course'.

'Mr Bartholomew was really worried about you. How did it happen?' Millie tried again.

'Well, it's a bit of a mystery. It was in the church but the police don't really have any idea who it was.'

'The police?'

'I'm on the flower rota. I do the first week every month, Jane does the next, then Vivienne and the last week is Lizzie. If there's a fifth week, one of us steps in. Last month I was doing it on Friday afternoon. I was on the floor with some greenery that I was sorting for the altar. I heard the door go and steps behind me but we've got restoration on the roof at the moment and there are people coming and going all the time, so I didn't think anything of it. I really don't remember anything else. Mr Bartholomew found me about three o'clock. I was unconscious, so I suppose I had been lying there for about a quarter of an hour.'

'You mean someone hit you?' Millie couldn't keep the excitement out of her voice.

'It was only a bump. They took me to hospital and did X-rays and made a fuss. They said I had a strong skull and not to drive for a few days. I must say it made me a bit shaky, but there's been several churches burgled in the last year and we always work in twos now. It's very inconvenient but Lizzie and I usually go together. She lives in the Manor up the hill. Oh, by the way, she said that we must ring when you're settled in and go to see her. You'll like the house and the gardens are beautiful; Mr Bartholomew does it all, and has done for years. Now, dear, can you help me get dinner ready for these students of mine, they're vegetarian and I'm running short of ideas. Do you think they could eat anything fishy? Because my cheese and vegetable dishes are quite exhausted.'

Millie thought an omelette would do but offered to make some suggestions when she had seen the contents of her grandmother's larder.

Chapter 2

Millie was in the small sitting room, helping her grandmother arrange the table for the evening meal when the students arrived. She had enjoyed her first afternoon in the kitchen, making pastry and cooking lentils, mixing herbs, grating cheese and slicing tomatoes. She was pleased with the result, it was a flan they would serve with potatoes and salad from the garden. Gran had complimented her on her cooking and they had discussed recipes.

There was the sound of voices outside.

'That'll be them getting their boots off,' said Gran.

Suddenly the door swung open and the room seemed to be full. Two boys in their late teens were in the sitting room one moment and gone the next. She could hear them running up the stairs and moving around above her head, chattering and laughing, followed by the sound of running water.

'Well, they certainly have arrived,' said Millie, unable to think of anything else to say.

'Yes, that's Matthew and Andrew. They probably want to clean up before they meet you properly.'

'Two boys?' Millie was puzzled.

'Yes, and they're so pleasant. Andrew's a bit reserved but you'll like them, they're very nice' her grandmother replied and went into the kitchen.

Millie continued to move the table and assortment of chairs, trying to arrange them so that all four of them could sit down.

'As it's a special occasion we'll use the good table linen,' Gran said.

Just as they finished arranging the brightly coloured floral tablecloth and plain napkins, the boys appeared at the doorway. They had obviously changed into their smarter clothes and hung back rather sheepishly.

They were both dressed in plaid shirts over jeans. The taller boy had dark curly hair and brown eyes. He was burly and had a ruddy complexion, like a rugby player, thought Millie. The other boy was skinny, he had ginger hair cut very short and a gold ring in one ear. He smiled nervously and held out a bottle.

'We brought a bottle of wine, we were keeping it and we thought you might like...' His voice trailed off

'Thank you Andrew, that was very thoughtful of you.' Her grandmother spoke like a teacher, kindly, not patronising but with the tone one might use with a child.

Both boys had to bend their heads as they came through the door.

'Millie, this is Matthew and this is Andrew,' she said, introducing first the dark haired one and then the one with the wine.

'Hi,' they all spoke together.

'I'll open the bottle,' said Andrew, escaping to the kitchen.

'I'll get the knives and forks,' offered Matthew and followed him, leaving Millie staring at the empty doorway with mixed feelings. They were very nice boys. Boys.

'I do believe they're a bit shy,' laughed Gran, 'They're not usually like this,' Again she sounded like a mother apologising for her children.

'We'd better get the flan out of the oven,' she added and disappeared as well.

Millie started arranging the mats and when Matthew and Andrew returned with the wine, cutlery and glasses, the three of them were bobbing round each other, apologising awkwardly for getting in each other's way. Gran carried in the salad and potatoes and went back for the flan, switching on two small lamps as she went.

'Shall we sit down?' asked Millie and they wedged themselves into their seats. With the table pulled out to the centre they seemed to fill the room. It was getting dull outside and the soft light of the lamps made a cosy scene as Gran returned carrying the large flan dish ceremoniously wearing a pair of large oven gloves.

The politeness continued as they passed round the plates with pieces of flan and offered each other the potatoes and salad bowl.

'This looks terrific,' said Matthew. 'What is it?'

'Lentil, cheese and tomato flan,' replied Millie, feeling pleased with herself. 'Gran said you were vegetarians.'

'Yeah, did you make it then?' asked Andrew.

'Yes.'

'It's very good,' said Gran.

Praise indeed, thought Millie.

Matthew poured the wine into the heavy glass goblets and, as she sipped, Millie relaxed for the first time since she had arrived in Yorkshire.

'Well, here's to your stay,' said Matthew.

'Yes, let's 'ope the weather stays good,' added Andrew. 'It's been very wet in the last few days. The rivers 'ave been really full and it's been boggy in the gill.'

Andrew had a London accent but Matthew sounded to Millie as if he came from somewhere in the north of England.

'What exactly are you doing up there?' asked Millie, meaning in the gill. She had warmed to them and really wanted to know.

'The impact of lead on the environment around the mines at Gunnerside Gill,' said Andrew, putting on a posh voice.

'That's the official title,' added Matthew. 'We're supposed to see if the lead tailings left up there are affecting the vegetation and water.'

'It's much more complex than that,' said Andrew, 'because we don't know what effect the mine water's 'aving.'

'It's far too complicated really.' said Matthew, leaning back in his chair and taking a long drink of wine. 'There's lead everywhere, in the ground, in the mines, and in the tailings, the waste material, and particularly in the hushes.'

'What?' asked Millie.

'Hushes,' repeated Matthew. 'Hushing is the way they used to collect the lead ore. They built a huge dam at the top of the fell and let it fill with water. They'd dig a trench down to an area where there was a rich vein of ore, loosen it off and then let the dam burst, suddenly, deliberately.'

'It must have been a 'ell of a whoosh when it went,' added Andrew, waving his hands and sending his glass flying. Fortunately it was empty and solid enough to survive.

'Why do they do that?' asked Gran.

'It carries the loose ore down to the bottom of the hush and makes it easier to collect,' replied Matthew. 'Then of course there was the smelting. The

- 12 -

chimneys went up the hills and they could be half a mile long. It must have been a fantastic sight.'

'They worked shifts, day and night, you know,' said Andrew.

Millie pictured the flames and heat, glowing in the dark. The sound of boots marching up the hill track to join the night shift, the bobbing lights of lanterns in the distance as they marched along.

'The kids used to clean the chimneys,' said Andrew.

'How awful,' said Gran. 'Making children work like that.'

'There were plenty of jobs for everyone here then,' said Matthew thoughtfully, as if suddenly coming back to the twenty-first century.

'So why are you doing this?' asked Millie brightly, trying to regain the happier atmosphere.

'It's our project for our final year at Uni,' said Andrew in a serious tone.

'Well we each have to do one, but we're doing the work together,' added Matthew. 'Andy is doing the effect on water and I'm doing the vegetation'.

'Vegetation?' asked Gran.' It sounds like potatoes and lettuces. Do you think my garden is affected?'

'No, Helen, it's grass, heather, bracken, the things sheep eat that might affect them,' answered Andrew.

It sounded strange to Millie to hear a younger person call her grandmother Helen. It made her suddenly aware that Gran was someone separate, not just her grandmother. Gran was obviously delighted to have Matthew and Andrew to look after and they must be good company to have around.

'I'll make some coffee,' Millie said, and went into the little kitchen, feeling very much at home.

Later, as she was washing the dishes with her grandmother, Millie thought about what the boys had been saying. It was very interesting, this work on the mines. She knew a little about mining but she hadn't realised how localised such work could be. The lead mining was carried out over a hundred years, the community had built up, schools had been filled, chapels and literary institutes, then it had disappeared, quite suddenly, all because there was no need for bullets.

'I wonder if I could go up to the mines with the students tomorrow?' she said.

'I'm sure they'd take you, dear. I could see you were interested in their work. I think they'd be pleased. There are some pamphlets in the bookcase. I bought them in the information place when I first came up. Go and have a look, I've nearly finished here.'

Millie went back into the little sitting room and looked along the bookcase. There were poetry books, classics like Dickens and Hardy, new novels just out in paperback. Her grandmother obviously found time when she was alone to read widely. On the next shelf were many books on the Dales, autobiographies like James Herriot but also books on geology, botany and the history of the Dales, especially Swaledale. 'Lead Mining in Swaledale', this was what she was looking for.

She settled down on the sofa with her legs curled round beside her and pushed the cushions into a comfortable shape. The students were looking at the most recent mining area in Swaledale, the Sir Francis Level. Millie found several pages devoted to it. The mine was begun in 1864. There were photographs in the book of a smelt mill and of an air receiver tank.

They weren't old photographs but recent black and white pictures of ruins and old rusty equipment. She went back to the description. It took thirteen years to cut the vein using boring machinery so nothing was mined until 1877. After that it operated successfully, with an ore dressing plant being completed in 1879. Millie made a note to find out what ore dressing was. Work was suspended in 1882 due to the low price of lead and although prices rose during the first world war, that was really the end of mining in Swaledale She was beginning to get really interested. She wanted to find out more about the earlier mining activities. After all, lead was mined in Roman times and the chapel at Low Row had been built for lead miners in 1691, so there was a lot to find out. She wanted to know more about ore dressing. All these things could be seen up in Gunnerside Gill and she would see it tomorrow.

In the kitchen her grandmother was sitting on a stool talking to Jasper, who was purring loudly on her lap.

'I think I'll go to bed now, Gran.'

'Do you want anything to drink?'

'No, but let me help you make up your bed, if you're sure you won't let me sleep down here?'

'No, I've got to be up first in the morning and I'll be quite comfortable. It will be a treat for Jasper to have me down here, he's not allowed upstairs.'

They had to push the table back to the wall to open out the sofa, but it all fitted and the bed looked very snug when they had put the duvet on it.

'Night, Gran.'

'Goodnight, Millie. Sleep well. I thought you looked very tired when you arrived today. Shall I wake you in the morning?'

'I think you better had,' she said, yawning. 'I am tired but I must wake up in time to go to Gunnerside Gill with the boys.'

'You do like them don't you? I hope you don't mind them being here but, to be honest, I like the company. When I first came up here it seemed very quiet sometimes. I'm used to it now but I'm glad to have them around.'

'I think they're very nice too,' said Millie, giving her grandmother a hug, and she meant it. 'Goodnight.'

Next morning Millie woke up to the sound of the curtain rings rattling against the wooden pole. Helen had brought up a mug of tea.

'It's only seven,' she whispered and disappeared, leaving Millie to wake up slowly, noting the blue sky and large white clouds. The house was quiet but in the distance she heard sheep bleating and dogs barked intermittently. Was it only Sunday? She felt as if she had been here for days. Leaning back on the wooden headboard, she looked across to the fells in the distance, and began thinking about what she would be doing that day. One day at a time. She would visit the lead mines today and see for herself the hushes, the ruined smelters and the chimneys.

Downstairs Helen was busy in the kitchen and Millie fell in helping her with ease. She knew where to find things now and could be helpful as they made a proper cooked breakfast for their guests. It was obvious that the students did not like getting up early and it was not until they had been called three times did they appear, dishevelled and bleary-eyed. Breakfast was eaten in silence except for requests to pass the marmalade. While the boys finished off a second plate of toast, Millie looked at the Ordnance Survey map of the area. She found Gunnerside and to the north traced Gunnerside Gill. At the top was Blakethwaite lead mines and Blakethwaite Dams; below that, further down the gill, was Melbeck Moor, another name that she recognised from her reading last night. The hills were criss-crossed with tracks.

'Which way do you go up to the mines?' she asked.

'You can go from here,' said Matthew with a mouth full of toast. 'There's a track that goes up past the Manor, we keep right up the gill and cross at Melbecks.'

'We sometimes come down to Gunnerside,' added Andrew. 'We 'ave to take samples all down the gill and it's easier on that side.'

'Is it OK if I come with you?' asked Millie.

'Yes, as long as you've got strong shoes,' said Matthew, looking at her as if he felt that she might not.

'It's alright, Millie,' said Helen. 'I've got some boots you can borrow and an anorak in case it's wet. I'll pack some food in the rucksack for you, same as the boys have.'

She disappeared upstairs and came back with thick red socks, large brown boots and a bright orange waterproof jacket. It reminded Millie of field trips she had made and feeling quite excited she went into her bedroom with her new clothes. She took out her thick jumper, which she was never able to wear at home because it was too hot for indoors. She pulled on the socks, then the boots. They felt strange but not uncomfortable, just a bit heavy. They made clonking noises on the wooden stairs, like clogs, she thought, the miners' feet.

The boys were already outside putting their boots on. Boots coated with dried lumps of mud that were banned from the house. They sat side by side on the bench in the sunlight, laughing and talking. Andrew was having trouble untying a knot in his laces and Matthew was helping him. When the lace was free, he ruffled Andrew's close shaved head and stood up to put on his rucksack, catching sight of Millie at the door.

'Are you ready?' he asked. 'Is your rucksack OK? If Helen has put as much food in yours as she does in ours it's probably rather 'eavy.'

'No, it's fine,' she said. It was fine now but she wondered how hard the walk would be and whether it would become a weight later.

Andrew had stood up and now had his rucksack on.

'Let's go then,' he said, and the three of them manoeuvred themselves through the narrow gate and set off up the road, towards the top of the village.

At the end of the road, only a few hundred yards from the row of cottages, was a derelict chapel and here a track began where vehicles had formed parallel furrows. There was no wall to the left and the open fields extended into the hills in all directions. The signpost indicated that the track went to Melbeck Moor. On the right was a high dry stone wall running along for some way and in the distance Millie could see a big stone building, hidden by shrubbery and trees.

'What's that place?' she asked, pointing in the direction of the house.

'That's Mossy Bank Manor,' Andrew replied. 'It's quite old I think, about seventeenth century.'

'I'd like to look round it,' said Matthew. 'It must be very interesting inside.'

'I think the owner is a friend of Gran's,' said Millie. 'Perhaps we will see it.'

As they drew level with the gates Millie could see a long drive curving round to a large house, with an attractive stone facade, stone mullion windows and a big wooden front door.

A dog came darting down the drive barking, a border collie with grey whiskers and dark brown eyes.

'Hello boy,' said Millie, reaching out to touch him, but the dog darted off again, presumably having established that they meant no harm.

They continued along the track in silence, a comfortable silence, broken only by occasional comments about the sheep or the sound of a curlew. Millie was getting hot in her jumper and took it off, only to find that the breeze was quite cool as they moved higher, without the shelter of the stone wall. After a while the main route turned off to the left, up the hill, and a less obvious path continued parallel to the gill. To her left, Millie followed the track as it climbed up past shooting butts to a small stone building in the distance.

'What's that place up there?' she asked.

'Old shooting Lodge, I think,' replied Matthew.

'So who has the shooting rights up here?' she asked, wondering if she had used the right terminology.

'I don't know,' replied Matthew. 'I'd assumed it was the old lady in the Manor. There is another farm on the other side of the village but I don't think it's theirs.'

They strode off along the path and Millie began to feel warmer as they gained the shelter of the valley. To her right she could see the river, Gunnerside Beck. There were piles of tailings on the other side of the beck and she could pick out the old stone buildings and other evidence of the mining activity. The path began to lose height and before long they came down to the beck, in an area where there were several old ruins and a small bridge.

'This is where we cross over,' said Matthew. 'We'll go up to the top of Blakethwaite Dam, if you like, and you can see how they did the hushing.'

'Great,' said Millie, as they crossed in single file.

'That 'ole up there is one of the smelters,' said Andrew, pointing back across the river, upstream of the bridge, 'and behind that is one of the tall chimneys.'

'I can't see anything,' said Millie, searching the skyline.

'It don't show very well,' said Andrew, 'but if you look carefully you can see the 'ole at the top, up the 'ill. They built the chimney in the 'ill so it runs right up, about 'alfway up.

Millie looked carefully across the valley and found the hole at the top of the chimney.

'It must have been a strange sight,' she said.

They continued along the track to the right of the river until they came to a small waterfall.

'This is where the dam is,' said Matthew. 'If we climb a bit further we can see the top of it.'

Millie was pleased that they were near the top. Her weekly aerobics class at college did not prepare her for this sort of exercise and she was glad of the prospect of a rest. They clambered up onto the flat ground where the miners had built the dam. Millie tried to imagine what it would have been like when it was full and turned to look down the valley. They had climbed a long way up and the view was impressive. Down below was the village of Gunnerside and over to the left was Swaledale stretching off to Reeth. To her right were moors covered with purple heather.

As she looked across at the shooting Lodge up on the hill opposite she saw a Land Rover moving slowly over the rough track down the hill away from the building.

'Do people live in the shooting Lodge?' she asked.

'I don't know, I don't think so. Maybe it's the farmer seeing to his sheep. I don't think anyone lives there,' replied Matthew, but he looked puzzled.

'Have they begun shooting yet?' asked Millie. 'Isn't it August when they start?'

'Yes, but not until the glorious twelfth,' said Matthew. 'We haven't heard any shooting yet.'

Andrew had undone his rucksack and was pulling out a package. He examined the contents carefully, replaced it and pulled out another. This time he found what he wanted and started eating a large piece of flapjack.

'That's a good idea,' said Millie, and she began investigating her rucksack. There were three packages. One was large and heavy and she guessed that these were sandwiches, the serious food best left until lunchtime. She moved onto one of the smaller packets; it contained a piece of fruitcake. It was very good and she recognised the flavour of her grandmother's 'special' fruitcake, which was only ever made on important occasions such as birthdays and Christmas. It tasted even better now but that could be because she was hungry and eating it out of doors. As a child she always looked forward to picnics but, with Dad fighting the camping gas stove and Mum flapping at the wasps, she had never really enjoyed it as much as she anticipated.

'Are you ready, then?' asked Matthew, and she tied her rucksack and got up.

'Where now?' she asked.

'We thought we would work our way down to Gunnerside.'

'It'll give you a general view of the gill,' added Andrew.

'Great,' she said, and they moved back down to the path they had walked up.

Before long Andrew stopped and pointed across the stream.

'You see that big thing that looks like a boiler over there?'

'Yes. I know that, it's an air pump or something,' she said, pleased she had done some reading.

'That's right!' said Matthew. He looked impressed. 'It's an air receiver tank.'

'What's it for?' she asked.

'I think it's to do with the compressor they used for boring a hole before they blasted through the mine, but I'm not sure,' he replied.

Millie made a mental note to find out more about how the machinery actually operated.

They carried on down the valley until they were back at the ruined buildings, where they had crossed the river.

'Do we cross back?' Millie asked.

'No, we'll go back down on this side,' said Matthew.

They had stopped at the large ruined building that looked like a house.

'This was probably the engine house,' explained Andrew. 'They used a hydraulic engine to pump out the water and to lift the cages carrying the miners and the ore.'

'It must have been noisy up here in those days,' said Millie.

Millie tried hard to imagine that quiet little valley full of people's voices, engines running, machines boring, blasting, the smelters roaring and the sound of huge volumes of water pouring down the hushes. It must have been hard work. In August it wouldn't have been so bad but the winters must have been dreadful. Now it was very peaceful, only the occasional bleating of one sheep to another.

'It can be noisy here now when the jets come over,' said Andrew. 'They practice over here from the RAF station near the coast. Watch out for 'em, they can surprise you if they fly straight down the valley.'

'Don't they frighten the sheep?' asked Millie.

'No, they're used to it, I suppose,' said Matthew.

They moved on down the gill, following a well-worn path and soon came to the area that Millie had seen from the other side of the river. Piles of waste, tailings they were called, thought Millie. They were piled up at the base of another set of ruins. This time the stone structure looked like a series of stalls.

'These are the smelting hearths,' Matthew pointed to the rectangular stalls. 'The lead was extracted by heating the ore and letting the molten lead pour out. It was collected in moulds at the bottom. This is where we expect to see most of the lead contamination.'

'And arsenic,' added Andrew. 'There's arsenic in the ore. We're looking for that as well. It's quite interesting to follow the line of the chimney, up the 'ill, because the lead would be vaporising all the way up. They used to collect it again by washing the chimney every so often.'

'How could they wash it?' asked Millie.

'By diverting a stream into the top,' explained Matthew.

'Do you mind if we spend a bit of time here?' he continued. 'I want to collect some samples along the path of the chimney. It won't take long.'

'That's fine,' said Millie. She was enjoying her morning and she had been wanting to find somewhere sheltered to have a pee.

She wandered down towards the pile of rubble and sorted through the stones. She spotted a white object and found it was the broken stem of a clay pipe. Pleased with her find, she put it in her pocket and made her way thankfully into the high bracken, out of view of the boys, who were busy on their hands and knees half way up the hill. Once she was out of the bracken, feeling more comfortable, she wandered further down to the river. Some hikers were marching along the track on the other side. They had heavy packs and were obviously carrying all they needed for more than a day. She pulled the map out of her rucksack and looked at the patchwork of footpaths. They could have come from Mossy Bank but more likely across from Keld at the top of Swaledale. It was on the Pennine Way and there was a Youth Hostel there. They must be heading across to Arkengarthdale or up to join the route of the Coast to Coast walk from St Bees to Robin Hood's Bay. Looking at the map again, Millie traced the track that she had followed from Mossy Bank. If they had stayed on the main track they would have gone up past the shooting Lodge and on to Keld. She might manage that one day, it would be a long walk but she could come back through Muker and along the bank of the Swale.

'Do you want to carry on or have lunch here?' Matthew shouted down from the spoil heap above her.

'Let's have lunch,' she called back. Looking at her watch she realised that it was only ten to twelve, but she was hungry.

Millie's legs felt stiff when they set off after lunch.

'Right then,' she said, breaking the silence, 'where do we go next?'

'We'll carry on down the beck,' said Matthew, 'and see the mine entrance. It's not far down here. It's one of Andy's sampling points.'

'Will you collect some water today?' she asked.

'No,' said Andrew. 'I 'ave to bring special containers otherwise I could lose some of the metals before I get 'em back to the lab. I 'ave to take 'em back quickly, so we do that when we've got a lift back to Uni.'

They were level with a stone arched entrance about three feet high, a tunnel disappearing into the hillside. Ferns grew round the entrance and water poured out of the mine. In the sunshine the tunnel looked inviting.

'Can I go in?' Millie asked.

'No way,' said Matthew. 'The mines are far too dangerous to explore.'

They carried on down the path, with bracken on either side like walls. They could hear voices below them, gradually getting closer, and a family of two small children, father and mother appeared on the path, chattering and laughing. The two groups exchanged greetings and parted, the boys standing to one side to let the family pass.

Millie wondered aloud how Dad and Fiona were getting on in Greece.

Matthew said, 'You live in London, don't you?'

'Yes.'

Millie explained that since her mother had died she had lived with her father and his girlfriend. The boys seemed embarrassed, unsure what to say, so she continued with amusing anecdotes about Fiona. It did her good and she felt better being able to talk to strangers about it all.

'My Mum's divorced,' said Andrew. 'My Dad left us when I was twelve.'

'That's sad,' Millie said.

'Yeah.'

'Do you see your Dad?'

'Not since 'e walked out on us.'

They continued in silence for a while, stopping only to climb a stile as the path changed into a wooded area. Millie was surprised how quickly they had descended. Now they were walking past a stone cottage and soon they were back by the river and on the path into the village. Washing hung on a line by the path and they emerged by a bridge.

'This is Gunnerside,' announced Andrew. 'We'll go back along the River Swale.'

They didn't start at the river but walked past bungalows and off across the fields, following the narrow path made by walkers. A signpost carved in wood asked them to keep to the path as the field was used for hay. The grass had already been cut and was now growing again. Reaching the other side of the hayfield, they walked along the edge of the next meadow, looking down on the river from high above. Each time they reached the other side of a meadow they went through a small wooden gate stile, just wide enough to squeeze through.

As they passed a large stone barn, Andrew asked, 'Have you noticed how nearly every field has its own barn? If you look back towards Gunnerside you can see them in the valley, there, away towards Reeth.'

By the next barn, they turned down a narrow path between giant butterbur and willowherb. It was dark and cool in the little wood and it smelt of aniseed. Crossing a narrow bridge, they climbed slowly up the other side, out into the village of Ivelet.

'We'll follow the road now,' said Matthew, 'until we come back to Mossy Bank. It's not far now.'

They walked in silence, each deep in thought, until they turned up to the village. Millie realised that she was quite tired and admitted to herself, no-one else, that she was glad to be back.

Millie was allowed to have her bath first. She spent a long time wallowing in the deep hot water and when she got out, she dressed slowly before going downstairs to join her grandmother who was busy in the kitchen.

'I hope I haven't taken all the hot water,' Millie said.

'It'll soon heat up,' Helen replied. 'Don't worry. The boys have gone down to see a friend of theirs at the bottom of the village. He's staying with his aunt while he's working at the pub in Reeth. So, did you have a good day?'

Millie described what she had seen, with enthusiasm.

'Well, I had a very nice time too,' said Helen. 'I went to church this morning, with Lizzie. She's asked us to lunch tomorrow, by the way. She drove and I stayed for coffee with her. I haven't done much this afternoon, except a bit of baking. I made an apple pie for supper. I've done a nice roast dinner for us, as the boys said that they would be happy to finish the flan. By the way, the church looks beautiful! There was a wedding yesterday, a big one, and it's all white - lovely, with the dark green foliage. It must have cost the earth. Flowers all round the porch, the door, every pew, windows, everywhere. We must go down tomorrow, before they fade.'

Helen chatted on about this and that as she prepared the vegetables and mixed the batter for Yorkshire pudding. Millie sat quietly, lacking the energy to join in.

Dinner was far more relaxed than on the previous night and the conversation flowed without pause. They talked about the day and what they would all do tomorrow. Andrew and Matthew had needed to take more grass samples and to start a proper scale plan of their sampling sites.

'Will you be coming, Millie?' asked Andrew. He sounded as though he hoped that she would.

'No, I've a lunch invitation with the lady of the Manor, tomorrow, and I'm going to see the church with Gran.'

'You don't *have* to, dear,' laughed Helen.

'I'd like to, Gran,' Millie felt guilty for neglecting her grandmother and was genuinely looking forward to a day with her. They seemed to be so relaxed with each other that she was beginning to enjoy her company.

'It will be interesting to see the manor house,' said Matthew, who clearly was keen to see it himself.

'Don't worry Matt, Mills will get you an invitation, won't you?' said Andrew, smiling at Millie.

'Of course.'

'I'm sure Lizzie would be pleased to show you round, dear,' said Helen. 'She would be glad of the opportunity. The house has been in her family for three hundred years and she's very proud of it.'

'I think, if you'll excuse me,' said Millie, yawning, 'I'll go up to bed now, I'm shattered.'

Everyone smiled.

'You'll get used to it,' said Helen. 'It's probably the air.'

The air, thought Millie as she climbed the stairs. The air *was* different up here, fresher. Yes, but it smelt different too. As she lay in her soft bed and looked at the stars through the gap in the curtains, she realised that she had hardly thought about Dad and Fiona at all since she'd been in Yorkshire. At the same time she thought they probably hadn't thought about her either. They were most likely enjoying themselves as much as she was. She wanted to write it down in a diary, so that she would remember it all, like she had as a child when she was on holiday. No, she would use the camera so she could show her friends the mines, the chimneys and the gill. She knew it wouldn't be the same, not very interesting for them, but next year she could bring them up here and show it to them herself. Next summer.

Chapter 3

The sound of rain beating on the window woke Millie. She turned over and picked up her watch from the bedside cabinet; it was ten past nine. Jumping out of bed, she felt the ache in the backs of her legs from the previous day's walking.

As she washed and dressed, Millie could hear her grandmother moving about downstairs. She chose a denim skirt and a sweatshirt in royal blue. Millie didn't want to look like a 'townie' but thought that she should dress up a little for lunch with Lizzie.

Her grandmother was vacuuming the sitting room as she came down the stairs and didn't react until Millie moved past her towards the kitchen.

'Hello,' she said, switching off the cleaner. 'I didn't wake you, you seemed so peaceful and the weather's awful today. I thought we should go into Reeth to get some bits and pieces and then, if there's time, we'll go to Muker to see the church.'

'Fine,' said Millie. She didn't like the sound of shopping but it was too wet to do much else.

'Where are Matt and Andy?' she asked.

'They've already gone. I think they're collecting today.'

'Won't they get wet?'

'Yes, but don't mind. They go out whatever the weather, unless it's misty of course. Now, what do you want for breakfast?'

'You carry on, Gran, I can make myself a piece of toast.'

By the time Millie had finished eating, Helen was ready to go to Reeth.

They parked on the green and hurried through the rain to the grocer's and then to the bakery, queuing for some time while an elderly woman discussed last night's television programmes with the man behind the counter. No-one was in a hurry and it gave Millie the opportunity to study all the different breads and cakes.

'What's that tart, Gran?' she asked in a whisper.

'That's curd tart, it's made with raisins, it's very sweet. Do you want to try it?'

'Yes, let's.' Millie was feeling hungry after her small breakfast. It would usually be sufficient but the exercise had given her an appetite.

'I'll have to watch my weight,' laughed Millie.

'Don't be silly, you must have walked about six or seven miles yesterday. You can afford to have a few extra calories.'

'Well, in that case, those doughnuts look rather good, as well.'

By the time they left the shop loaded with brown paper bags containing a range of samples, it had nearly stopped raining.

'Where now?' asked Millie.

'I thought that we could go home and drop these off and then go to Muker.'

'But we'll have coffee?' Millie wanted to taste the curd tart.

'There's a nice place in Muker. I'm sure they'll serve curd tart there,' teased her grandmother.

Parts of the countryside were now familiar on the journey back; the wooden seat at the junction in Healaugh, the pub up on the bank at Low Row and the bridge at Gunnerside, where they had walked the day before. Soon they were back in Laurel Cottage unloading the groceries and packing them away in the fridge and the walk-in larder.

It was only two miles to Muker. They parked in a little car park on the opposite side of the river. In the village was the sort of teashop that Millie liked, serving good coffee and home made cakes. Her grandmother suggested that she tried some parkin.

'Well, how have you enjoyed your first couple of days in the Dales?' asked Helen, as they finished off their cakes and poured a second cup of coffee. It was quiet in the teashop since they were the only customers, and the smell of lunch was beginning to waft from the kitchen.

Millie wanted to tell her how happy she was, how welcome she felt and how relaxed she was up here.

'I feel great actually.'

'Do you? Good. I hope you're not missing your Dad?'

'No way!' Millie immediately regretted being so honest. 'Do you never get bored or lonely up here, Gran?'

'No dear, I don't. When the boys are staying I have company but they're not here all the time and I have a number of friends, like Lizzie, who are on their own like me. We meet up for coffee or lunch and then we go into Richmond and even to York sometimes; but I am very happy just pottering around at home and in the garden. And what about you, Madeline? Do you get lonely?'

Millie was surprised by the question. She hadn't considered herself to be in the same situation as her grandmother, but it was true that she no longer had a Mum to confide in.

'Not really.'

'You should make the most of your stay here to relax and forget about Fiona. You did look exhausted when you arrived and already you seem much better.'

'Thanks Gran, I'm really having a good time.'

They finished their coffee in silence, waiting for the girl to bring the bill.

When they stepped from the teashop the rain had stopped, and they walked up to the church in sunshine.

'The church is very old, it was first built in the sixteenth century. Now just look at those flowers!'

There were white blooms and dark green foliage decorating the porch and, when they went into the church itself, Millie was surprised by the number of flowers decorating every corner of the building.

'Isn't it beautiful!' she exclaimed.

'It certainly makes my job easy this week.'

Millie was reminded of the attack on her grandmother and asked her to show her exactly where and how it had happened.

They walked up to the front of the church, level with the pulpit.

'I had laid out all the greenery on newspaper on the floor, so I was kneeling with my back to the door. I heard the door closing and someone must have walked up the side to the right, because I would have seen them if they'd come up the aisle. The next thing I knew, I woke up in the ambulance.'

'Where were you hit?'

'Just here.' She pointed to the left side of her head. 'I had a terrible bruise for sometime.'

'And how was it that Mr Bartholomew found you?'

'Ah, well, he had been to the pub in Muker at lunchtime. He was coming back when he saw Lizzie's Jaguar outside the church. I parked it outside because I needed to carry the leaves and stuff in. He'd apparently seen it when he arrived and thought it odd that it was here at all. It was good he came when he did.'

'Why were you driving her car?'

'Mine was being serviced. She suggested I used it. At first I was a bit nervous but it's quite easy to drive, it's an automatic you see.'

'And there was nothing taken from the church?'

'No, the police think it must of frightened them, seeing me unconscious.'

The church door banged and they both jumped and turned round. A young couple were coming in.

'Tourists,' whispered Helen. 'Gosh, look at the time, it's nearly twelve, we'd better get to Lizzie's at once.'

They drove straight past the cottage in Mossy Bank and up the rough track at the end of the village. Helen turned the car into the gravel drive of the Manor and pulled up behind Lizzie's maroon Jaguar. As they climbed out of the car, the front door swung open and the border collie flew out at them. This time it didn't run away when Millie put out her hand but sniffed it expectantly and then wandered off to cock its leg against one of the dwarf conifers ornamenting the drive.

A tall woman in tweed skirt came towards them. She had white hair tied in a bun and twinkling blue eyes. Millie judged her to be about sixty-five, maybe nearer seventy, certainly not much older than her grandmother.

'Hello Helen darling, and you must be Madeline. I've heard so much about you, I feel I know you already.'

'Millie,' muttered Millie under her breath.

'Oh Lizzie, don't embarrass the poor girl,' laughed Helen.

'Bernie! Stop that at once!' The dog had his leg raised, ready to mark out another bit of territory. Bernie lowered his head and skulked off behind the house, as if upset at being scolded in front of strangers.

'Come inside and sit down. I thought we would have a drink before lunch and maybe wander round the garden this afternoon, if it stays warm.'

They followed her into the house, through a hall of dark polished wood with an attractive carved staircase, and into the drawing room, as Lizzie called it. There, they sank into soft floral armchairs while their hostess poured sherry into cut glass. Millie silently admired the paintings and rugs and hoped that she might have such a room one day.

'So what do you think of Mossy Bank? Don't you think Helen has done wonders with the cottage? I was so pleased when she decided to move in.'

'I think it's lovely, the village I mean, and the cottage, of course.'

'Good. I hear that you've been out with our students. Did you visit Gunnerside Gill?' asked Lizzie.

'Yes. I want to go up again, and to visit Keld.'

'I think it's so nice that the young people these days take such an interest in the environment, don't you Helen? We never bothered at all, did we? Imagine my great-great grandfather being concerned about whether mining in Swaledale was a healthy occupation. So long as it paid, he wouldn't care.'

'Did your grandfather own the mines up here?' asked Millie, hoping to discover some of the history of Lizzie's family.

'Well, some of the land. He was in partnership with another man who worked further down the dale and his father before him. In fact, this house has been in the family for several hundred years. Some of the land has been sold off. It used to stretch in all directions and included most of this part of the dale. Now it only goes down to Low Farm and up to the Lodge on the track to Keld.'

'I've seen the shooting Lodge. Do you rent it out for people who shoot in the season?' asked Millie.

'That is a moot point. I'm having a bit of trouble in that area at the moment. It used to work well in my father's time. Then, of course, it was weekend parties and the county set, so we used to have local families making use of the shoot, and my own family did quite a lot of entertaining. Then the gamekeeper died and father got too old to look after the business side, so he got an agent to sort it out. At first it was no problem at all because all the usual visitors still came but gradually the families stopped entertaining and companies, business corporations started making use of the moor. They like to entertain by bringing important clients for a few days shooting. It's more of a business thing.'

'I should think it's better isn't it?' asked Helen.

'Not at all. I don't know them and they have little interest in the shooting. The moor is maintained by a keeper who is employed by the agent and I never see him. They book the expensive country club type hotels to house their guests and the Lodge is only used for luncheon when they are up there. Oh! Gosh, lunch! I must go and check that it alright.'

Lizzie rushed out leaving Helen and Millie smiling at each other.

'She has some lovely things, Gran.'

'Yes. I keep telling her that she should get a burglar alarm fitted but she doesn't listen. She says that Bernie is better than an alarm.'

'We're OK,' said Lizzie, as she entered the room. 'Another few minutes, I think. Time for another quick sherry,' and she filled up their glasses. Millie, who thought sherry was disgusting, had hardly touched hers but Helen offered her glass for a top-up.

'So no-one lives in the Lodge now?' prompted Millie, interested to hear about the building which intrigued her so on her first day out.

'No. I would like to let it as a holiday cottage, like I do for Ivy Cottage - has Madeline seen it, Helen?'

'No.'

'It's in the grounds, at the side of the house,' she explained.

'Why don't you? Let it, I mean.' Millie was curious.

'I can't. It's so silly. I asked the agent last year and he said that all the shooting had been booked by a Dutch company and that they insisted on having the use of the Lodge. I couldn't understand it because they didn't use it very much and, in fact they very rarely came to shoot last year, maybe three or four times. I shouldn't complain because the income is good but it seems such a waste, I'd rather see a family enjoying it.'

'I saw a Land Rover coming down from it yesterday,' said Millie.

'I stopped it a few weeks ago to ask the driver why he was using the Lodge now but he wouldn't discuss it. He just waved his arms and shouted abuse and drove off. They seem to think I'm interfering but it worries me. Sometimes they go up and down at night and Bernie starts barking, which makes me think there is someone prowling about. I've made my decision now and told the agent that I want to put a stop to these people and not to renew their contract for this season, even if it means no shooting this year.' Lizzie had become quite flushed during her speech and paused while she caught her breath. 'Now, I think we should have lunch. I hope you don't mind eating in the kitchen.'

She led the way into an enormous stone flagged kitchen with low beams and leaded window panes. It overlooked a walled garden, planted with vegetables, presumably tended by Mr Bartholomew. They sat at a dark oak table decorated with a large bowl of old fashioned roses. The bare wood was highly polished and reflected the silver cutlery laid out for the three of them. The meal was simple but delicious, poached salmon, a green salad and potatoes cooked with mint. Afterwards she produced a large china bowl of strawberries and a jug of thick cream.

'Are these your own strawberries?' asked Helen.

'Yes, and the cream is from Low Farm. My tenants are very pleasant people aren't they Helen? The Price family, they rent some land from me. His father had the farm before him and I must say, with more modern methods David has made a success of it. Of course, the milk side is not very profitable but he has a good trade locally. Sheep are his main business and his wife has hens and ducks, she sells the eggs to the local stores. He has a big flock and keeps four working dogs. One of them is Bernie's brother, not that Bernie is any good for sheep, that's why I got him; he was too naughty! Now, I think we should have a potter round outside before I put the kettle on.'

The kitchen door led straight out into the walled garden. It was neat and tidy and full of vegetables: runner beans climbing up long rows of canes, neat rows of lettuces and peas, large green plants covered in tender young courgettes.

'Gosh, it must be a full time job to keep this garden so smart,' exclaimed Millie, thinking of her father's plot at home which contained two wigwams of beans and five courgettes plants, but looked a shambles for the entire season.

'Bert Bartholomew does it all. He spends a lot of time up here, usually early morning, but he enjoys it and he can take as much produce as he needs for his own consumption. He's worked for the family all his life and of course in this line of work there's no pension, so he carries on, even though he really should be retiring now.'

'Those tomatoes look interesting,' said Helen, examining a plant covered in small yellow fruit.

'They must be a new variety that Bert is trying. I don't know the name, you must ask him. Try one.'

They wandered up and down the neat beds, admiring the vegetables and sampling the herbs. In the greenhouse were yet more varieties of tomatoes, celery, cucumber, peppers and aubergines.

There was a wooden door in the end wall leading out into the main garden, behind the house. The path led them through the apple, pear and plum trees into a formal rose garden.

'This marks the end of the Bartholomew domain,' said Lizzie with a laugh. 'I much prefer a simple garden.'

The rest of the garden was surrounded by a high laurel hedge. The borders were full of country flowers presenting sweeps of colour from deep blues to purples, into mauves and through to pink. The effect was natural and simple, yet clearly took a lot of work and careful planning to achieve the effect. There was little lawn but any areas not covered with flowers and shrubs were paved with York stone or gravel. They wandered through paths and patios back in the direction of the house. Stopping under a wooden pergola covered in a mass of old fashioned climbing roses of cream, Lizzie suggested they rested on a wooden bench while she fetched a tray of tea. Gazing at the attractive house and its surroundings, Millie mused on what would happen to the Manor when Lizzie was no longer able to look after it, but she didn't feel she should ask her grandmother such a tactless question. Instead she pointed out the butterflies visiting a buddleia nearby as they waited politely for Lizzie to return.

'Does Lizzie have any family?' she finally asked, unable to curb her curiosity.

'Yes, she has a son who is a teacher in Edinburgh. Her daughter and son-in-law died in a boating accident, very sad. They left a girl in her teens and a younger boy.'

'Do they come to visit?'

'Not often. I think she is closest to her granddaughter who's studying medicine. She visits in the holidays sometimes.'

Bernie appeared, trotting down the path in front of his mistress, who was carrying a large tray.

'He's seen the biscuit tin,' she shouted.

Millie fed Bernie, which was clearly the way to win his attention. He sat at her feet while they drank tea from bone china cups, and Helen updated Lizzie with the latest village gossip.

'Irene Jackson is nearly going mad with her nephew staying. He's working at the pub in Reeth and doesn't get home until about midnight most nights. She says she can't sleep until she knows that he's back but she gets up at six to make Jim's breakfast.'

Jim apparently helped out at Low Farm and had to be up early.

'You're lucky with your two lads then,' said Lizzie. 'Although I was wondering how you manage now that Madeline is staying as well? It must be difficult in that tiny cottage.'

'We manage,' Helen said with a smile.

'And I have so much space here. It's a shame that Ivy Cottage isn't free this week or they could have had that, just for the time being,' she added quickly, aware that Helen would not want to lose them permanently.

'Never mind.'

'Look, why don't they stay with me in the house, just while Madeline is here. That way you'll have a bit more space, less to worry about, cooking and so on, and they can move back when she has to go.' She paused for a response. 'In fact,' she went on when Helen didn't answer, sensing that further persuasion was required, 'I would be grateful to have them about until this business with the shoot is sorted out. I didn't like the way that man in the Land Rover spoke and I'd feel happier with them around.'

'Do you think so?' Helen sounded uncertain.

'Go on, Gran, you know that Matt and Andy would be as pleased as punch to have the chance to stay here for a week or two.'

Millie liked the idea of a bit more time on her own with her grandmother. 'We can still have them round for a meal now and then.'

'Alright then, it's settled,' Lizzie ordered. 'You tell them to move over here tonight. They can cook for themselves if they like or I can ask Irene to do extra for them. Irene is Bert Bartholomew's daughter, she cleans and cooks for me when I need help,' she added by way of explanation to Millie.

She collected the cups and saucers onto the tray and they walked slowly back to the house, with Bernie at their heels. It was growing cool in the garden and Millie noticed that it was nearly five o' clock.

'If you look to your right,' said Lizzie, nodding her head in that direction, 'you can see Ivy Cottage. I've got a family in there at the moment. They've got two small children but they're very sweet, you wouldn't know they were there. I feel sorry for the parents. The mother asked me if I knew anyone who would baby-sit but I don't because young Rosie in the village is on holiday herself, in Cornwall. It must be disappointing not to be able to go out in the evening when you're away with the children. They only wanted to have a pub meal in peace one night this week. I would offer to do it myself but, to be honest, I wouldn't know what to do with a two year old now.'

'Madeline would do it, wouldn't you, dear?' Helen looked at her questioningly.

It was not something she would have volunteered to do but it was difficult to refuse gracefully.

'I suppose so.'

'Would you, dear? How kind you are. We'll go and see if they're in now if you like. Let me just put the tray in the kitchen.'

They walked along a narrow shady path behind the house and through a high wrought iron gate onto the front drive. To their right was a small wooden gate, that Millie hadn't noticed when they parked the car. A stone path took them to the porch of a cottage covered in ivy. Just as they reached the door a small child, about four years old, appeared from the side on a tricycle.

'Hello,' she said.

'Is your Mummy or Daddy home?' asked Lizzie, bending down to speak.

'I'll see,' she replied and pedalled off back behind the cottage.

They heard the gate click behind them and saw a thin girl carrying a small child asleep in her arms. She was nervous-looking with long straight blonde hair and large grey eyes.

'I was just getting William out of the car. We've been shopping in Hawes. Jeff's locking it up,' she explained.

'Hello dear. This is my friend Helen and her granddaughter. I brought them over because Madeline has offered to baby-sit, if you still want someone.'

'That would be nice but...' she seemed to hesitate, perhaps suddenly apprehensive about leaving her children with a complete stranger.

'I do a lot of baby-sitting at home,' said Millie. It was how she got away from Fiona's constant presence. 'Please don't worry, they'll be quite safe.'

'It's my birthday tomorrow and Jeff said he'd take me to that pub where they filmed James Herriot if I could find someone.'

'Well, that's settled then. What time should I arrive, about seven?' Millie asked.

'Half past would do, then they'll both be ready for bed. We'll be back by eleven, honestly. Thanks for offering.'

'Good, we'll leave you in peace,' said Lizzie and they turned back down the path.

'We really must be off,' said Helen when they reached the drive. 'Thanks for a lovely afternoon.' She gave Lizzie a kiss on the cheek.

'Yes, thanks a lot, it's been lovely,' added Millie.

'Well, we must do it again, before you go back, Madeline.'

'Yes.'

As they climbed into Helen's car, Millie caught sight of the husband peering into the Jaguar. He was a very large man, built like a wrestler, with tattooed arms, a shaved head and a tasteless tee-shirt over dirty looking jeans.

'Good heavens!' whispered Helen.

'He's rather big isn't he?' said Millie, hoping he hadn't got his eye on Lizzie's vehicle.

The evening was spent moving Matt and Andy into the Manor. They seemed highly delighted with the plan and Helen appeared happier once she saw that they were pleased with the arrangement. Millie helped them ferry their cases and outdoor gear across and Lizzie showed her the room she had given them. It was large and overlooked the walled garden. She could see Mr Bartholomew picking runner beans, presumably for his tea.

Chapter 4

Millie was happy to rest in the comfortable glow of the fire. She fetched the book on mining in Swaledale and re-read bits of the first chapter. It made more sense now she'd seen the remains of the workings. The next section concerned life in the dale and she soon found herself gazing into the fire, with the book on her lap, imagining the owner of this very cottage getting ready to go to work at the gill. He was dressing up against the drizzle, which seemed light but would quickly soak him to the skin. His wife was packing the children off to school. They would go across the fields, the way she had come with Matt and Andy on Sunday. Father was off up the track in his big boots, carrying his lunch in a tin box, not to be seen again for perhaps twelve hours or longer. Maybe never, if one of the fatal accidents happened on his shift.

Her imagination was getting out of hand and she tried to think about something else but the cottage seemed to be conjuring up its past. Millie got up and looked out of the window, thinking to blow these ideas away with a brisk walk up the road. It was still raining but if she dressed up in her jacket it had a hood and she wouldn't get too wet.

As she opened the front door the wind pushed against her. She walked up the track, past the Manor. Further on it became wilder and she had to work hard, leaning into the wind as she fought her way along. The hood kept falling over her eyes and so she pulled it back off her head and marched along, hair whipping round her face in wet strands. There was no-one out on the fells, only the sheep sheltering at the bottom of the stone walls. Millie struggled on. The exercise helped the stiffness in her legs, and reduced the feeling of claustrophobia she had felt in the cottage. There were no ghosts out here. Coming to the fork in the track, where the smaller path led across to Gunnerside Gill, she stopped and turned back to face the village. Smoke billowed from the cottage chimneys and the windows were lit. A cosy picture to the solitary walker with hair plastered to her face. Nevertheless, instead of returning home she continued up the main track, resolving to carry on as far as the old shooting Lodge before coming back. She marched on with her eyes fixed on the Lodge, no smoke and no lights; it was grey and uninviting in the distance. Getting hot inside her jacket, feeling sweaty under her woolly jumper, Millie wished that she hadn't worn denim jeans; they were wet and rubbed her legs as she walked.

As she got nearer, Millie could see that the Lodge had been an attractive building. It was made of stone on two floors and the main part was in good repair, with sash windows, a stone roof, chimneystack and a stout wooden front door. But to the sides of the Lodge, the outhouses lay in ruins giving a dilapidated air to the place. She approached with curiosity. Peering through the window, it was too dark to see inside. Millie tried the front door but it was locked. So, looking round to check that no-one was watching, she picked her way through the rubble of the ruined barn and sheep droppings to the back, jumping as she disturbed a sheep sheltering against the wall. It bleated and walked clumsily away. There was no door but she could see through the window into what appeared to be the kitchen. The sash shifted slightly as she leaned on it to get a better look and, pushing harder, the window opened. Millie couldn't explain why she did it, but at the time it didn't occur to her that she shouldn't. It was an empty house, no-one to object. Without thinking twice, she climbed onto the low sill and clambered in across the draining board.

The small kitchen looked very old-fashioned with a stone sink. Dirty mugs in a layer of brown water. There was a stove covered in grease but no food except a half empty jar of instant coffee and an old milk carton. The wooden table with an overflowing ashtray was covered with maps in a foreign language. Through the door was a hallway with bare boards leading to a sitting room at the front of the house. The room was bare except for an old sofa, an armchair, a dining table and odd chairs. No television or bookshelves, no telephone. The staircase went straight up from the hall with no carpet and Millie's boots echoed as she climbed them slowly, feeling her way in the dim light. The first room upstairs was the bathroom. She ran her hand through the dust on the edge of the cold enamelled bath. The bedroom had an iron frame bed with dirty grey blankets, no other furniture. An old coat hung on the back of the door and she noticed the faint smell of stale tobacco smoke from an old tin ashtray on the window sill.

The view from the window was down the valley to Mossy Bank. There was smoke coming from the chimney at the Manor. A movement on the track alerted her to the Land Rover. It was slowly heading up towards the Lodge. Running down the stairs to the kitchen, thinking that she would slip out of the window, Millie saw her muddy prints on the draining-board and panicked. What if they saw her running off? It would be so embarrassing to be caught snooping round someone's house. Perhaps she should just explain and apologise. Not knowing what to do she pushed the window shut and ran through the hall to the front door. The sound of the vehicle was drawing closer and she rushed back up the stairs, into the bedroom, but there was nowhere to hide.

The engine stopped and two doors slammed, one after the other, bang, bang; there must be at least two people. Voices shouting to one another.

'So what time does the boat leave?'

'They'll send a message when they're ready.'

One voice had a Yorkshire accent but the other sounded foreign. Millie froze on the stairs as a key was fitted into the lock and front door swung open.

'What the hell are you doing there?' the Yorkshireman shouted when he saw her.

'Cleaning.' It came out as a squeak. Millie could feel her face turning a bright red and her legs were shaking.

'What do you mean "cleaning"?' sneered foreign accent. He reminded Millie of Mr Turner, her geography teacher, tall with blond hair and metal-rimmed glasses.

'Lizzie, Mrs Banford, asked me to clean up a bit,' she stuttered, looking at the ground.

'Get down 'ere!' barked Yorkshire accent. He was dark and unshaven. He moved backwards, still staring at her and without turning round, felt for a switch high up on the wall. There was a click and all the lights came on at once.

'Let's 'ave a look at yer,' he grinned.

'I have to be going now.' Millie surprised herself with how strong she sounded, despite her legs. She had no duster or broom, how could they possibly believe her?

'Get out and stay out,' snarled foreign accent, slowly. 'I don't ever want to see you in here again. Do you understand? Or else…' On each word he moved a step closer.

Millie could hardly release the handrail, she'd been gripping it so tightly in her sweating hand. Now she nearly fell down the stairs, she was moving so fast. The two men parted as she dived for the open door and raced away. She only turned round to see if they were following when she reached the track to Gunnerside Gill. The Land Rover was still parked in front of the Lodge and there was no-one about.

Thinking that the boys might be working down there, Millie continued towards the gill. When she heard the sound of an engine she threw herself down in the bracken and it was with relief that she watched the Land Rover make its way back down the main track towards Mossy Bank. To Millie's surprise it slowed down at the bottom of the hill just as it reached the Manor. She watched waiting to see who got out, but it just sat there for several minutes before moving off into the village and out of sight.

Millie retraced the route she had taken with Matt and Andy the day before but there was no sign of them. She passed the spot where they had had lunch and eventually came to the ruined buildings and large waste heaps. She spotted the mine entrance about a metre high, a dark tunnel disappearing into the hillside. Ferns were growing round the arch and water poured out. It looked far less enticing than it had in the sunshine on the previous day. The boys had said that it wasn't safe and she had no idea where the tunnel led. Millie looked hard into the black hole until her eyes were accustomed to the dark. She could see a spot of white moving and wondered if a sheep was sheltering in there.

'Hello!' she said, thinking that it might bleat or make a noise in return. There was no sound but the white patch moved again. Millie walked gingerly into the opening. It took her about a minute to become accustomed to the dark and while she stood there she could feel icy water filling her boots. There was a form, which she was sure was a sheep, lying further into the tunnel.

'Hello,' she said again, and this time it made a sort of squeal. Millie moved about five metres further, feeling her way with her hands along the cold wet stone until it was so dark she really couldn't see at all. Reaching out she felt something soft and moving her hands over it she could tell it was alive, even though it was very cold and wet. Unsure of what to do she simply pulled and tugged and shoved the animal up the tunnel. It was hard work and she thought that it must be a very large sheep. Several times she rested and then started again, hauling it about half a metre at a time. As Millie reached the entrance and grew accustomed to the light she saw that it wasn't a sheep but a sheepdog and it had a large rock attached with rope around its neck. The dog was very frightened. It was soaking wet and must have been frozen lying in the stream of icy water pouring from the tunnel. Millie pulled the circle of thick rope over the dog's head and gave the boulder a shove with her boot so it rolled down the hill into the river, with the rope still attached to it flying round as it went.

'You poor little thing,' Millie said hugging the dog. She rubbed it vigorously and removed some of the water that saturated its hair.

'Can you walk?' she asked, but it lay still looking up at her apologetically.

Millie couldn't understand how anyone could be so cruel as to dispose of an unwanted dog that way. She knew that sheepdogs were not pets and that they had to work for their living but surely they were not got rid of like this when they were no longer useful?

If she got it back to the village, her grandmother would know what to do.

'Come on then.' Millie talked softly to the dog and tried to lift it into a standing position. Clearly it was injured and there was no alternative but to carry it. She didn't know how much it weighed but she was going to find out! If she carried on down to Gunnerside she might meet the students on the way. At least she might get a lift or there might be a vet in the village, with luck.

'OK, I'll carry you then.'

Millie picked up the sodden bundle, clutching it in front of her and was surprised to find that it was not too heavy, at first. When she got to the first stile she lifted the dog over and rested. Continuing down the track, the stops became more frequent until the village was in sight. At the bottom of the path, just before the village, she stopped once again.

'Poor old thing,' she said gently. 'What are we going to do with you? Doesn't anyone want you?'

She wondered what would happen to him. He may be badly injured and this carrying might not help... As she picked him up again she wished that Andy and Matt would miraculously appear round the corner.

There was no-one around in the village. Cars passed her at regular intervals as she sat at the edge of the road but she couldn't expect someone to give her a lift with a soaking wet dog. There was a phone box across the bridge.

'What on earth's the matter, Madeline?' Helen sounded concerned when Millie started crying into the phone.

'I found this dog, someone tried to drown it. Can you come and get us?'

'Where on earth are you, dear?'

'In Gunnerside. In the phone box.'

And that is where Helen found her, clutching a bedraggled dog, that was slowly licking her hand as tears streamed down her face.

Millie had wanted to dry the dog and give it some warm milk but Helen suggested that if it was injured the priority was to get him seen by a vet. As soon as they arrived home she rang the local surgery and was told to bring the animal in straight away. When Helen ordered Millie to stay behind and have a hot bath, she insisted on accompanying them.

The surgery was in a large house at the edge of the village. It was out of hours and the door was locked when they tried to get in. Helen rang the bell and immediately a young girl in a green uniform appeared.

'Come in, Mr Evans is expecting you,' she said with a smile. But then she looked anxiously at the dog cradled in Millie's arms.

They followed her along the corridor and into the surgery where a tall man was washing his hands at a sink in the corner. Turning as they entered, he looked at the dog and said, 'Hello, put him on the table. Is it a him?'

'Yes,' said Millie.

She explained how she had found the dog, while the vet examined him. A young man in green stood by looking intently at the animal.

'Well, I think his back leg might be broken,' he went on, 'and I'd like to do an X-ray and give him a very thorough examination. Best keep him in for a while, Helen, and find out who he is. He needs a good rest and some warmth and food. He'll be as right as rain in no time. By the way,' he added, waving an arm towards the boy, 'Have you met my new student assistant, Pete?'

'I'd like to know who he belongs to,' said Helen. 'Whoever it is should be punished for what they've tried to do.'

'I agree,' said the young man, Pete, smiling down at Millie. 'If it wasn't for your efforts he would have been dead quite soon. He must have been a weight to carry all that way.'

'Yes,' she replied, aware of the warmth in his dark brown eyes.

As they were leaving the girl assistant followed them into the car park.

'Mrs Johnson, I thought that the dog looked a bit like Bernie. I suppose Bernie is alright is he? Is he with Mrs Banford?'

'Don't worry, Jenny, I'm sure I would have recognised him if he is Bernie but I'll check with Lizzie when I get back.'

They drove in silence on the way home. Millie was contemplating the horrible way some people treat animals and hoping that the dog would be alright. As soon as they got in, Helen rang the Manor but there was no answer and they assumed that Lizzie was out somewhere. Millie had a hot bath and felt a lot better after a cup of tea and a sandwich.

At about twenty-five past seven Millie was knocking on the door of Ivy Cottage. There was quite a commotion of shouting and crying going on inside and when the door finally opened it was the thin girl, looking quite distraught.

'Come in. I'm afraid we're not quite ready yet.'

Millie followed her into the tiny cottage. It was a lovely place, beautifully furnished, except that it was cluttered with toys, clothes and all the paraphernalia of a family with small children.

'We won't be long.' She disappeared into the back of the house. There was obviously a room upstairs because Millie could hear heavy footsteps, presumably the husband's, overhead. A child was crying and whenever it became too loud the father shouted at it to stop.

Millie found a teddy bear on the chair and picked it up. She was sitting with the bear on her lap when a little girl, dressed in a flowery night-dress, looked round the door, shyly

'You've found Fifi!' she said.

'Is his name Fifi?'

'Yes, William won't go to bed without him, he's been crying for ages.'

'Why don't you take Fifi then?' Millie said, offering the bear to the little girl.

It took only a few seconds for the crying to stop. The mother now re-appeared dressed in a short pink dress that Millie thought was probably a bit over the top for a local pub.

'You look nice.'

'I 'ope it's not too posh but I like to look, well, nice when I go out with Jeff.'

Jeff appeared behind her. His black tee-shirt commemorated a heavy metal band concert some five years previously and was probably his best outfit too.

'Right then, we're off out,' he said gruffly.

'The kids will be fine. We've told them to behave themselves,' his wife added, and they were gone.

Millie sat in the overcrowded room in the sudden quiet. She needed to tidy up a bit, to introduce some order into the place, at least remove the piles of clothes from the sofa. She peered into the kitchen. On the wall nearest the door were some hooks and she hung up the coats and jackets. The shoes and a potty she placed on the floor underneath them. There. This immediately cleared the sofa and the tiny room looked twice the size. It was getting chilly and she wondered whether it was alright to light the fire. In the kitchen was a door leading into a sort of utility room, with bags of coal and kindling. It took her several attempts to start it because the newspaper was damp but finally she had a blaze that glowed pleasantly.

She hadn't brought anything to do. There was no television and no sign of any books. Millie wandered through the kitchen in search of anything of interest but the only other room on the ground floor was the bathroom. She climbed the stairs to check on the children and found them both in one of the little bedrooms. William had fallen asleep exhausted, clutching Fifi, but the girl was lying looking at her when she peered in.

'Hello,' Millie whispered.

'Hello,' said the girl quietly.

'I'm Millie, what's your name?'

'Samantha, but they call Sam.'

'Samantha's a pretty name.'

'Yes.'

'Are you OK?'

'Yes.'

'Do you want anything?'

'No.'

'Goodnight then.'

'Goodnight.' She smiled and waved as Millie turned to go back downstairs.

On the landing was a bookcase of old paperbacks and she selected a dog-eared Agatha Christie.

Half an hour later she crept up the stairs and found Samantha sleeping soundly. Hopefully this was going to be a quiet evening.

By eight-thirty Millie was nearly asleep when she heard a knock. At first she thought she had imagined it but there it was again. Leaping up, she opened the door quickly in case it got louder and woke the children. On the step was a man of about thirty, who looked as surprised as she must have done.

'Ay. Hi. I'm David Price from Low Farm.'

'Hello.'

'Mrs Banford, suggested I came t' tell thee about t'auction on Friday.'

'Right.' Millie played for time, hoping it would become clearer.

'She thowt t'kids would like to see t'sheep and cows and ...' he seemed to run out of animals rather rapidly.

'Ah. No. Sorry. I'm Millie. Madeline Sanderson.'

'Sorry?'

'I'm baby-sitting for the parents. They've gone to the pub.'

'Oh. I see.' Millie could tell that he wasn't too sure.

'Look, why don't you come in for a minute.'

Millie thought that she ought to explain who she was and it seemed odd talking on the doorstep. He followed her into the tiny room and sat down on the sofa.

'This is reet cosy,' he said. 'Tis such a cold house. Never gets t'sun you see.' He looked as though he could stand the cold. As though he spent much of his time outdoors, on the fells, tending his flocks, Millie thought.

'Doesn't it?' she asked.

'Nay. Too many trees.'

'Well I'm only visiting. My grandmother is Helen Johnson. In the village.'

'Ay, I know Helen. Well, so she's thy nan.' He examined her face. 'Don't see any family resemblance!' he said grinning.

Millie blushed.

'Does thee know these folks renting t'cottage, then?' the farmer asked.

'No. My grandmother and Lizzie offered my services. I didn't really want to do it but anyway, it's only one evening and there's nothing else to do.'

'Thee must come and see us one evening, down at t'farmhouse. Jean would like that. Someone to chat to. She gets reet fed up sometimes.'

'That would be nice.' Millie blushed again.

'Saturday then.'

''What, this Saturday?'

'Ay, or are thee busy?' He suddenly looked worried.

'No, that would be nice,' Millie lied, desperately trying to think of an excuse.

'Grand. Must be going now. Got t' feed dogs yet.' He got up.

As she opened the door, Millie remembered the reason he came.

'What did you say about the auction?' she asked.

'Auction mart at Leyburn. It's on Friday. Theers this seasons lambs and there'll be calves. Mrs Banford, said kids might like it; I'm going, so if thee want to go I can give thee a lift.'

'Thanks, I might do that.'

'Grand. Give me a call if thee do.'

'Bye,' and he strode off.

Millie made a cup of coffee but still found herself dozing over her book. She was woken by the slamming of car doors and the crunch of steps on the gravel as the revellers returned. The door crashed open and in came the husband. He marched straight through the house and into the bathroom without a word. The wife followed looking very unhappy, she had obviously been crying.

'We're back earlier than we thought.'

Millie looked at her watch, it was only a quarter to ten.

'Jeff had an argument with the barman and he asked us to leave.' She burst into tears and ran upstairs.

Jeff came out of the bathroom and was crashing about in the kitchen.

'I'll be off then,' called Millie.

There was no answer.

'Goodnight then?' she called.

Still no answer. Millie made sure that the guard was in front of the fire and let herself out.

It was a clear evening and cold but still light enough to see where she was going. As Millie made her way down to the village she wondered whether she should go back in the morning to see if everything was alright. They hadn't actually paid her and she hadn't been able to tell them about David Price's visit. She wondered, as she closed the gate and opened the door of her grandmother's cottage, whether the farmer would be capable of disposing of an unwanted sheepdog on the fell.

Chapter 5

It was only half past eight when Millie marched down the drive of Mossy Bank Manor. Helen had suggested that it might be too soon to visit the family in the holiday cottage but Millie had reminded her of how early young children woke in the morning, particularly when they're in strange surroundings. She had another reason for wanting to get there. Millie was already missing the opportunity to involve herself in the work that the students were doing and hoped that she would bump into them on their way from the Manor to the gill.

She stopped at the gate to the cottage and noticed that the curtains downstairs were drawn. Perhaps they were still in bed. She looked back down the drive and saw that their old car had gone. Maybe they'd already left for the day. Deciding to see if they were in anyway, she knocked on the door and waited, half expecting to hear the shouts and cries of last night but there was silence. Turning and leaving the little garden, instead of retracing her steps down the drive, she carried on up to the big house. She was surprised not to see Bernie rushing down to meet her but perhaps he stayed in for breakfast with Lizzie. Millie could hear the doorbell echoing in the big hall. Who would answer? If it was Lizzie, she would ask if the family had left and had the boys gone up to the gill yet? If Andy or Matt answered, she would tell them that she thought she would go for a walk and were they going in the Gunnerside direction today? Millie stood for a while waiting, puzzled that she could hear no-one, not even the dog. Several minutes passed. After ringing the bell three times, she gave up and trudged back down the drive. The Jaguar was parked in its usual place and she wondered if Lizzie was working in her garden. Uncertain whether to go round to the back of the house, she decided to give up and come back later.

She returned at eleven. The house looked the same as it had done earlier; the Jaguar was in the same spot and the curtains were still drawn in the cottage. She rang the bell for the fourth time that day and waited. No answer. This time she strode confidently to the back of the house. After all, it was late morning and more likely that Lizzie would be out there. Millie opened the wrought iron gate and stepped into the vegetable plot. She knew the kitchen door led into this part of the garden and kept close to the house until she reached it. Looking through the window she could see that the kitchen was empty. She tried the door but it was locked. There was clearly no-one around and turning to retrace her steps, she bumped into Bartholomew.

'Oh, hello. I was looking for Lizzie, I mean Mrs Banford.' Millie blushed.

'Oh ay. And did thee find 'er?' Bartholomew asked staring at her.

'No. She seems to be out.'

'Well, 'er car's 'ere.'

'Yes it is. It's been here all morning. Do you think she's alright?'

'Ay. 'Appen someone's given 'er a lift.'

'Oh, of course,' said Millie, with relief, carrying on towards the drive and then she remembered the dog.

'Mr Bartholomew,' she called. 'Would she have taken Bernie?'

'No, she leaves 'im on account of 'is being too boisterous.'

'Would he be here then?'

'Ay, she leaves 'im in t' kitchen.'

'Can we see if he's there?' she asked.

'If thee wants.' He shrugged.

They walked round to the back door and Millie peered through the window again but the gardener took a key from his pocket, opened the door and went in. The kitchen was empty. There was a wicker basket in the corner next to the Aga but there was no sign of the dog and Mr Bartholomew called out.

'Anyone at 'ome?'

There was no sound but the loud tick of the grandfather clock coming from the hall.

'Well I'm blowed. 'Appen she's taken 'im this time.'

He went into the hall and Millie followed close behind, so that when he stopped abruptly she walked straight into him. At first she couldn't see why he didn't move and squeezed between him and the door frame. The hall seemed empty but then Millie saw Lizzie lying face down at the bottom of the stairs.

'Oh Lord, is she gone?' he asked, grabbing the wall for support.

Millie didn't answer. She ran over and knelt down beside the body.

The gardener remained where he was in the doorway muttering to himself.

The old woman was lying with her arms out on either side of her body, her legs straight. Millie gently lifted the head and the old lady's glasses fell to the floor. Her head was heavy and Millie was sure that she was dead. The body was cold and she felt for a pulse, knowing it was pointless.

'Could you call the doctor?' she asked. Bartholomew didn't reply. He seemed to sense that it was too late for any assistance and stood motionless, cap in hand.

'Why don't you sit down in the kitchen,' Millie said, 'while I phone.' She led the man slowly towards a chair at the big oak table. She was too busy looking after him to think about her reactions. She didn't know the number of a doctor and automatically rang her grandmother.

'Gran? It's Millie. I'm sorry, it's Lizzie, there's been an accident. I think she's dead. What do I do?'

'Oh no! Stay there I'll get the doctor and be right over.' She rang off abruptly and Millie stood by the door staring into the garden.

'Just sit there Mr Bartholomew. Gran's coming.'

He muttered something under his breath and kept his hand over his brow, shielding his eyes from her.

Millie went back into the hall and looked once more at Lizzie's body. She had never seen anyone dead before and didn't know what to expect really. The woman looked as if she'd fallen from a great height and landed flat on the floor with her limbs spread-eagled out beside her. Could she have fallen? Surely not from the top of the stairs, unless she had jumped. Millie found a light switch. There was no sign of distress, in fact she looked very peaceful, lying tidily on the wooden floor in her blue tweed skirt and matching fine wool jumper. Looking closely she could see a trickle of blood on her forehead to the left side of her face. Had she fallen? Millie hoped that she hadn't been in pain before she died.

There was nothing she could do so she waited in the kitchen with Bartholomew and it was about ten minutes before she heard a car in the drive. Going to the front door, she saw her grandmother in a grey Morris Minor with an elderly man in tweeds. They both looked worried as they came in and the doctor went straight over to the body. Millie took Helen in to see Bartholomew and the three of them sat in silence, waiting for the doctor.

'I'm afraid she's dead. It must have happened late last night or early this morning.'

'The lights weren't on,' said Millie.

'Well early morning then.'

Millie thought of her first visit, how Lizzie must have been lying there while she had been ringing the bell. Perhaps she'd heard her. If only she had persisted.

'How did she die?' Helen asked.

'Probably caused by a heart attack. She was quite elderly you know. Is there a telephone?'

She showed him the phone in the kitchen. He talked quickly in a soft voice.

'I've rung the undertaker,' the doctor said, putting down the receiver. 'If you could stay here until they come, I'm afraid I have some urgent house calls I must make.'

'That's alright James,' said Helen and she walked with him to the front door.

'Millie I think you should see Bert home safely,' she said, when she came back.

'Yes, of course. Shall we go now Mr Bartholomew?'

The old man stood up and sat straight down again, then got up for a second time.

'I'll be all reet,' he said slowly. 'just give me time.'

They walked in silence out into the garden and round to the front of the house. They made slow progress down the drive and into the road.

Bert Bartholomew lived towards the end of the village on the opposite side of the road to her grandmother.

'Thee can leave me 'ere,' he said, stopping at the gate of a neat cottage with a well kept front garden. He said it firmly and Millie let him make his own way up the path to the door. She could see a figure looking out at them and, satisfied that someone would look after him, she turned back up towards the Manor.

When she got back her grandmother had found a plaid blanket to cover the body. They sat in the kitchen for perhaps two hours. Helen talked about Lizzie's friendship in quiet measured tones and Millie encouraged her, with questions and comments. She made a cup of tea and they sat calmly waiting for the sound of a car on the drive. When eventually it came Millie got up and walked through the hall to open the door. A discreet black van was parking outside, close to the front of the house. This was the unpleasant part. They both sat in the kitchen while the undertakers took the body away and then they came back to ask Helen to complete some paperwork. The house was finally empty. Millie was worried about the boys returning to the house unaware of what had happened.

'Shall we leave a note for Matt and Andy?' she asked her grandmother.

She found a pad of paper obviously designed as a shopping list and scribbled a note for them to come and see them at Laurel cottage.

Millie was still puzzling over why the holiday family had not returned and she looked for a key to Ivy Cottage, but there was no sign of one. When they left, Helen locked the kitchen door using Bartholomew's key, and they walked slowly back home.

'Is that it?' asked Millie as they sat in the garden that afternoon. 'Is that all that you do when someone dies?'

'No, certainly not. There are a hundred and one things to do but *we* can't do them. It's up to Lizzie's relatives. I've rung her granddaughter in Halifax and she is contacting her uncle in Edinburgh. He's a teacher and so he's probably free to spend a bit of time sorting out the arrangements.'

'Was her granddaughter very upset?' Millie asked.

'Well of course, but she is training to be a doctor so I suppose she will cope.'

'I hope Mr Bartholomew will be alright. It really was a shock for him.'

'Yes, he seemed very shaken.' Helen sounded worried.

'Gran, that dog, do you think it might be Bernie?'

'It can't be. No-one would do that to him.'

'But if it's not, where is he?'

'Mm. We'll go down to the surgery tomorrow and see.' Helen answered distractedly.

'It's all very strange. First the family disappears, then Matt and Andy, then I find the dog and then Lizzie. It's very odd.'

'I'm sure there's a simple explanation.' Helen looked tired.

'Do you think we should tell the police?' Millie tried unsuccessfully to gain her grandmother's attention but she sat gazing into the distance.

'Tell them what, Madeline?' she asked after a pause.

'That they're missing?'

'Perhaps, if they're not back in the morning.'

'I think we should see if the family has come back. They ought to be told about Lizzie. I'm going to see if they're back.' And without waiting for her grandmother's reply she jumped up and went to get her jacket.

Millie was glad to be moving, doing something, but she didn't like returning to the Manor and regretted it when she turned down the drive. The little car belonging to the family had not returned but there was a light on in Ivy Cottage behind the closed curtains and Millie decided to try again. Still there was no answer and after waiting only a short time she turned and hurried back home.

'What time is the vet's surgery this evening?' asked Millie.

'Six until seven,' said her grandmother looking at the clock. 'It's only just past six thirty, I could ring to see how he is if you like?'

'No. We'll go along.'

'It's not necessary to go all the way there, Madeline.'

'Please, I want to. Can't we go?'

'Of course, but it's been a long day. I feel exhausted. I'd like to go and have a bath.'

'We won't be long, honest.'

Millie told Helen to rest in the car while she popped into the surgery. The waiting room was full of people with dogs on leads and cats in boxes. When the young man called Pete came out to fetch the next patient, she asked him how the collie was.

'Oh, hello, I didn't recognise you,' he said with a smile. 'Did you want to see him? He's much happier now.'

As they turned down a corridor marked private and through a door into a room full of large cages, Millie thought that she must have looked a sight when she brought the dog in. Pete went over and opened a cage at floor level, gently coaxing the dog out.

'Come on then, Bernie,' he said, 'There's a good boy!'

The dog wagged his tail gently.

'Hello boy,' said Millie. Slowly the dog came over to her and licked her hand.

'It is Bernie then?' They were both crouching down over the dog and Millie stood up, embarrassed.

'Oh yes, definitely. He has an identity chip. And, of course, he answers to his name. I'm sure Mrs Banford will be pleased to see him. We tried to ring her but she isn't in yet.' He smiled at her again and she noticed his brown eyes for the second time.

'Lizzie, Mrs Banford, died today I'm afraid.' It came out all wrong.

'Oh no. But that's awful. What happened?'

'The doctor thinks it was a heart attack.' Pete looked so sympathetic that Millie was anxious she might cry. That would be too dreadful to contemplate.

'So what will happen to Bernie?' He seemed to know that she didn't want to talk about it.

'We'll look after him. I mean, Gran or someone. What are the rules, what do we do?'

'I think we'd better ask Mr Evans,' he said, putting Bernie back in his cage.

He led Millie into the surgery where the vet was peering into the mouth of a small white poodle. They stood in silence while he explained dental hygiene to a lady who obviously doted on the animal.

'Well, have you come to see the patient?' he said smiling at Millie.

'Yes but she has some bad news,' said Pete.

'It's Lizzie, she's dead,' blurted out Millie.

'Oh dear. That is bad news. I'm sorry to hear that.' The vet looked concerned.

'What will happen to Bernie?' asked Millie.

'Well I'm sure he'll find a good home.' The vet looked over his glasses at her.

'I thought, that is, if it's alright, I thought perhaps...' She felt awkward asking him.

'Would Helen be able to look after him, for the time being?' he asked. 'There's nothing broken but he's very badly bruised. He needs lots of attention and good food.'

'We can look after him. I mean I'm sure Gran will be happy to.'

'That would be perfect. Perhaps we can pop out and have a look at him at the end of the week?' Millie hoped that meant that Pete would come too.

'Yes that would be wonderful.' Millie felt that it was time to go and turned to Pete who had been standing silently by.

'Should I take him now?'

'If you'd like to. I'll get him.' And Millie followed him out, leaving the vet examining the poodle.

Bernie seemed pleased to be leaving and trotted out into the car park quite happily.

'Oh, Madeline!' Helen exclaimed when she saw the two of them but Millie explained that it was Bernie and she simply helped bundle him into the car.

'Gran, can I just have a look in the pub to see if Andy and Matt's friend is working tonight?' she asked as Helen drove towards the centre of Reeth. 'He might know where they are.'

The pub on the village green was quiet. It was just before seven and there were a few families with small children eating in the lounge. A couple of farmers were sitting through in the public bar. Millie could see a young lad behind the bar with an earring in his ear and thought he looked the most likely one.

'Hi, what can I get you?' he asked as she went towards the bar.

'Actually I'm looking for someone,' she said.

'Ah.'

'Do you happen to know Matt and Andy?'

'Oh, yeah. Is it them you want?'

'Yes.'

'Andy's over there, I've just brought him back from Lancaster.'

He was sitting at a table by himself, wiping his plate clean with a piece of bread. Millie went over and sat down opposite him.

He looked up in surprise. 'What are you doing 'ere?' he asked, peering worriedly at her.

'It's a long story. I thought I might find you here. Where's Matt?'

'In Lancaster. 'E's getting some samples analysed and 'e's seeing his supervisor tomorrow. D'you want a drink?'

'No, Gran's in the car. Would you like a lift back, we need to tell you something.'

He drained his glass, picking up his holdall and a cardboard box. Millie took his carrier bags for him.

'Cheers mate!' shouted his friend from the bar and they struggled out with the packages.

Millie opened the door of the car to put the bags in the back with Bernie. He wagged his tail when he saw her but bared his teeth and growled at Andy.

'Steady old boy.' said Andy, putting out his hand but the dog crept back into the corner continuing to growl.

'I expect he's a bit upset after his experience,' Helen said.

'Hop in the front,' said Millie, 'I'm sure he'll be alright.'

On the way back, when Helen told Andy what had happened to Lizzie, he seemed quite shaken and sat quietly.

The dog eventually calmed down but even when they reached Mossy Bank he was still looking very unhappy.

Back in the cottage Andy rang Matt to explain the situation. Helen made up their room and suggested that he collected his belongings from the Manor the following morning. Then she went off for a bath, saying she wasn't hungry. Millie had a few biscuits and a mug of hot chocolate. As she drank it she realised just how wound up she had become as the day had proceeded. She needed to talk to someone about it all and Andy was the ideal person. She started at the beginning with the family in the holiday cottage disappearing. Then she told him about how she had found Bernie. Finally, the worst bit - Lizzie.

Andy didn't say much while she was relating the story. He nodded and shook his head and muttered the odd exclamation of surprise or sympathy but even when she had finished he didn't seem to be able to think of any suitable remarks to make.

Finally he said, 'What should we do?'

'I think we should contact the police about the missing family but Gran isn't worried.'

'Pr'aps they were going anyway?'

'Maybe.'

'Millie, do you think there's a connection between the family leaving and the dog being taken?'

'No. It's probably a coincidence but maybe Bernie was out loose, if Lizzie was, well, dead. He could have got upset by her lying there and run off.'

'Was the door open?'

'No. Mr Bartholomew had to unlock it.'

'Well that doesn't make sense then, does it? Bernie couldn't 'ave gone out and locked the door!'

'But you weren't there this morning?'

'No. Nick gave us a lift back to Lancaster late last night. I wanted to go today but 'e said 'e 'ad to be back at work 'ere, so we 'ad to go yesterday. That's why Matt ain't 'ere because 'e stayed to see 'is supervisor tomorrow.'

When Helen came back down she clearly wanted to go to bed and suggested that they all had an early night. The cat wandered in expecting to settle down but left rapidly when he saw the dog lying comfortably on the rug beside the fire. Millie noticed that Bernie had relaxed visibly when Andy left the room and as she went upstairs to bed she wondered why the dog was so upset by him.

Chapter 6

By the time Millie was down in her dressing gown looking for coffee, Helen had put on some washing, had her breakfast and was sitting reading the paper.

As she kept an eye on the old toaster, which has a tendency to burn the bread, her grandmother told her how restless Bernie had been.

'Where is he now?'

'Dozing in the sitting room, bless him.'

'Perhaps you should do the same.'

'Well perhaps later. I do feel very tired, I must admit.'

Helen went up to wake Andy and before long he and Millie were ready to collect his belongings from the Manor.

As they walked through the sitting room to the front door Bernie jumped up and began barking at Andy again. Helen held him tightly while they left, promising that she would try to get some rest herself.

It was a pleasant day, fresh but warm. Only nine o'clock and it promised to be a fine day.

'That's good,' said Andy. 'I want to collect a few more samples before I go back to Uni.'

They turned into the drive. Only the Jaguar stood outside the house and the curtains of Ivy Cottage were still drawn.

'You know it's very odd that the family haven't come back,' said Millie.

'Maybe they're ill?'

'I wonder if someone should contact them. It seems strange that they went at the same time that Lizzie, well, died.' She hadn't thought about yesterday and finding the old lady, until that moment, and it gave her a rather creepy feeling to be going back into the house.

'Do you have a key, Andy?'

'Yes, she gave us each one.' He searched in his pockets and produced it, unlocking the heavy front door. There was a newspaper poking through the letter box and a brown envelope on the floor. Millie left them there. Her eyes were drawn immediately to the foot of the stairs where the body had been lying. Now it was gone and the house looked perfectly normal again.

'Where's your room?' she asked.

'Up the stairs and on the right. I won't be long.'

Millie followed him up the dark wood staircase and onto the landing. He went down the corridor to a room at the far end and Millie wandered in the opposite direction and peeped into the rooms. The one at the far end was the bathroom, rather old fashioned with brass taps and a high level cistern. The next room was very neat and rather empty, probably the spare room. Next was the master bedroom that clearly had belonged to Lizzie. The large bed was unmade, with sheets and blankets thrown back in disarray, a blue night-dress on the top. There was a tray with teapot, cup and saucer on the bedside table, as if she had only just got up. On the bow-fronted chest of drawers was a jug of wilting roses. Already some of the petals had dropped. Millie picked up the jug and carried it carefully along the corridor to the room where Andy was throwing his clothes into a holdall.

'I'm just going to tidy up Lizzie's room a bit,' she said.

'OK. I won't be long.'

She started down the stairs with the jug, watching the flowers for falling petals.

'Who the hell are you?' a man's voice boomed. She jumped and the jug flew from her hands, landing at the foot of the stairs. It smashed and there was water all over the wooden floor.

'Who are *you*?' she asked angrily, upset by the shock of his appearance and nervous of his threatening tone.

'I'm Daniel Banford. What are you doing here? You're not the usual cleaner. Where's Irene?'

'I'm Millie Johnson. My grandmother is, I mean was, a friend of Lizzie. I'm sorry, I was just tidying up.'

'We've got a cleaner in the village, there's no need for you to come in here.'

Millie was gathering up the prickly stems dabbing at the parquet tiles with a paper tissue she found in her pocket. She had gone very red and felt like bursting into tears.

'Where's a mop or a cloth to clear it up?' he demanded.

'I'll go and look for something,' she muttered and ran into the kitchen without looking at him.

She hunted around until she found a roll of kitchen towel on the inside of the larder door. Back in the hall, Daniel Banford was peering down at the floor. Millie soaked up as much of the water as she could with the paper towel while he stood watching her. She noticed Andy on the landing, hanging back, uncertain what to do. The man had obviously not seen him and Millie didn't say anything.

'That's fine. I'm sure it'll dry,' he said impatiently.

She collected up the balls of sodden paper and cleared the bits of broken china away to the kitchen.

'Shall I make some coffee?' Millie asked, trying to improve her relationship with the man who must be Lizzie's son. She didn't want him to think that she was in the house prying.

'Do you know your way around here?' he asked in surprise.

'Not really,' she said. 'I met your mother on Monday. My grandmother is a friend of hers and I'm up here on holiday. It was me who found her yesterday, with Mr Bartholomew.'

Yes, I see,' he said solemnly. He paused while he considered her reply and appeared to realise that he had been rather rude. 'Look, I'm sorry, I must have appeared rather brusque. I'm Daniel, Daniel Banford. My mother, well you know. I've come down to sort it all out. It was rather a shock, you coming down the stairs like that.'

'Yes it must have been.'

She found a jar of instant coffee and two mugs. Then she remembered Andy. She went to the kitchen door and shouted his name, but he was already on the stairs with his bags, waiting for the right moment to make his entrance.

'I'm here,' he said, with a grin.

Daniel was rather cool towards Andy. He was pleasant enough but regarded him with suspicion and seemed surprised that his own mother would provide lodgings for anyone, never mind a man wearing a gold earring. They sat rather awkwardly drinking their coffee.

'By the way,' said Daniel. 'Where is the family that is supposed to be renting the cottage? I thought there was a booking for this week.'

'There was,' said Millie, 'but I haven't seen them since Tuesday. The curtains are still drawn and the car has been gone for two days. Perhaps there's a key?'

'Must be, somewhere. I'll have to look. There's an agent that looks after the bookings, in Hawes. They'll have to sort it out. Thank goodness they pay in advance.'

Millie was going to express her concern about their welfare but he didn't attract confidences so she kept quiet and indicated to Andy that it was time to go. As she stood in the hall, waiting for him to gather his possessions together, there was a knock at the door. Daniel rushed from the kitchen.

'That'll be Penny,' he shouted with obvious relief and opened the door to a smartly dressed woman who had blonde hair sculpted into a beautifully kept style of the Princess Di type that Millie secretly admired. Her make-up was immaculate and she was dressed in a simple suit of emerald green.

'Hello dear, come in, let me take that.' He took a carrier bag from her. It bore the name of the grocer in Reeth.

'I had to wait hours to be served. Two old biddies discussing the weather!' she exclaimed with a loud sigh and stepped into the hall. Andy was just coming down the stairs again and by the look that crossed her face he could have been a seal balancing a ball on its nose, making his way into the hall.

Millie looked at Daniel and Daniel looked at Andy.

'Ah,' he said. 'Darling, this is the young man who has been staying here and this is the girl who found Mother.'

'I'm sorry,' said Millie. Having apologised for their presence, she just wanted to get away.

'How nice to meet you,' said Penny, offering her hand. Millie shook it and said quickly, 'We just came to collect Andy's things. We should be going.'

'Right,' she replied and this time her smile seemed more genuine. 'Perhaps we'll see you at the funeral?'

'Yes.' They hurried out into the sunshine and Daniel shut the door behind them without further comment. They walked in silence down the drive; there seemed little to be said. Neither had felt comfortable with Lizzie's son and daughter-in-law and Millie was embarrassed by their reaction to Andy. She hoped they didn't think his presence had anything to do with Lizzie's death.

'What are you going to do this afternoon?' she asked, wanting to change the subject.

'I thought I'd collect some water samples so that they're fairly fresh when I take them back. I'll probably take them over to Uni later. D'you want to help?'

'I would, but I'd better see what Gran's doing. She may need a hand.'

'OK.'

The offer was very attractive. It was a nice day and Millie wanted to get away from the oppressive feeling she had since visiting the Manor again. She hoped that she would have the opportunity to join him. Perhaps she could encourage her grandmother to have a sleep after lunch. When they reached Laurel Cottage it was empty except for Bernie, who barked furiously at Andy. He suggested popping down to catch Nick at his Aunt's before he went back to work, since he would need a lift back to Lancaster at some stage. Millie was sure that this was an excuse to avoid Bernie's aggressive behaviour towards him, which obviously upset Andy.

Left to her own devices, Millie went out into the tiny garden with Bernie, who was happy to lie in the sun and watch the insects. Millie pondered on what had happened in the last couple of days and puzzled over the disappearance of the family from Ivy Cottage. She wondered if she could find out by contacting the letting agents but she didn't know who they were, only that they were in Hawes. She found the telephone directory in the kitchen and looked up estate agents. There were several but one, Hope and Longthorn, listed lettings particularly. She decided to start with them.

'Good morning, Hope and Longthorn, how may we help you?' The voice was that of a young woman.

'Yes, I'd like to, that is, I want to know if you can help me. I'm trying to contact a family who are staying at Ivy Cottage in Mossy Bank.' Millie hadn't thought about what to say and she hoped that the girl didn't ask her why. Before the girl could answer she added, 'I need to contact them over a family matter.'

'Well, just a minute.'

She could hear the girl consulting someone else in the office.

'It's that family from Ivy Cottage - someone wants to talk to them. What shall I say?'

'Tell them they've gone,' replied a gruff voice.

'Hello?' she came back on the line.

'Yes?'

'I'm afraid they've gone home.'

''Oh dear,' said Millie. 'Do you know why?'

'No, I'm afraid I can't say.'

'But they're alright?'

'I don't know.'

Millie felt that she was going to get no further and, thanking the girl, put the receiver down. She went back out into the garden and sat down in a deck chair.

'Well, Bernie. Whatever next?' she said aloud. 'It's a bit outrageous making phone calls like that don't you think?'

He was stretched out in the sun and ignored her. Although she was not much further forward, she had established that the family were not lying in a pool of blood in the cottage. She had not really thought that anyway because it was so quiet and the car was gone. However, it would have been nice to have been able to take a look round the cottage. No doubt Daniel and Penny would be doing so fairly soon. She wondered where Gran had got to, since she was supposed to be catching up on her sleep. Bernie was making up for his lost rest and was totally relaxed, lying in the sunshine.

It was nearly one o' clock when Helen returned, and she was not alone. With her was a girl with long, brown, wavy hair and bright blue eyes. She was dressed in jeans and a man's chequered shirt. Bernie leapt up to greet them and to Millie's surprise it was the stranger he rushed to, wagging his tail excitedly.

'Bernie! Sweetheart!' the girl cried, kneeling down and making a fuss of him.

'This is Naomi, Millie. This is my granddaughter Millie. Sorry I'm late,' she continued. 'We've been down at Bert Bartholomew's. He came up here this morning. In fact I was having a rest when he

- 81 -

knocked. He was in such a state. He kept going on about being responsible for what happened.'

'I told him, if it's anyone's fault it's mine,' said Naomi. 'I promised Grandma I would come over for this week and next, but I got tied up and didn't make it.'

Millie realised that this must be Lizzie's granddaughter, recognising the bright blue eyes of her grandmother. She was looking up, rubbing Bernie's chest as he lay on his back with his paws in the air.

'He's a soft old thing.'

'Did Gran tell you what happened to him?' Millie asked.

'We've been with old Bert most of the morning. I popped in to thank Helen for everything she, and you, have done and Bert was here. He was so wound up that I thought we should get him back home but we were still there after about an hour. He really seems to have taken it badly. He feels that it's all his fault but I can't see why.'

Helen had gone into the kitchen and Millie used the opportunity to tell Naomi about exactly how she had found Bernie. Naomi was as mystified as she was and expressed the view that Bernie was unlikely to be wandering the hills on his own. He was devoted to his mistress and would not have gone off alone. He was not a great explorer and took no interest in sheep or rabbits.

'It's yet another mystery,' said Naomi. 'I think Grandma's death is rather odd, to be honest.' She looked up, waiting for Millie to answer, judging her by her response.

'It was rather sudden,' agreed Millie, cagily.

'Well I spoke to Dr Mellor; he's convinced that it was a heart attack and says that there's really no need for a post mortem. He should have been more interested. You saw her, how was she found?'

Millie explained how Lizzie was at the bottom of the stairs; she was dressed; she was wearing her glasses but they'd fallen off because she was lying face down.

'But she only wears reading glasses and she knows not to wear them on the stairs; it's something she's usually very careful about.'

At that moment Helen came back and they stopped their conversation as if they both understood that she would not approve of their discussions.

'I've made a few sandwiches,' she said, coming in with a plate piled high with food. Naomi grinned at Millie, she also, it seemed, had been fussed over in the same way by Lizzie.

'Did Andy collect all his things?' asked Helen.

Millie described how they had met Daniel and Penny during their visit to the Manor.

'Oh you met Dan, did you?' said Naomi in a tone which indicated that she did not get on well with her uncle. 'And his immaculate wife?'

'She did look very smart,' agreed Millie.

'I shouldn't be so rude about her, it's probably jealousy, but she always looks so perfect! They're not that well off but she is always beautifully turned out. Mind you the kids are more normal.'

'Do you have any brothers or sisters?' asked Millie.

Naomi laughed. 'Yes. A younger brother.'

'I wish I had a brother!'

'Well I can assure you, it's no picnic.'

'I don't know how you manage,' said Helen admiringly, as she passed round the sandwiches. 'Naomi is training to be a doctor you know.'

She bit into her sandwich while Helen went on about how hard her studies must be.

'Will you be staying long in Mossy Bank?' asked Millie, deliberately changing the subject.

'No. I came to help sort things out before the funeral but Dan has beaten me to it. He and Penny are arranging it all and so I am going back at the weekend.'

'Will they be here for a while?' Millie asked.

'Yes. Dan's a teacher so he's free at the moment. He'll stop at the house and Penny will be in her element sorting it all out. I really ought to go and see them soon.' She pulled a face, indicating that she did not relish the encounter.

'If you need any help, Naomi,' Helen offered.

'I will let you know, certainly. Thanks so much. It's lovely that you are here in Laurel Cottage.' She got up and gave Bernie a friendly pat. 'Bye Bernie, I'll come and see you again soon.'

Then she turned to Millie. 'Why don't you pop over later and we can continue our chat. I'll be there all afternoon. Dan and Penny are going out at about four.' She made the remark in a pointed way as if to indicate that it would be best to come after that.

'Yes I will. See you later then.'

Helen accompanied her to the front door and Millie could hear her telling Naomi that the local ladies had the catering under control. When she came back into the garden Helen smiled. 'She is such a nice girl. She'll be a wonderful doctor and she's had such a difficult time with her family.'

'It didn't sound as if she likes her young brother very much.'

'Well, she had a lot of problems with him. Drink and drugs. She virtually brought him up after her parents died. She's helped him through rehabilitation, is that what they call it?'

'How dreadful.'

There was a noise in the kitchen and Bernie jumped up. Andy had come back. Expertly Helen grabbed the plate of sandwiches and took them inside, trapping Bernie in the garden. When she returned Helen reported that Andy would eat inside and that he had persuaded Nick to take him back to the university but he would not go until the following day. This meant that he wouldn't be collecting samples today but he would be doing a map of Gunnerside gill with the sampling points on to save time tomorrow and that she would be welcome to come.

'That would be nice,' said Millie looking at her grandmother's reaction.

'You go. I'm going to try and catch up on my sleep this afternoon and this time I'll ignore the doorbell!'

Millie and Andy were soon making their way up the track towards the mines. She wanted to escape from the confusing number of questions that worried her, none of which had been answered so far. How did Bernie end up in the tunnel? Did Lizzie die of natural causes? Why did the family leave Ivy Cottage? And where was Matt? She had learnt that often one had to be patient in order to solve problems. She decided that this afternoon would be a break from it all and she threw herself into the work in hand. Andy wanted to make a map of Gunnerside Gill with all the mine workings located on it. They had to go up to the top and work down so it was almost two-thirty before they began walking down the track along the side of the gill.

As Andy marked on the map the workings on either side of the stream, they decided where the best sampling points were to monitor any sources of pollution. Next time Millie looked at her watch it was a quarter to four and they were only about half way down the gill.

'Have you got to get back?' asked Andy. He looked disappointed.

'No, not really. I said I'd see Lizzie's granddaughter but I can go any time.'

In fact Millie was enjoying her afternoon and did not want to cut it short. She would go later when they got back. The sun was still high in the sky and there was no wind on the fells so it was still very warm. It was supposed to be a holiday after all, she told herself, sitting down on a clump of soft grass to watch Andy making some additions to the sketch map.

'Will you get all the sampling done tomorrow?' she asked.

'I think so. Nick is going to give me a hand. He's taking me back to Lancaster with the samples as soon as they're collected.'

'That's nice of him.'

'Yes, it is really. I don't know why he's always so keen to go back to Uni.'

'Perhaps he still has friends there.'

'Yeah.'

'When are you coming back?'

'As soon as Nick does. Probably on Saturday morning early. He works weekends.'

'Will you see Matt there?' Millie was curious why he had disappeared off the scene.

'If he's there. I expect so. It's time he came back. Anyway we best be getting on,' he said, picking up his rucksack. Millie jumped up and followed.

They continued to work systematically right the way down the gill to Gunnerside itself. By then it was nearly six o'clock but still a pleasant summer evening and there were several families sitting outside the pub, enjoying the last few hours of the day, as they walked by on the way to Mossy Bank.

When they reached the cottage Helen was up and about, having spent the afternoon resting. She shut Bernie in the kitchen and the three of them were able to eat together. Helen was interested to hear about their afternoon and they spent much of the evening talking about the lead mines and Andy's project. Millie's enthusiasm for the mines had been rekindled by being up the gill again and she sat reflecting that she wanted more than anything else to be able to work on a project like Andy was doing. Was it such a foolish idea? She wasn't sure but she didn't say anything aloud because she thought it might be.

As they were going to bed, Helen asked her if she had popped in to see Naomi on her way back. Millie had a pang of conscience when she realised that she had forgotten but told her grandmother that it had only been a casual invitation. She would go the following morning, Millie said.

Chapter 7

The telephone rang early and Millie could hear her grandmother talking excitedly downstairs, then footsteps on the stairs and the bedroom door burst open.

'That was young David from the farm. He said you wanted to go to the auction mart in Leyburn.'

'Yes.'

'Well, he's leaving in about fifteen minutes and he'll come up for you. I'll get you some toast.'

Millie looked at her watch. It was just after eight.

Ten minutes later she was munching toast and taking gulps of hot tea. Helen was giving her a list of things that she wanted from the market including cheese and a scrubbing brush. Millie grabbed her rucksack and opened the front door just as an old Land Rover turned into the lane. It was pulling a trailer and she could see the anxious black faces of the sheep inside.

David leant over to open the passenger door and as she climbed in she met the gaze of a boy aged about nine or ten.

'Hello,' she said to David.

'Morning. Sorry about t' rush but thee said thee wanted to come. Justin decided he did too, so I reckoned thee'd keep each other company.'

'Fine.' Millie thought it sounded more like baby sitting but wasn't too concerned. Justin didn't look as if he needed much supervision. He glowered at her from under his baseball cap and continued to flick through some football cards.

David manoeuvred the Land Rover and trailer round in the narrow lane and they sped off along the dale. He was obviously used to the lanes and Millie found herself hanging on to the side of her seat anxiously. The route took them through Reeth and on to Grinton, over the large bridge and onto a narrower road which began to rise up over the moors. It was a clear morning and the views across the dales impressed her.

'Are you selling some sheep today?'

'Well, I haven't brought 'em for t' ride!' said David.

It was meant as a joke, she knew, but the tone suggested that he didn't suffer fools gladly.

'What sort of price do they fetch?' she asked.

'Well enough.'

It was going to be hard work.

'Are you enjoying the school holidays?' This time she aimed her question at the boy, hoping that he would be more chatty.

'Not really.'

'Have you been farming long?' One last attempt with David before she gave up.

'Since I were a lad. My father owned the farm and his father before him.'

'When did you take it over?'

'When 'e died. It must be ten year now. My brother wasn't keen, he drives a wagon for the quarry. When I took it over it were really on its last legs, the farm. You've got to be on the ball in farming these days. No good being a small fry, you've got to think big.'

'So you've expanded it since then?'

'Yes. I've got more sheep and gone into cattle. I bought some meadows when a farm were sold and then I got some land close by, I'm gradually expanding.'

He continued to tell her enthusiastically about his plans to get more acres as they became available.

Millie remembered Lizzie telling her that David farmed her land and she wondered if David's plans included that. She didn't like to ask directly and he didn't mention it.

Leyburn was busy when they arrived and they queued for their turn to unload the sheep. There were Land Rovers and trailers everywhere and animals were being herded into pens. Once David's sheep were safely unloaded he started chatting to the men working in the market and to other farmers as they arrived. Justin stood with him, so Millie wandered round watching the activity as the stock arrived. She was leaning against the railings of a sheep pen, watching a farmer persuading his animals to stay while he shut the gate, when David returned with his son trailing behind him.

'Would you keep an eye on this young 'un while I attend to some business?' and he was off through the doorway leaving Justin looking grim-faced.

'What would you like to do?'

'Nowt.'

'Well, I've got to get some shopping for Gran, why don't we go into town and see what there is in the market?'

They walked past the cars queuing to find a space, to the town square filled with people swarming around the stalls. There was everything from fruit and vegetables, to clothes and carpets. Millie spotted an ice-cream van and suggested that Justin might like one. His face expressed assent, which was as well since he remained silent. He cheered up with a '99' in his hand and Millie was able to buy the items on her grandmother's list.

'I'd die for a cup of coffee,' she said, looking round the square.

'There's a café at the auction,' said Justin.

'Ah.' Millie imagined the type of place it might be and hesitated. It seemed churlish to reject Justin's suggestion and she thought that it might be interesting to sit and listen to the farmers' chatter. Millie packed her purchases in the rucksack and they went back up to the auction building. The café was clean and bright with chequered cloths on the tables and paper napkins. A cheerful woman gave her a coffee.

'Hello Justin, are you with your Dad today?'

Millie felt that she should explain who she was but the woman carried on talking to the boy, asking if David was selling or buying.

'I'll expect we'll see him later,' the woman said, giving Millie a smile.

There were one or two farmers sitting talking but mostly they were busy inside the auction, so Millie and Justin sat looking at each other as the boy drank his cola and consumed a large chocolate biscuit.

When she had finished her coffee, Millie bought some more chocolate bars as insurance against Justin's continued good humour and he showed her where the auction rings were. They walked past the pens where the animals stood patiently waiting their turn and into a hall where sheep were being herded into position at the side of the ring. There were perhaps forty or fifty people looking on. They were nearly all men, middle-aged or elderly. The exceptions were easy to spot, there were two mothers with their young charges in push chairs, a bright young girl with curly red hair and tight blue jeans carrying a baby and two young men standing at the edge of the ring, talking earnestly together. Everyone seemed to be in deep conversation. Farmers, leaning on their tall sticks comparing notes on each other's stock, wore a uniform of chequered shirt, braces, cloth cap and working trousers of brown or green. There were variations, trilbies instead of caps or an absence of braces, but here were farmers enjoying their work and taking the opportunity for a bit of gossip and light-hearted banter.

Millie climbed up the steep tiered rows and sat on a small bench at the top with Justin beside her. Some of the farmers stood, some sat on the benches and others, presumably those buying today, stood at the edge of the ring leaning over the high rail. The auction ring itself was perhaps thirty feet in diameter. At the back was an opening large enough for two people to sit at the auctioneer's desk overseeing the proceedings. It was at a height that meant that someone communicating with the auctioneer could just see over the desk. With gateways on both sides like the wings of a theatre stage, the expectant atmosphere resembled that of an audience waiting for the performance to begin. Millie looked at her watch. It was almost eleven o' clock. She noticed that several men were already taking up their positions inside the ring and the sheep were waiting to one side. A moment later the auctioneer took his seat and a woman sat down beside him. Although there was a certain amount of anticipation among the assembly, the talking continued and Millie noticed that the constant level of chatter did not cease throughout the auction.

The first entrant was a calf, all alone. It came in hesitantly and stood looking puzzled. The auctioneer started the bidding and a man chivvied the calf around the ring using a thin stick, in a gentle fashion, to keep it moving. Try as she might, Millie saw no-one bidding. Clearly someone was because soon the calf had been sold and it was herded off through an exit. Several more were sold in succession and then ten sheep came tumbling into the ring as the gate to the left of the auctioneer swung open. As each new batch of animals entered the ring, they were driven round by the owner, using his or her stick to keep them moving and looking lively.

She noticed David standing with a group of farmers. He was watching the sale and taking an interest in each lot that appeared. Finally it was his turn. As six sheep were hustled into the ring, he joined them and moved about like a ringmaster. The auctioneer started his patter and the figures went up. Millie couldn't make out the amount, it sounded too much for one sheep but not enough for six. She whispered to Justin but he was busy with his second chocolate bar. The bidding eventually stopped and someone, Millie had no idea who had bought them.

Millie assumed that David would come and find them when he was ready to leave and so she sat quite happily watching the proceedings. She liked observing the farmers who were busy scrutinising their neighbours' sheep, remarking on the prices they reached, comparing notes amongst themselves. Some of the watchers had changed and Millie saw three men who didn't fit her stereotype. None had chequered shirts or cloth caps, but all were dressed in denim trousers and polo shirts. They were deep in discussion, ignoring what was happening in the ring.

The change that took place when the next lot came in was quite noticeable. The three men almost stood to attention. Five sheep were being moved around by their owner, a large farmer with a red face and a beer belly. Millie could tell that the blond man in the group of three was bidding. The figures increased quickly and she sensed that even some of the farmers were stopping mid-conversation to watch the progress. She still couldn't follow the figures but she could tell from the atmosphere in the hall that these sheep were getting a higher than normal price. As the blond man turned to talk excitedly to his friends, she realised it was the foreigner that had been so aggressive when he found her in the shooting Lodge. Millie made a mental note to ask David about him afterwards. She looked round but there was no sign of him and the three men were heading for the door.

'Come on,' she said briskly, 'let's see if we can see your Dad,' and grabbing Justin's hand she jumped down the wooden tiers and almost ran out of the hall.

The three men had gone off towards the pens and now stood talking in a tight group. Millie walked casually past but they lowered their voices and she couldn't hear what they were saying. She saw the Yorkshireman was in the group as well and slowed down in case they recognised her.

Justin was running towards his father.

'Well that was all reet,' he said and Millie could tell that he was pleased with the price he had got for his sheep.

'I couldn't make out exactly how much the sheep were selling for but there were five that seemed to get more than the usual price in there,' she said, pointing towards the other ring.

'Ay. It's the foreign buyers, they always push the price up.'

'But why?'

'I don't reetly know. They know what they want but I can't say that I can see it.'

'I think it was that man behind us, the blond one talking to two others in jeans.' She hoped that David would identify them.

'Oh the Dutchman. He's a regular. Small batches but regular. Always pays over t'odds.'

'Is he a farmer then?'

'I only know 'im from the shooting, He brings a party over now and then. I find beaters for 'im.'

'Does he stay at the Lodge on the fell?' Millie's heart was beating fast.

'Not stay. I reckon theer in the best hotels but they use it when theer up in the day.'

'Can we go now?' asked Justin, who had obviously had enough.

'In a minute, lad. I've just got to see old Sam from Keld about some land 'e's letting,' and David disappeared back in the direction of the rings, leaving the reluctant companions alone once more.

Millie had a strong desire for more information about the men standing not far away. She wandered slowly back towards them, keeping her head turned away and looking with deep interest at the cows as she walked along.

'Oh look, Justin, isn't that a lovely cow?'

'It's a bullock.'

'Oh yes, well it's a lovely colour. And this one, hasn't he got lovely eyes?'

She took her camera from her rucksack, a difficult task since she couldn't put it on the floor, which was covered with urine from the animals.

'Smile!' she took photographs of the animals and of the boy, trying to alter the angle gradually to include the group of men who were still deep in conversation. Justin was not co-operative but she continued until she was sure that she had managed to get part of the group into one or two shots. The men didn't take any notice of her and she moved along the rails, edging closer, slowly, until she could, if she listened very hard, catch a few words and phrases.

'..tomorrow... earlier the better...' said one, in a Yorkshire accent.

'wait... routes not clear... customs...' He sounded foreign.

'settled...(or was it Settle?).....complete...next time....' The Dutchman. He definitely had an accent.

'We're going now.' It was Justin. David was waving from the door that led outside. 'Come on,' and he was off.

Millie could hardly stay and listen, although she desperately wanted to. There was nothing odd about their conversation, presumably they were arranging the transportation of their five sheep.

As she reached the door she looked back and saw that the trio had been joined by someone else. A young man was shaking hands with the Dutchman and smiling. He seemed familiar and she suddenly realised it was the student assistant from the vet's, the one with the brown eyes. Surely he wasn't part of the gang?

'Come on,' shouted Justin insistently and she followed them out to the Land Rover.

They sat in silence on the way back over the moors until Millie could not contain her curiosity any longer.

'I suppose,' she announced, 'the man who bought those five sheep is from Holland.'

'Ay.' said David.

'I suppose,' she continued, 'he must take the sheep back to Holland.'

'Ay,' said David, 'I suppose so.'

'And how would he do that?'

'In a trailer, same as I do.' David sounded fed up with her questioning.

She sat and considered the matter. Why did she have such an odd feeling about this Dutchman and his comings and goings? He buys sheep, he organises shooting parties and the uses the Lodge. And he wanted to buy the Lodge from Lizzie, in fact he was quite aggressive about it. What had she said? That he had been quite persistent and made her feel quite uncomfortable. Perhaps Millie was overreacting but maybe she was right to be curious about him.

As they drove across Grinton Moor, she could see the shooting butts in a line across the hill. When did the season start? The glorious twelfth?

'Is it the start of the shooting season tomorrow?' she asked.

'Ay, but theers not a lot goes on until later in the year.'

'Do you shoot?'

'No, only rabbits. Not in that league. I just do t'beating if they need a hand.' He sounded slightly bitter and she was sure that he would like to be in that league. He was an ambitious man.

'Perhaps one day,' she said.

'We'll see.'

When she got out of the Land Rover Justin surprised her by thanking her for the sweets. She in turn thanked David and said that she supposed they would meet at Lizzie's funeral on Monday but he corrected her.

'No. Thee's coming to us tomorrow night.'

She remembered the night when she had been baby-sitting and David had come to ask about the auction. He had suggested dinner then and she had forgotten.

'Of course!' she said, blushing. 'What time should I come?'

'Oh, about eight, I suppose. Bye!' and with that he turned the vehicle round and disappeared back down the lane.

The front door of Laurel Cottage was open and in the small sitting room Helen, Naomi and Andy were sitting eating sandwiches and drinking tea.

'Hello Millie,' said her grandmother, jumping up from her chair, 'Have you had anything to eat? No? You must be starving.' She rushed off and came back with a plate, cup and saucer.

'There's cheese or ham. Sit down. I'll get you some tea.'

'There's no rush, Gran. I'll survive for a minute or two.' Millie smiled, embarrassed, at the other two, who made meaningful faces at her. They both had grandmothers, although of course Naomi didn't now and perhaps would miss the one person who never stopped treating her as a child.

'Did you enjoy the auction?' asked Naomi. 'I used to go when Grandad was selling his lambs on. I don't suppose it's changed much.'

Millie told them all about the auction and its atmosphere. Andy had not been there himself and by the time Millie had finished describing it both agreed they should visit it sometime.

'Have you decided what you're doing this weekend, Andy?' Millie asked.

'Oh nothing much,' replied Andy, going almost as red as his hair.

Millie thought of the glorious twelfth. He wouldn't be shooting but beating, perhaps. As vegetarians, surely the students wouldn't take part in any of it - or was that why he was so embarrassed?

'And what about you Naomi?' she asked to save Andy from further probing, 'Will you be staying here over the weekend?'

'No, unfortunately, I have to go back to get some work done. But I have to go into Hawes this afternoon, Millie,' she said with a meaningful look at her. 'You would like to come, wouldn't you?'

'Oh yes,' she replied, wondering what was going on.

'Right. I'll go back home and get the car. See you in about twenty minutes.' She got up and thanked Helen for the lunch.

'It's nothing, dear. It's nice to see you again.'

When her grandmother had gone into the kitchen, Millie asked Andy if he had heard from Matt. She knew that he hadn't but she wanted to know what was happening.

'No. It's as if 'e's disappeared off the face of the earth. That's why I want to go back if 'e's not here tomorrow. I was sure 'e'd have come by now.'

'Can you tell me what it is that you're doing tomorrow?'

Andy blushed again.

'Is it to do with the start of the shooting?'

He blushed even more. 'I'd rather not say.'

'That's OK, I just wondered, I'm sorry - I shouldn't have been so nosy.'

'I would tell you if I could but I shouldn't talk about it.'

'OK.'

Millie emptied her rucksack in the kitchen and prepared for her trip to Hawes. It involved further requests for provisions from her grandmother. This time it was groceries, which required a single stop in one small supermarket, Helen assured her, as she climbed into Naomi's car.

'I'm sorry about the mystery,' began Naomi as they left the village. 'I popped into Ivy Cottage this morning and it really looks as though the family left in a hurry. It got me thinking about Grandma, how they left the same night or day that she died. It sounded a bit melodramatic to talk about in front of Helen but I thought we should go and see the agents, see if they can help us.'

Millie was taken aback. On one hand this was exactly what she wished to do herself but couldn't and on the other, she had already contacted the agent. They wouldn't recognise her but they might mention that someone else had been enquiring. Should she admit to Naomi that she had been interfering?

'Look, it sounds awful to say but I did try to find out the other day.'

'What?' Naomi turned round at her in surprise and then looked quickly back at the narrow lane.

'I'm sorry, I shouldn't have.'

'No - what happened? What did they say?'

Millie explained how she rang them up and asked about the family.

'Well, at least we know that they are safe and we should be able to get their address to find out more. I could suggest that we are considering a rebate or something.'

'So you don't mind about me interfering?'

'Of course not. It's a relief to know that you found it odd. I was beginning to think that I was over-reacting. I spoke to Grandma's GP and he sees no cause for believing that it was anything other than a heart attack. I began to think I was going mad, trying to find an alternative to natural causes,' she laughed. 'Anyway, it's sensible to check all possibilities, don't you think?'

The road to Hawes was as impressive as the route to Leyburn. It wound up a valley with thin waterfalls glinting in the sunlight on either side. Once over the top, they dropped down into Wensleydale and the bustle of Hawes. Parking at the top of the town, Naomi led the way through the shoppers in the main street and along to the estate agents. The girl on the desk looked about sixteen and Millie recognised her voice.

'Good morning. Can I help you?' she asked.

'Yes. My name is Naomi Carter. My grandmother has just died and when I was sorting out her belongings I noticed that I had not found any references to the letting of Ivy Cottage over this summer. Do you have a bookings list or something similar that I can use to work out what use has been made of the property?'

The girl sat motionless throughout Naomi's speech.

'Right,' she said and then paused while she worked out what to do.

'Just a minute.' They heard her in the next room. 'Someone about Ivy Cottage,' was the brief message she gave.

A man appeared in the doorway and smiled.

'Can I help you?'

Naomi gave her introduction again. This time she embellished it, emphasising the need for full details for tax purposes.

'Of course,' he said. 'Cheryl, get the file for Ivy Cottage please.' And the girl disappeared behind the desk and began rifling through the filing drawers.

Using the opportunity of talking to someone in authority, Naomi continued, 'I notice that there is no-one in the cottage now.'

'Is there not? Perhaps it wasn't booked this week.'

'Oh I think it was,' she said.

'Well, we can check when we have the file. Have you found it yet, Cheryl?'

Cheryl produced a well-worn file containing a pile of papers. The agent flicked through them, pulled out a sheet and read it carefully.

'These are our summer bookings for this year. It should be occupied by the Barnes family, husband, wife and two children, both under twelve.'

He went over to the photocopier and made a copy which he gave to Naomi.

'They left, early,' Cheryl said importantly. 'She wanted a refund.'

'Did she say why she left?' asked Naomi.

'Oh no,' replied Cheryl.

Naomi took the list and checked it. It obviously had all the information she wanted because she said, 'Well, thank you so much for your help,' and then she turned to leave.

'I told her we didn't do refunds,' was Cheryl's parting comment as they left.

'Did it have the address on the list?' asked Millie as soon as they were out in the street.

'Yes and telephone numbers. We can ring as soon as we get back home.'

'I've got shopping to do first, if that's alright?' said Millie and they arranged to meet up in half an hour. Naomi had to go to the bank anyway.

Millie liked Hawes. It was a busy market town with shops, pubs and cafés, all bustling with locals and visitors jostling together down the narrow pavements. She found the grocer, who stocked a variety of local cheeses that she never saw at home, including Swaledale cheese made from cows' milk and from ewes' milk. She had ten minutes to spare after shopping and she browsed in the antiquarian book shop, hoping to find something on the lead mines. Unsuccessful, she dragged herself away and met Naomi in the teashop they had selected earlier.

As they sat with tea and scones, Millie mentioned Bernie's lucky escape again.

'I can't imagine why anyone would want to take a dog half way up the gill to drown him,' Naomi said. 'Why not dump him in the nearest rain barrel? It is a strange coincidence.'

'I wondered if someone wanted him out the way because he could identify...' Millie hesitated. Until now they had talked about the possibility of Lizzie not dying of a heart attack. Neither of them had actually said what the alternative might be. Millie couldn't say 'your grandmother's killer.' It was ridiculous but what was the alternative?

'I know what you mean,' said Naomi. 'Let's pay the bill and get out of here. We need to discuss this rationally.'

They didn't talk until they were back in the car and had driven up to the open fell. Naomi parked the car at the viewing point and stopped the engine. There was another car parked some distance away and an elderly couple were unpacking their picnic table and chairs.

Naomi began, 'Right. Let's think about what we know and try to make some sense of it.'

'Right,' said Millie.

'First, Grandma is dead and the GP says it's a heart attack. Do we have any evidence of that? No. What did you see?'

'She was at the bottom of the stairs on her front. She was wearing glasses and she was dressed.'

'OK, so that's the first problem. Why was she wearing her glasses, her reading glasses, coming down stairs?'

'Perhaps she was reading and was disturbed, came down to open the front door...'

'Was the door bolted?'

'Yes.'

'OK. So she hadn't let anyone in that morning?'

'Presumably not.'

'Was the back door locked?'

'Yes. We had to open it with Mr Bartholomew's key.'

'So it wasn't bolted?'

'No, why?'

'Because at night she always bolts back and front doors, she always has.'

'So the back door must have been unbolted at some stage, perhaps to let Bernie out! And then Bernie is out on the hills...'

'Except that Bernie will not go outside the garden without Grandma and she wouldn't lock him out.'

'Oh.'

'Was the key in the back door when you arrived?'

'No, there was no key there.'

'I don't understand it.' Naomi sat for some time in silence. 'What about these students? The one I met at lunch seemed nice enough but could they be involved in this?'

'No, I'm sure. They'd gone to Lancaster the night before.'

This was the other thing which coincided but she dared not mention that to Naomi. She had not seen Matt since then. Granted, Andy had come back but not Matt. Surely this was just an unfortunate coincidence?

They fell silent. The elderly couple were boiling their kettle on a camping gas stove and the woman unpacked plates and cups onto the table.

'Oh well, let's phone the Barnes family,' said Naomi, with a sigh as she started the engine again. A few spots of rain landed on the windscreen and as they reversed back onto the road to Swaledale, the couple were busy packing everything into their car again.

By the time they reached Mossy Bank the rain had settled in. Naomi suggested they rang from the Manor and Millie felt a twinge of expectation as they turned into the drive. Only the Jaguar was parked there.

'Is your uncle around?' asked Millie.

'Oh God, yes and his wife. I don't know why I find them so difficult to cope with but I do. Fortunately they've gone off to Skipton to see the family solicitor today. Dan's hoping to find out what share he's getting of the estate.'

The phone was in the lounge and Millie perched on the edge of the settee as Naomi relaxed in an arm chair with the phone on the table next to her. She sat for a few moments and then said, 'Hello.' She looked puzzled and repeated 'Hello,' and after a pause she gave Millie an exasperated look, 'I think it's one of the kids.' Then she asked 'Can I speak to Mummy?'

'Hello Mrs Barnes. My name is Naomi Carter. You booked Ivy Cottage this week, it belongs, belonged, to my grandmother... I know... Yes, I know... No, it's alright but I wondered, well, I wondered what the reason was. Did you not like the cottage? I see. Your husband didn't like it? Ah, so it wasn't the cottage, then?' There was a long pause. 'No, I'm sorry, as the girl said, they don't do refunds. One other thing, can you tell me what time you left? About twelve? I see. Thank you. Goodbye.'

'It seems,' said Naomi, putting down the receiver, 'that her husband didn't like the local hospitality. Something about some men in the pub being heavy?'

'Oh yes, she told me about that. Seems he was asked to leave a pub in Askrigg.'

'Well, whatever it was, it upset him so much that he didn't want to stay. Dragged them all out at midnight and drove home. Apparently he's still like a bear with a sore head.'

'I feel sorry for her and the kids,' said Millie.

'Well then, they can be eliminated from our enquiries I think, don't you?'

'I guess so,' agreed Millie. She was secretly disappointed because it did not help clarify their unanswered questions, but it did demonstrate one coincidence and perhaps the other disappearing figure was also a coincidence - Matt.

'I don't suppose Grandma knew they'd gone,' said Naomi. 'The light was still on in the cottage and the curtains drawn.'

'Wouldn't she have heard the car leave?'

'Not from the back of the house where her bedroom is.'

'Would Bernie bark?'

'I don't know. I suppose he was used to strangers coming and going at the cottage. I would have thought he might have done at a car leaving at midnight.'

'You know we're no further forward after all this.'

'Yes we are. The next thing to investigate is the students. You can do that while I'm away this weekend. It seems very suspicious that they went off that same night.'

'I've told you, they both went back to Lancaster the night before with their friend who has a car.'

'Well at least you can find out why one of them hasn't come back!'

'I'll try, I promise.'

When Millie left the Manor she felt depressed. It seemed that a friend was under suspicion and she didn't know how she would be able to grill Andy about it. As it turned out she didn't have an opportunity. He left the house soon after she returned and didn't come back until very late in the evening.

Chapter 8

It was the first evening that they had spent together alone since Lizzie's death and Millie was pleased to have the opportunity to sit quietly with her grandmother and chat about what had happened in the last few days. Bernie was lying on the rug and appeared to have settled into his new surroundings.

'Is he feeling better, do you think?' Millie asked.

'I think so. That young Pete who works with the vet rang yesterday to ask how Bernie is and suggested that he might drop in on Sunday to see him. I must say Bernie does seem more relaxed now that the house is emptier.'

Millie remembered how impressed she had been by the vet's assistant in his green scrubs, at a time when she was feeling particularly vulnerable.

'Bernie was pleased to see Naomi,' said Helen. 'I wondered if she might like to have him, although I suppose she has rather a busy life.'

'You could ask her. But wouldn't you like to keep him yourself?'

'Oh Millie, I don't know. He does seem to have settled in here, I must say.'

'Well, we'll see.'

'I think Naomi is marvellous, the way she is coping. Her grandmother was always so proud of her but she seems so, so competent.'

And I suppose I'm not, thought Millie. 'Did she say what time the funeral is on Monday?' she asked.

'Yes, twelve o' clock. A sensible time. We can have lunch afterwards and it's not too late for people travelling back. I was wondering if you had anything suitable to wear? I've probably got something you can borrow.'

'Thanks Gran.' Millie certainly hadn't got anything suitable herself. Her clothes were strictly holiday style. She hadn't expected to attend a funeral. It was almost one week since she had arrived in the village and it felt as though she had been here for months. Looking back she considered what had taken place and wondered how it all fitted together. She would have liked to have discussed the various aspects with her grandmother but she felt inhibited, partly worried that it would upset her but more because she actually wanted to forget about it all herself for one evening. What had started as an intriguing mystery with puzzles to solve was now a serious concern growing more worrying by the day.

'So what are the plans for tomorrow?' Millie asked, thinking that a day out might be just the thing she needed.

'I'm going to do some cooking for Monday.'

'Aren't they having caterers?'

'No, I told you, we're all going to contribute. Lizzie would have done the same. In fact she did. When Eileen died last month, it was Lizzie who suggested that we all did the food, as a kind of gesture really. I'd like to pop into Reeth to get some bits but after that I'll be busy in the kitchen.'

'Would you like some help?'

'Perhaps. If you're not busy. You seem to have been out and about a lot this week.'

'I'm sorry Gran. There seems to have been a lot going on.'

'Oh don't be silly. I'm glad to see you busy. It makes a nice change and I don't need you to myself. Anyway, there is another two weeks yet.'

Millie agreed but thought to herself that two weeks was not long at all.

'Just a minute!' said Helen jumping up so quickly that she made Bernie start. 'I've got an idea.'

She went upstairs and Millie heard her moving about in the bedroom overhead. She re-appeared with a dress on a hanger. It was grey, it had short sleeves and hung loosely with a drop waist.

'This is ideal,' she said, 'I bought it in Richmond but it's far too young for me.'

Millie thought it looked rather old-fashioned for her.

'Try it on, Millie.'

She went up to her room and changed into it. Even standing in her woolly socks it looked nice. She felt that it suited her and walked downstairs to show it to her grandmother.

'Oh yes, that's lovely. I thought it might do. I'm not sure about the socks though!'

Bernie moved stiffly over to where she stood, sniffed her feet and wagged his tail.

'He obviously approves,' she added. 'I expect Fiona would approve as well. She must take an interest in clothes, hers and yours.'

'She likes the fashionable stuff, although she doesn't criticise what I wear.'

'I think that's nice. Nowadays I think parents and children have a different kind of relationship. It was different when your mother was young.'

'Was it?'

'Of course. We only had the example of our parents and that was almost Victorian, wasn't it? Children should be seen and not heard. You weren't expected to question anything. Do as I say, not as I do.

'Yes. I remember that. Grandad used to say, "When you're grown up you'll be able to do what you want but now you must do as you're told." I used to hate that.'

'I don't think it made children any better behaved then. I think they grow up more quickly now, that's all.'

Bernie had settled down on Millie's feet and he jumped up as she moved to go upstairs to change out of the dress.

'I believe he's much happier now,' said Helen. 'He may even be able to go out and about soon. How about some tea then Bernie?' and she moved towards the kitchen with the dog following closely behind.

As she changed back into her jeans, Millie could hear her grandmother chatting to Bernie while she opened the tin of dog food.

So the preparation of the evening meal began. They opened a bottle of wine and talked about old times, when her mother was alive. Millie found that she was able to tell her grandmother about how she had felt growing up, her relationship with her mother and how she missed her. She also found herself talking more openly about Fiona and how she didn't really like her. How she'd be glad when she could finish college and leave home.

'And what are you going to do in the future?' asked Helen.

'I know it sounds silly but I really would like to do the sort of thing that Andy and Matt do, research. I could get a degree.'

'Yes,' said Helen, thoughtfully. 'You'll have to work hard for that. Your father needs to pay more attention to your education and less to that Fiona.'

Millie kept to safer topics during the rest of the evening. They discussed the plans for the following day, including Millie's dinner party with David and Jean. Helen didn't know Jean well but thought that she was pleasant enough. They decided to make an early start and went to bed at half past ten.

They were in Reeth by nine o'clock but there was already a line of customers outside the bakery as they drove into the centre of the village.

'I'll go and queue. You stay and keep Bernie company,' ordered Helen.

'OK.' Millie was happy to sit in the car and watch the world go by. And it seemed as if the world *was* going by this morning. There were vans and Land Rovers driving through the village at high speed and, judging by their dress, they were either shooting or beating. There were lads hanging out of the backs of Land Rovers and other vehicles. She noticed a police car parked on the green with two policemen sitting inside. Even more curiously, a large minibus arrived full of uniformed police officers and this drew up beside the patrol car. Then a van drove slowly past, full of young men, some with handkerchiefs covering the lower parts of their faces, like cowboys. She couldn't believe her eyes. The van speeded up when the driver spotted the police and an unmarked car parked beside the police car, pulled out and followed them down the road. Clearly there was something happening and it was connected to the first day of the shooting season.

Another Land Rover passed, with a van full of youngsters in pursuit. It looked as if the 'bandits' were following the beaters, presumably with the aim of disrupting the shooting. Animal rights people probably. The police were obviously expecting trouble and another car followed the convoy as it disappeared in the direction of Grinton.

When Helen returned from the bakery, she was able to tell Millie that this activity had been going on since early that morning and that it wasn't the first year that the animal rights people had tried to prevent the start of the shooting season.

'Do you think we'll see them in Mossy Bank?' Millie asked.

'No, I don't think there's any shooting on the fell, is there?'

'It looked as though they were heading for Grinton.'

'Yes, that's where most of the grouse moors are, anyway.'

As they drove back they passed a van of youngsters parked in a lay-by. They had binoculars turned on the fells towards Grinton. Millie looked carefully to see if she could spot Andy or Matt but there was certainly no-one with red hair in the vehicle.

It was quiet in Mossy Bank and there was no sign of the excitement that they had witnessed in Reeth. Millie helped her grandmother with some cooking and in the afternoon she tried to take Bernie for a short walk. He was happy to hobble along for a short way but he didn't want to go past the Manor and refused to go onto the fell road at all. Once they had turned round he moved quite quickly back to the cottage. At least he seemed to be healing physically. She automatically looked down the driveway of Mossy Bank Manor. The house looked quiet and rather sad.

The late afternoon and early evening dragged. Helen was bustling about in the kitchen, very much in her element. Millie wandered about aimlessly, picking up books and putting them down again. At half past five she went to have a long bath and felt so tired when she had soaked in the hot water that she wished she was not going out at all. By seven o'clock she was dressed and had applied some makeup, the first time that she had bothered since she had come to the Dales. She had chosen a dress that she had brought with her, especially for such an occasion. It was a simple sleeveless dress with thick straps crossed at the back. She liked it although she could tell that her grandmother thought it rather 'loud'. It was quite cool in the cottage and she put a thick Arran sweater on to keep warm while she waited for the clock to move round to at least seven forty-five.

'I expect you'd like a lift there and back, Millie?' Helen asked, coming into the room.

'I suppose so. Is it far?'

'No, it's only down the lane but the track down to the farm is quite long and it will be very dark coming back.'

'Right.' She hoped it wasn't going to be a long evening, particularly if Jean turned out to be anything like David.

Helen almost missed the turning altogether at the farm. Driving slowly, they wound through a couple of fields and parked in front of a large stone farmhouse. A dog began barking as Millie climbed out of the car and picked her way across the farmyard and knocked at the front door. There was no answer and she stood for some time before knocking again. Still no-one came. Then she saw another car making its way towards the farmhouse and thought that perhaps the Prices were only just arriving home. She waited until an old estate car pulled up and Pete climbed out

'Hello. I didn't know you were coming,' he shouted across to her. 'We can use the back door.'

She followed him round to the side of the house where there was a stable door that clearly led to the kitchen. She could see through the window into where a blonde woman in denim jeans and a sloppy sweater was whisking something, perhaps cream, in a bowl. Pete opened the door and ushered her in.

'Pete!' exclaimed the woman. 'And this is?' she flashed Millie a welcoming smile as she waited for his answer.

'I'm sorry, I don't know your name,' said Pete, looking at her quizzically.

'I'm Millie. You must be Jean,' she answered, hoping she sounded natural although her heart was still thumping and she couldn't prevent herself from blushing.

'Oh I'm sorry!' Jean said with a laugh, 'I thought you must have come with Pete. Oh dear, what a silly mistake!'

'Don't apologise, Jean,' he said, 'I'm flattered.'

'Do you two know each other?' she asked them.

'No,' said Millie, at the same time as Pete said, 'Yes.'

'Millie brought Bernie to the surgery,' he added. Millie couldn't think what to say, so she kept silent.

'David! David! They're here,' Jean shouted and David appeared looking rather harassed.

'I've told him he can read for a bit and Lucy's asleep.'

'That's fine,' she replied. 'Take them into the sitting room, David, and get some drinks.'

They moved through a small hallway into a cosy room. There was a log fire which pleased Millie since she felt rather exposed when David took her jacket. She realised that she was a little overdressed and wished that she had come in something more casual.

'Jean's cross with me for not getting down sooner,' said David. 'She wanted to be changed before thee came but I'm sure no-one minds.'

Then he added, 'What do you want to drink? Millie, wine?'

'A glass of wine would be lovely, thanks.'

David disappeared and they stood in silence looking at the fire. Millie was wondering what Pete had been doing talking to the Dutchman at the auction and she didn't trust him at all. David returned almost immediately with a bottle of red wine and gave them each a glass.

'Well, how was business yesterday?' asked Pete, looking at David. 'I saw you in Leyburn.'

'Not bad.'

'Were you working there?' Millie asked Pete, trying to sound casual.

'Yes, helping Mr Evans. I saw you there Millie, did you enjoy the auction?'

'Yes it was very interesting,' she replied, reddening a little.

'It's more fun when they're doing the big events but there's always something interesting going on.'

'Do you mainly work with farm animals?' she asked him.

'Theer's more money in it, isn't that reet Pete?' David asked.

'Yes, around here anyway.'

Pete turned to Millie, 'How is Bernie? He was in quite a bad way when I first saw him.'

'Oh he's much better now. Quite frisky really.' She wanted to explain about Bernie's fear of going onto the fells but she didn't know whether it was wise to say anything about it to Pete. So she changed the subject. 'There was a lot of activity in Reeth today, police and vans of youths with masks.'

'Animal liberation crackpots,' said David. 'They'd better not come round 'ere, that's all I can say.'

'Do they? Come round here?' asked Millie.

'We've not had them over this way, have we?' said David looking at Pete.

'There was a lot of activity towards Grinton today. I hope it didn't turn nasty,' said Pete.

'Serves them hooligans reet if they get a shot or two at them,' said David vehemently.

'Has anyone ever been hurt?' asked Millie, wondering what lengths the grouse-shooting fraternity would go to, in order to protect their sport.

'Not that I know of,' David replied. 'But it certainly disrupts t' shooting.'

'Do you have any shoots arranged in the next few weeks?' asked Pete.

'Theer was going to be a group this weekend but it was cancelled at t' last minute. Bloody annoying.'

'Good thing really, if it meant trouble.'

'Well now, is everyone comfortable?' Jean came in with bowls of crisps and placed them by her guests. She had changed into a long green skirt and a white blouse with a high collar. Her long hair was tied back with a black velvet ribbon.

'Anyone else coming?' asked Pete.

'Well, Nick and Samantha were supposed to,' she replied. 'My sister and brother-in-law,' she explained, turning to Millie. 'They couldn't find a baby-sitter.'

'All the more for us!' said Pete with a grin.

Millie wasn't sure if she was pleased or disappointed. She would have felt even more alien in a larger group of friends but the foursome was a bit too cosy and still emphasised the fact that she was a stranger.

However, Jean made every effort to make her feel welcome. She asked after her grandmother and talked about how much part of the community Helen had become. Jean herself was clearly an active member of the village and knew everyone. When Millie asked if she was born in the area Jean explained that her father farmed in Wensleydale and that she had known David as a boy. Millie was relieved that Jean had to go back into the kitchen and so didn't press her about her own family, since she didn't want to talk about her mother and inevitably her Dad and Fiona in this environment. It was warm and she was already feeling the effects of the wine on an empty stomach.

'Dinner's ready!' called Jean from the kitchen and David stood up.

'Follow me and bring your glasses,' he said and led them out of the warmth of the fire and into another room. It was smaller, with a table that nearly filled the entire room. There was just space to squeeze onto the chairs. The walls were lined with books and at one end stood a bureau with a computer balanced precariously on top.

'This is my office by rights,' said David. 'The table is usually folded down with my pc on it but she insisted we did it properly. It's cold in here. Are thee warm enough?' he directed his question at Millie.

'I'm fine, thanks.' She had goose bumps on her arms but she was not going to let Jean down. She had obviously gone to a lot of trouble with silver cutlery and white linen napkins on the polished wood table. A small bunch of wild flowers was placed in the centre, in a delicate blue vase.

'There,' said Jean, as she came in bearing a large tureen of soup. It took some time to ladle it out and Millie's had begun to cool by the time everyone had been served. It was home made vegetable and still warm enough to be very acceptable. As they ate, David explained to Pete how he planned to expand the farm.

Jean listened in silence and then said, 'I keep saying to him that we have enough to do as it is.'

'And I keep saying that we have to expand to survive. She won't listen.' David was raising his voice and his guests shifted in uncomfortable silence.

'It's just that you work so hard already, dear. That's all.' Jean smiled at them.

'No it's not. Thee don't like me doing better than your Dad. Thee think it embarrasses him.'

It was Jean's turn to raise her voice. 'No I don't. I don't like getting into so much debt, if you must know!'

'Now that's just damn silly, isn't it Pete? Everyone knows that business is run on overdrafts. Anyway thee have to take chances, grab opportunities when they arise. Look at the Banford place.'

'I don't know,' said Jean bringing the conversation back to a calmer tone. 'It will probably all go to Daniel.'

'Well, he won't want it will he? He's no farmer, he's a school teacher isn't he?' David was almost sneering and sounded quite nasty.

'I'll bring the plates out,' said Millie and she collected the empty soup bowls and followed Jean out.

'I wish he wasn't so ambitious,' Jean said suddenly, in the kitchen. 'It really worries me sometimes. I don't know where it will all end.'

'It's better than having no ambition at all,' Millie replied, with feeling. 'My Dad's just the opposite.'

'Oh he's dynamic alright, but it doesn't seem to make him any happier, somehow. Perhaps he's not cut out for farming in the Dales.'

'What else would he do?'

'Oh I don't know. Estate management? He was offered something in Holland a couple of years ago year. Mind you I'm glad he didn't take it. Can't speak Dutch you know!' and she laughed. 'Come on, let's get some food down them.'

Millie helped her carry in the roast lamb and vegetables. David carved while they discussed the attributes of local meat. Millie tried to change the subject by asking Pete about his veterinary training. He was working as an assistant in the surgery, so he would have as much experience as possible. His parents lived in Leeds.

'It must be worst in the winter, working out in the cold,' said Millie.

'Yes. I sometimes get up in the middle of a cold winter night if Mr Evans is called out to a arm for something like a cow with colic!'

'Better than treating a poodle with piles,' scoffed David.

'Just as painful for the animal concerned,' replied Pete good-naturedly, winking at Millie. They had obviously gone over this ground before.

'I suppose sheep dogs are different though,' said Millie.

'Depends. You could say a dog like Bernie is no different to a poodle,' said Pete.

'I meant working dogs.'

'Bernie was useless,' said David. 'I remember him. Thee could put him next to a herd of sheep and he would look t'other way, or even run away. Unbelievable. His mam was a brilliant dog, in fact she's still about here and she's had five others, all working in t' area. But Bernie,' he shook his head, 'hopeless.'

'Is that why you gave him to Lizzie?' asked Millie. She remembered her telling them about how Bernie had come from David as a lost cause.

'Nowt else to do but drown him.'

Millie glanced at Pete and she could see that this was another topic they didn't necessarily agree on.

'Has everyone had enough? Then I'll serve pudding in the sitting room. It's beginning to get a bit chilly in here,' said Jean pointedly.

As Jean left the room, David and Pete began to laugh.

'What did I say?' asked David.

They sat with bowls of trifle on their laps in the glow of the fire. The comfortable surroundings made everyone more amiable and David stopped his abrasive responses to his wife's remarks and turned his attention to Millie.

'So what have thee been up to since thee arrived in sunny Mossy Bank?' he asked.

'Not a lot,' she replied. 'but I have been exploring the lead mines quite a bit, with Andy and Matt.'

'Are they the students, lodging at your Gran's?' asked Jean. 'They seem very nice.'

'Oh very!' said David and raised his eyebrows. Millie couldn't think of a response and hurried on to explain about their research.

'Lead? Arsenic?' asked David. 'Are they making out we're poisoning our stock or summat?'

'No, not at all. It's just interesting to see what levels occur naturally and what is contributed from the workings,'

'Sounds as though they ought to get a proper job. What will they do with those qualifications?'

'They could do anything I should think,' said Jean. 'Everything's the environment now, isn't it?'

'It's certainly a growing area,' Pete agreed. 'Have you seen the crushing mill over at Grinton?' he asked Millie. 'It's in good repair and the chimney is almost perfect. It's the best example you'll find in the area.'

'I'd love to see that!' she exclaimed.

'I could take you up there tomorrow, if you like,' offered Pete.

Millie was taken aback and there was a brief silence. She hoped she hadn't sounded too eager. It wasn't like she was asking for a date or anything.

Jean smiled at her. 'Well, there's an offer you can't refuse,' she said.

Millie blushed. 'No, of course. Thank you.'

'Good.' Pete looked pleased.

There was a shout from upstairs. 'Mu...mmy!' and Jean got up.

'Sounds like someone's awake!' She disappeared upstairs.

'It's probably Lucy,' said David. 'She wakes Justin up and he calls us.'

'How old is Lucy?' asked Millie.

'She must be about six weeks now.'

Jean came in with a tiny baby wrapped in a white cellular blanket.

Millie was torn between the desire to ask if she might hold the little bundle and a wish to retain her more sophisticated image.

'Millie, would you mind taking Lucy while I get Justin a drink?'

'No, of course not,' and Millie took the baby willingly.

The men were chatting about the latest cricket scores and she sat happily rocking the baby, which was fast asleep again. The clock read ten-forty and she remembered that she had agreed to ring Gran by eleven for a lift unless the Prices offered to take her back. Farmers got up early and she doubted whether Jean would want them to stay much longer. So when she re-appeared Millie handed Lucy back to Jean and said quietly that perhaps it was a good time to go.

'Well, if you're off to Grinton tomorrow, you'll not want to be too late,' she said with a mischievous grin.

Pete heard her and said, 'Yes, I'll come over at about ten. I want to have a look at Bernie. Anyway, I can give you a lift home.'

'Right then.' Millie wondered if she had accepted too quickly.

The night was cool after the heat of the farmhouse and Millie shivered as Pete escorted her to his car.

As he pulled up outside Laurel Cottage he said 'So. I'll see you tomorrow then. Ten o'clock.'

'Yes,' she replied, fumbling to open the car door. As she jumped out, he started the engine, turned the car round and drove off. She stood watching him disappear, leaving the village in darkness. Well, she thought as she opened the front door and was greeted by Bernie. What about that!

Chapter 9

'He's taking you where?' When she told her that the vet's assistant had invited her to go to Grinton on the Sunday, Helen had laughed and looked quite pleased.

'To the crushing mill at Grinton,' repeated Millie, simply.

'A strange place for a date,' her grandmother had said teasingly.

'It's not a date,' she objected. 'He knew I was interested in lead mining and wanted to show me the mill.'

By the morning Millie was beginning to have doubts. She lay on her back looking at the ceiling, wondering if she was doing the right thing. There was no choice at the time but she could pretend to be ill or suggest it was not good weather. Unfortunately it was a beautiful sunny day and, after all, he was pleasant enough; it was just that she was worried about his motives. Was he in league with the Dutchman? Perhaps they wanted to get rid of her and leave her at the old crushing mill. It hardly seemed plausible on such a lovely day.

Millie thought desperately whether she might find someone to come with her but apparently neither Andy nor Matt had re-appeared, Naomi was in Halifax and she knew no-one else. This morning she was not going to be ready and waiting and she tried to hurry herself to get dressed. She took care to wear her ordinary walking clothes but she did apply some eye-shadow and tried to get her hair to look under control. Really it needed washing and would have been better tied back but she combed it behind her ears and smiled weakly at herself in the mirror.

'He's here!' shouted Helen up the stairs, and Millie heard her rush to the front door, fussing round him. She let them chat while she put on her socks and then padded downstairs. They were in the kitchen and Pete was down on the floor looking at Bernie.

'He seems better, Mrs Johnson, but I shouldn't let him do too much to begin with.'

Bernie looked up solemnly and wagged his tail, as if to say 'Thank you.'

Pete straightened up and turned round. 'Hello Millie.'

'Hello Pete.'

'Well. You've got a nice day for your walk,' said Helen, brightly, smiling at Pete. At the word 'walk' Bernie leapt up and they all laughed.

'Not this time, Bernie,' Helen said, patting him. 'Well, off you go then,' she urged.

Millie picked up her boots and carried them outside. Pete waited until she had got them on and then went to the car. In the back were two border collies. Millie was surprised, she hadn't expected dogs but she supposed it was natural for someone who was training to be a vet to have pets.

'These are Jess and Blackie - and before you ask, I didn't choose their names. They're rescue dogs. They're very intelligent and good friends. Get in.'

She climbed into the passenger seat of the old estate car. It smelt of dogs and the floor was muddy.

'Do you still want to go to Grinton?' he asked, as he started the engine.

'Yes, if you're happy.'

'Good,' and he turned the car round.

They didn't talk much on the way but Millie sat wondering what they were going to do. Would they spend the day together or was this just a quick trip out to the mill? Did he have other plans for the rest of the day?

'Do you have to work at weekends?' she asked, hoping for a clue.

'Sometimes. I generally help in the surgery on a Saturday but I don't usually work on a Sunday unless there's a call out.'

Soon they were in Reeth. It was quiet except for a few walkers sitting on the green. Taking the road to Grinton, over the bridge past the pub, they left the Richmond road heading straight past the church and up the hill, towards Leyburn. As the road climbed steadily they reached a bend and Pete pulled the car off the road onto the open moor.

'Well, here we are.' Pete opened the back door and the dogs jumped out, waiting patiently for him to lock the car. He set off down the wide track and Millie followed.

'It's not far,' he called over his shoulder.

They were quite high up now and the view back down the valley was peaceful. No grouse shooting, no animal liberation protesters and no police. The dogs walked quietly beside Pete and appeared not to notice the sheep.

'They're well-trained,' Millie said.

'Yes, I won't have them any other way,' he said.

In front of them was a neat building, a barn. As they approached, some sheep jumped up and ran out bleating.

'This is the crushing mill,' Pete explained. 'They used it to prepare the lead ore. It would be brought here from the fells. If you come and have a look down here, you can see where the beams were for crushing the ore.'

They moved round the side of the building where there was an opening, a window, overlooking the inside of the mill.

'Behind us is where the crushed ore was passed into the smelter.' He pointed to a covered tunnel and beyond that to the chimney opening. 'The chimney goes right up the side of the hill. You can see how far it is.'

Millie looked up the hill and followed the line of the chimney. To the left were two arches.

'What are they?' she asked.

'I'm not sure, other storage areas I think. I'm not very familiar with how it all worked.'

'You sound as though you know all about it! Gran's got some interesting books on it all.'

'I haven't been here for ages. I'd forgotten how good it is. Let's go up to the top of the chimney.'

They walked along the side of the chimney which was built up the hillside - a chimney lying down. There were holes in the stone work but most of it was intact. They stopped and investigated areas where a white deposit covered the stones. At the top, Millie stood and looked around. There was a slight breeze but it was pleasant in the sunshine. The dogs came chasing through the heather and sat down at their master's feet.

'This is really very nice,' she said.

'You like the Dales then?'

'Oh yes. I really think it is the nicest part of England. Do you come from this area?'

'Oh no. I was brought up in London and all over the place. My father worked for a bank and we moved around a lot. At the moment they're in Leeds.'

Now that they were talking about him, Millie was nervous of asking further questions, in case it became too personal. On the other hand it was difficult to converse without exchanging these details, she found. She decided to stick to the veterinary job.

'How did you choose to be a vet?' she asked.

'I don't know. I think I drifted into it really. I liked animals as a kid; I always had small pets around like rats and mice, hamsters, cats. I was never allowed a dog and I think I probably did it to irritate my mother; she didn't like any of them.'

'What does she think now?'

'Oh she's very proud of me. Tells everyone how clever I am; she irritates me now!'

'Let's look at those arches,' she said, deliberately changing the subject in a hearty fashion, leaving no doubt that she did not wish to discuss her mother, and she marched off towards them with the dogs bounding at her heels.

'I seem to remember that they were for storing something.' said Pete, catching her up. 'But I can't remember if it was ore or some sort of dressing they used. You'll have to look it up for me!'

'Yes. Or I could ask Andy.'

'Is that one of the students lodging with Helen?'

'Yes.'

'I haven't met them but they sound interesting. Are they doing research?'

'Yes, at the university. It's a project.'

One of the dogs started barking and they turned to look. Both dogs were racing through the heather towards the stream that ran by the mill, a rabbit raced just ahead of them.

Millie followed Pete back down towards the chimney and followed the line down to the mill. The dogs were still running about in the bracken on the other side of the stream. On this side of the mill was a large entrance and inside the floor was thick with sheep droppings that squashed under Millie's boots as they went inside. It took several seconds for her eyes to become accustomed to the darkness. She turned and bumped into Pete, who immediately jumped back, apologising. She was embarrassed but relieved that he had reacted in that way and reminded herself that last night she had been nervous of even coming out alone with a friend of the Dutchman.

As they walked back out into the sunshine she said casually, 'What sort of work do you do at the auction?'

'Oh, this and that. The auction people like to have a vet available to monitor animals and be on hand for any of their customers, so I go with Mr Evans to observe.'

'I found it all very interesting, particularly the way people come from so far to buy.'

'Yes.' He was busy trying to attract the dogs' attention, or was he avoiding any talk about foreigner buyers, Millie wondered. She began to take some photographs of the mill, thinking to herself that she might be able to make a study of it later.

'You really are interested in the mining aren't you?' said Pete, when he had got the dogs back to heel and found her photographing the chimney entrance.

'Oh yes. Why? Did you think I wasn't?'

He didn't answer at once but after a pause said slowly, 'I didn't realise that it was a serious interest.'

Millie wondered what he meant by that. Surely he wouldn't have invited her if he didn't think she was interested in the mill, would he?'

'I thought we could go back down to Grinton and have some lunch in the pub. It's a bit early but we could have a look at the church until it opens.'

'That's a good idea,' said Millie with a smile, she was beginning to feel more comfortable again.

They strolled without speaking back to the car with the dogs racing backwards and forwards along the track. The inside of the car was hot and the doggy smell was overpowering. Millie opened the window and enjoyed the breeze as they drove back down the hill. Pete parked the car in the pub car park, making sure that the dogs were in the shade, and left the window open a little.

'This way. We'll go and see if there's a service on.'

It was a pretty church that had been repaired recently by the look of the new stone and mortar work. It was empty and they walked quietly round, examining the simple interior. Once it had been the only church that served this part of Swaledale, until the miners arrived and chapels and churches were built in villages up and down the dale. Millie had read how the dead were carried in wicker coffins all the way from Keld to Grinton to be buried. The funeral procession followed a very old road beside the Swale called Corpse Way. She remembered that the journey could take two or more days.

The cool of the church was pleasant and flowers gave it a cared-for look. Millie thought fleetingly of her grandmother and the attack in Muker church. She swung round quickly but Pete was down by the door peering at the postcards and looking at his watch. She decided that she was perfectly safe and, feeling rather foolish, she walked down the aisle and back into the sunshine. Outside there were some very old gravestones, dating back to the eighteenth century. They wandered round reading the epitaphs and commenting on the names. As they opened the gate there was a fire engine parked on the bridge.

'Oh dear, not a cottage on fire, I hope,' said Millie.

'No. I think they're filling up at the river. Let's have a look.'

They walked down and across the road to where a couple of firemen were standing beside their vehicle.

'Yes, they must be refilling,' said Pete. 'Perhaps there's a fire on the moor. Come on let's go and eat, I'm starving.'

There were people sitting outside the pub watching the fire engine while they drank their beer but Millie said that she preferred to sit indoors. She asked for a tonic water when Pete offered her a drink and he came back with a menu.

'There's a fire on Grinton Moor. It's surprising we didn't see the smoke. So what would you like to eat?'

She was far from relaxed and couldn't decide what she should have.

'I suggest the roast, unless you would rather eat later,' he said.

'No, that's fine,' she said gratefully. After all it was Sunday. But what did he mean, later?

'Good, and some red wine?'

'OK then.' Perhaps she should lighten up.

It was inevitable that eventually they would begin to chat about their respective domestic arrangements and with a roast beef dinner plus several glasses of wine, Millie was telling Pete all about her mother. She even told him about Fiona.

'Pudding. They do super sweets here.' He cheerily changed the subject and persuaded her to have a sweet, although normally she would have refused.

It was three o'clock when they left the pub. Another fire engine, or maybe the same one, was just arriving to fill up again.

'Let's go for a walk by the river,' suggested Pete.

'Are you sure you haven't got to go?' Millie asked, not wishing him to feel that he had to.

'Go where? I told you, Sunday is my day off.'

'OK, but we'd better take the dogs, hadn't we?'

'You're right. Are you OK here, while I fetch them?'

'Of course.'

She watched him as he walked up the road and round the corner to the car park behind the pub. He was nice, she thought, and she was enjoying his company. She smiled to herself and thought how strange it all felt.

A few minutes later, round the corner came two dogs on leads pulling Pete. He ran down the road and they all stumbled down the path to the river.

'I'll keep them on the leads in case we meet any livestock,' he explained.

'I'll take one,' Millie offered and was handed a lead.

'Here, you have Jess. She doesn't pull as much as Blackie.'

'So who did name the dogs?' she asked as they marched along.

'The owners of course. Jess belonged to a little old lady in Richmond. She couldn't cope and the only problem was that she wasn't properly trained.'

'The dog or the owner?' Millie joked.

'Both.'

'And Blackie?'

'Ah, well, he had a collar on and that was his name. No phone number or owner's name so we couldn't trace his home.'

'The owners must have been daft.'

'He's an intelligent animal. He'd obviously been trained well and he's never been a problem except where loud noises are concerned. There must be something to cause that.'

'Do you do doggy psychology in your training?'

'No, not really. But I think I'll understand them better after working with them.'

The path led along the bank, sometimes they had to cross a stile or go through a gate in the wall. They met no-one and it seemed as peaceful as it could be anywhere. Big trees shaded the path on the side of the river and it was cool.

'Shall we sit down for a minute?' asked Millie. Her boots and socks were hot and she thought she might have a paddle if they stopped.

'Yes, sure. We can let the dogs off here. There's nothing about.'

Millie untied her boots and pulled the socks off her hot sweaty feet. 'That's better.'

There was not a lot of water in the river here. The dry weather had emptied the streams so that parts of the Swale were quite low. In fact the river looked a bit scummy just by the bank and debris hanging from the lower branches of the willows showed how much higher the water level would be when the river flooded. The dogs went down to the edge and paddled in the shallow water. Pete pointed across the river.

'Look, there's smoke on the tops. It must be where the fire is.'

Millie could see smoke but not where it was coming from, it was out of sight behind the fell.

'What would cause that?'

'The shooting, perhaps. It's very dry despite more rain recently. Picnickers, maybe. Difficult to know.'

'Will they be able to put it out?'

'It will probably go out by itself eventually. It's difficult for the engines to reach some of the fires on the top of the fells.'

They were sitting on the bank now under the shade of a large oak tree. Occasionally there was a splash and Millie would look in time to see just the ripples where a fish had jumped.

'Do you go fishing?' she asked.

'No. I don't really enjoy it and it's not good for my professional image.' They both laughed.

'What do you do then?' she continued to probe.

'Nothing really. I don't seem to have much time. I see Jean and Dave sometimes but not often. I'm studying mostly. So, what about some tea then?' he asked, changing the subject.

'We've only just had lunch!' she said.

'No, I'm thirsty. Let's find some tea.' He jumped up and called to the dogs. She put her socks and boots back on and they retraced their steps. Millie discovered that he was able to identify all the wild flowers and he pointed out a dipper on the river, on the way.

'I wonder if I should get back now?' she asked. 'I didn't give Gran a time and I feel a bit guilty; I've hardly spent any time with her since I came up here.'

Helen was out when they got back so she invited Pete in for a cup of tea. She suggested that they sat in the garden and as they went through the kitchen Pete noticed the trays of sausage rolls on all the available surfaces.

'Having a party?' he asked.

'No, they're for Lizzie Banford's funeral tomorrow.'

'Oh dear, yes of course.'

Bernie was dozing in the garden. He was delighted to have a second visit from his veterinary assistant in one day and sat at his feet looking up expectantly, hoping for a biscuit or just a pat on his head. They were still waiting for the tea to brew when they heard the front door open and Millie jumped up,

'That must be Gran.'

Bernie began barking and snarling. 'No, it's Andy,' she said and went through in time to see him going upstairs. 'Hello Andy,' she shouted.

'Hi,' he replied and slammed the bedroom door.

'Does Bernie always bark at your grandmother's lodgers?' asked Pete.

'No. It's odd. It's only Andy and only since I found him in the mine.'

'Perhaps there's something about him, you know, like the person who took him? It's like dogs who bark at anyone in a white coat because they don't like vets.'

'I see.'

'What does he look like?'

'Andy? Well he's got ginger hair.'

'Aha! Does Bernie bark at anyone else?'

'No, but there's no-one else with ginger hair.'

'Right then, that's probably it.'

'Should we look out for someone with red hair then, to test your theory?'

'Yes, we ought to catch that bastard if we can.'

Millie was surprised by the tone of his voice. He obviously cared passionately about animals. Certainly there's no way that he could have been involved in Bernie's abduction.

'I must be off,' he said. He stood up and drank his tea quickly. 'And I hope the funeral tomorrow is not too grim.'

'You're not going then?' she asked as she followed him through the house.

'No, I can't. It's surgery tomorrow.'

'Well thanks for a lovely day,' and she meant it.

'I enjoyed every minute of it.' He smiled. 'We must do it again,' and he rushed down the path, almost bumping into Helen.

'Hello, I'm sorry I must go. Bye Mrs Johnson,' jumping into his car he was off up the lane to turn round.

Millie and Helen stood watching until he re-appeared and they waved as he went past. He waved back and shouted goodbye through his open window. The dogs were leaping about in the back.

'So, have you been busy then?' asked Millie as they walked back into the house. 'There's some tea made,' she added.

'Lovely. I'm exhausted but everything's done and we're all ready for tomorrow. Lizzie would have been proud of us.'

'By the way, Andy's back,' Millie told her grandmother.

'Yes I know. I saw him walking down past the Manor when I was just coming out. He didn't see me. He looked very fed up.'

Just as she spoke the bedroom door above them opened and they heard his steps on the stairs.

'I'm going out,' he said gruffly.

'Oh Andrew, I've got some spare puddings left from the preparations and I was going to defrost one of my spinach lasagnes tonight.'

Her offer was clearly tempting.

'I'd like to have a chat, Andy,' said Millie, 'I haven't seen you for ages.'

'Profiteroles,' Helen added.

'OK.' He was obviously exhausted and they went into the small sitting room and sat down. Andy looked like a guilty party waiting to be cross-examined.

'I'll get some wine,' said Helen and retreated tactfully.

'Are you alright Andy?' Millie began. 'You look very tired.'

'Didn't sleep well last night.'

'Oh?'

He lowered his voice. 'I was in a police cell.'

'Oh Andy!'

'You sound like my Mum.'

'I'm sorry.'

'That's OK.'

'Were you arrested?'

'That's the usual reason for being in a police cell.' Andy had clearly had enough.

'I'm sorry.'

'Stop saying I'm sorry. It's me that should be sorry.'

'Why were you arrested? Do you want to talk about it?'

'Causing an affray.'

'Were you with the animal liberation people?' guessed Millie.

'Yeah but 'ow did you know?' He looked up, as if he suspected her of following him.

'Put two and two together, it was August 12th yesterday and I saw the vans in Reeth.'

'Well, I joined them at Grinton. We'd been told to keep clear of Reeth in case they recognised us.'

'We?' Had Matt been with Andy?

'Some mates from Lancaster.'

'Matt?'

'No.'

'Have you seen him?'

'No. I don't know where the 'ell 'e is.' Andy looked distraught. His face tightened into a frown as two deep lines furrowed his forehead. He looked as if he was going to burst into tears.

'Here we are.' Helen arrived on cue with a tray and three glasses of wine. It was chilled and tasted wonderful. It cheered Andy up sufficiently for Millie to risk telling Helen about Andy's escapades. 'You don't mind Gran knowing do you?' she asked but she was sure that he would feel better if it was out in the open. In fact he seemed relieved to have made his confessions,

'Have you heard from Matthew?' Helen enquired, ignorant that Millie had already asked.

'No'

'When will he be back? Do you know?' asked Millie. She felt her heart pounding and tried to sound casual.

'Tomorrow. That's all I know. If 'e comes back 'ere.' Andy sounded like a petulant child.

Helen got up and went to the kitchen to start dinner. Millie hadn't the heart to say that she wasn't hungry so she sat and told Andy about the smelting mill at Grinton while her grandmother chatted to Bernie in the kitchen. Millie was reminded of her first night in Laurel Cottage. Everything the same except that Matt was missing, Lizzie was dead and now Bernie lived there too.

Chapter 10

Andy looked very smart in a suit and Millie noticed that he had taken the gold ring out of his left ear-lobe. Helen remarked that when her brother was his age the trend for long hair meant that it was impossible for young men to look tidy, even in a suit and tie. Andy was embarrassed by the fuss made of him by everyone, particularly Bernie, who was thoroughly taken by his new appearance and did not even growl under his breath at him. Millie remembered her conversation with Pete and decided that it must have been the clothes that turned Bernie against him previously.

Millie was pleased with the effect of the dress she had borrowed from her grandmother and Helen looked younger in a black linen suit. They sat about waiting until it was time to leave for church. The funeral was at noon and although they were parking at Muker by eleven forty-five, the church was nearly full when they arrived. Helen joined her friends in the row behind the front pew but there was not room for all of them and Millie and Andy took seats at the back. It gave Millie the opportunity to study the congregation while they waited for twelve o'clock. Naomi was in the front pew with her uncle and aunt. No sign of their children. On the opposite side of the aisle, at the front, sat some elderly men and women who were probably other relative's of Lizzie. Behind them she could see Bert Bartholomew sitting next to an elderly woman, who Millie assumed was his wife. On his other side was a middle-aged woman who might be the daughter who cleaned at the Manor.

Across the aisle were Lizzie's friends, including Helen. She could also see David and Jean, about half-way down the church. They were sitting next to an elderly couple and Millie guessed that they were Jean's parents. The whole church buzzed with lowered voices that did not subside until the doors opened and the coffin was carried down the aisle. It was a simple and moving ceremony. Friends read passages from the bible and favourite poems. The vicar clearly knew Lizzie well and it was a very personal tribute to her life that left the congregation sad but satisfied that she had had 'a good send-off'.

As Millie and Andy moved out of the church and drifted round to the burial area, David and Jean caught them up. They spoke to Millie ignoring Andy totally. She felt embarrassed but he had not seemed to notice the snub. Millie found the burial very upsetting. All her relatives had been cremated and the ceremony had always left her feeling that it was a strange arrangement. The burial, on the other hand, was such a simple affair. The digging of the grave and the filling in afterwards had been carried out for thousands of years and therefore held a dignity. Naomi and Derek were outlined beside the grave while the other mourners held back, distributed amongst the headstones, and Millie couldn't hear what the vicar was saying. She stood watching everyone, wondering if any of these people knew something about Lizzie's death. Bert Bartholomew was certainly upset, his daughter had her arm round him and his head was bowed very low. Most of Lizzie's women friends were dabbing their eyes. It was a moving sight and Millie wished that they were walking back to the car and off to the relief of the refreshments afterwards. Andy had wandered off to look at the headstones.

Eventually the crowd began to drift away from the new grave towards the churchyard gate. Millie watched her grandmother rush ahead with her friends to reach the Manor before the guests arrived. As she waited for Andy to make his way through the graves, she saw Jean bearing down on her.

'Millie. Would you and your friend like a lift to the Manor? David had to go back now but I'm going there.'

'Thank you,' she answered, surprised by the offer.

They walked together in silence to the car park. Andy climbed into the back of the small car and Millie sat next to Jean in the front.

'I thought it was a very nice service,' said Jean.

'Yes, it was,' Millie replied.

There was a silence.

'Thanks very much for Saturday night, Jean. I did enjoy it,' said Millie, trying to sound friendly.

'Oh yes! And how did Sunday go?' she added with a grin.

Millie blushed. 'Oh fine. It was a nice day,' Then she added, 'Sunny I mean.'

'Well, Pete is nice,' said Jean.

They were turning the bend towards Mossy Bank when Millie saw a familiar figure walking along the road towards them and Andy shouted, 'It's Matt!'

He was dressed in a dark suit and tie although the collar of his shirt had been loosened and the tie hung over his shoulder, as if he had been running. He looked hot and tired. Jean pulled the car over and stopped as Matt reached them and he peered through the windscreen at them. Millie got out and lifted the front seat so that he could climb in behind her, next to Andy.

'You're too late,' said Millie lightly. 'The funeral is over.'

'I'm sorry.' He sounded exhausted. 'I came as quickly as I could.'

'I'm sure she'd have forgiven you,' said Jean. 'Were you out enjoying yourself?'

'No. I've been working,' he replied indignantly.

'Working?' asked Andy.

'I'll tell you later.'

They were silent for the rest of the short journey and remained quiet as they climbed out in Lizzie's drive. Jean went to go to the front door but Millie indicated that they should go round to the back garden. She couldn't face that hallway and the other guests would probably be outside in the sunshine. She had pleasant memories of tea in the garden with Lizzie. Millie was right, they were all gathered at the back of the house chatting and laughing, a relief after the solemnity of the service. Lizzie's friends were enjoying their duties as hostesses on her behalf and Millie could see Helen handing round trays of sausage rolls.

Bert Bartholomew was sitting alone under a tree but the younger woman that Millie had identified as his daughter was walking purposefully towards him with a plate of sandwiches. Jean was already off in the direction of Daniel and his wife, presumably to express sympathy and Millie suggested to Andy and Matt that they went to get some food. The students had not spoken to each other since they had arrived and she thought that they might need some time alone. She was intrigued to find out where Matt had been and thought that once Andy knew, he might confide in her. She wandered over to Bert and sat down beside him. His daughter had given him the sandwiches and left him alone. He was solemnly munching one without any sign of pleasure.

'Hello, Mr Bartholomew.'

'Hello.'

'How are you?'

'Well as can be expected.'

'It's always sad when someone dies,' she replied not knowing what else to say. 'Is that your daughter who was with you at the church?' she continued.

'Ay.'

'She used to clean at the Manor, didn't she?'

'Ay.'

'Does she clean for anyone else?'

'Ay. She does for most folks who can't do it for themselves.'

'Such as?' Millie wondered if Bert thought her too inquisitive.

'Oh, many about. 'Bout five in Gunnerside, three in Muker. One or two others. She fits in round the young 'uns.'

'How many does she have?'

'Three.'

'How old are they?'

'I don't rightly remember. The lad's about six, Tommy. The big lass, Jade, left school and t'other is between 'em, 'bout twelve, that's Rosie.'

'Quite a family then.'

'Ay, them's a 'andful all reet.'

His daughter was marching over with a boy in tow. 'Ere Dad, look out for Tommy. 'E's being a reet nuisance.'

'I want to look at the fish.' The boy had his arms folded tightly, head down and a scowl on his face.

'I'll take you to see them if you like,' offered Millie, thinking that a chat with Tommy might be interesting.

'No need. 'E can sit 'ere with 'is grandad,' the woman replied sharply.

Bert's daughter scowled at her and Millie saw the family resemblance. Then she marched off.

'Grandad. Can I see the fish? Please?' Tommy was obviously used to getting his way with Bert.

'In a minute lad, when yer mam's gone,' he said quietly. 'Thee can have my sausage roll if thee likes.'

Tommy sat down next to Bert and finished off his plate of food.

'The garden looks lovely,' Millie said. 'The roses are a picture.'

'Ay. It's been a full-time job up to now. I don't reetly know what'll 'appen now she's gone.'

'Where's she gone, Grandad?'

'To heaven Tommy. She were a good lady.'

'What 'appens if you're not good, Grandad?'

'Then you go to 'ell. God knows if you're good or not.'

'I want to see the fish, Grandad.'

'Well, if you're good, I'll take you.' Bert got up unsteadily and made his way slowly towards the house with Tommy's hand in his, leaving Millie sitting admiring the garden. It did look wonderful with roses everywhere, climbing the pillars and posts around the edge of the lawn. They were pale pink and cream. Old fashioned roses with strong scents that filled the warm air. Bert's daughter seemed a grim sort of woman, thought Millie. Not the kind of cleaner she would want around the house.

'Hello Millie.' Naomi was standing in front of her, with a dark-haired man dressed in a grey suit and black shirt.

'Hi,' said the man.

'Millie, this is Neil, DC Neil Clark, but don't tell anyone else.'

'Hello,' said Millie, unsure whether he was a friend of Naomi's or not.

'Neil is based in Halifax. He's a mate of mine.'

'So she says,' he added with a grin. 'She's invited me to come down for a few days. But I suspect ulterior motives.'

'Don't be silly, Neil. You said you needed a break and I've got to stay most of this week. It seemed a good arrangement.'

'Millie,' she added, as they watched an elderly woman coming towards them. 'here comes Aunt Edith. Will you stay until they've all gone, I'd like a chat.' Then she moved round pulling Neil with her. 'Aunt Edith, let me introduce Neil...'

They drifted off and as they turned Millie noticed that Neil had a neat but long pony-tail tied at the back. Not the sort of policeman she was used to at all. Perhaps he was in the vice squad or undercover work, she was certainly going to wait to find out why he here. She felt sure that Naomi had something in mind when she had invited him, something to do with her grandmother's death.

She looked across the lawn and caught sight of Matt and Andy talking to Helen. She was pleased that Matt had re-appeared but he had some explaining to do. Jean was close by, chatting to the elderly couple that she was sitting next to in church. Millie decided that she would go and talk to her and find out who they were.

'Hello Millie,' said Jean, 'Do you know Dr and Mrs Mellor?'

'We have met,' said the doctor. 'This is my wife.'

He didn't give her name and Millie simply nodded at her and said 'Hello.'

It didn't seem polite to mention the circumstances under which they had met before and Millie hesitated, unsure how to continue. Dr Mellor, on the other hand was not so squeamish and said, 'We met when she found Lizzie on Tuesday. Rather distressing for you, my dear.'

'Yes,' answered Millie, weakly.

'Had Lizzie been suffering from a bad heart? I know it was a heart attack, in the end.' Jean's voice trailed off, she obviously felt that the topic was not really appropriate.

'No, but sometimes there are no obvious signs. Very usual in the elderly. Now we really must be off,' said the doctor, and the couple left.

'Well, I suppose it's time to go,' said Jean. 'By the way, I hope you do like Pete. He seems to lead such a lonely life. It's nice if you two get along, even for a couple of weeks. Bye Millie, enjoy your holiday.'

Well, really, she'd been set up! They saw her as an ideal person to cheer up the lonely while she was here. It was her holiday after all. She was irritated and unsettled, left standing, munching the remains of a sausage roll, flakes of pastry depositing themselves on her grandmother's dress.

Millie heard Naomi calling to her and she joined her in the shade of a large apple tree.

'Millie, this is Mr Norwich. Millie is Helen's granddaughter,' she explained to him.

'Ah yes. Delighted. But please call me Ian, Naomi. Are you enjoying your holiday Millie?'

'Yes thank you. Of course it has been a sad day today.'

'Yes, you're right. It was a great surprise to us all. I was actually expecting to see Lizzie last Friday. She had rung to ask for an appointment.'

Millie was puzzled. He couldn't be her doctor, unless he was some sort of specialist.

'In fact Naomi,' he continued. 'I would like to have a chat with you as soon as possible. Would you be able to come to the office tomorrow?'

'Yes of course, Ian. What time?'

'Would eleven o'clock be suitable?'

'Yes certainly.'

'And now I think I should be taking my leave. Very nice to meet you Millie, Neil. Goodbye Naomi!'

'That's our family solicitor,' explained Naomi, as soon as he was out of earshot. 'He said that he needed to talk to me. I suppose it's about the will.'

Neither Millie nor Neil replied. It was family business.

'I don't think there's anything funny about it. Just the normal stuff. I think Uncle Dan gets the house and I'll get some cash and jewellery, I suppose.'

'Don't you mind? I mean him getting everything?' Millie asked.

'No, not really. As long as he keeps the house in the family and doesn't go selling it off to the first person that comes along. I couldn't bear it to become a holiday home.'

'I know what you mean,' Millie said. 'It must be wonderful having a house like this in the family.'

'The trouble is that Dan and Penny are unlikely to want to move from Edinburgh and so it'll be empty for most of the time. It'll cost money to keep up.'

'What you need is a housekeeper,' said Millie, thinking of her grandmother's proximity.

'How long has it been in your family, Naomi?' asked Neil.

'About two hundred years, that's all.'

'That's all!' he roared with laughter. 'My folk have been in our place for fifty years and we think that's a long time.'

'Not round here Neil. You have to have lived in the village for a long time before you're considered a local.'

'I think it's amazing how quickly Gran's become part of the community here,' said Millie.

'Well, there are exceptions and Helen contributes a lot to the village, that's why. Come on, let's see how the ladies are getting on.'

They walked slowly across the lawn to the open kitchen door. Only Helen and one other woman were left cleaning round the kitchen surfaces and hanging up damp tea towels.

'There, that's better,' said Helen with a sigh. 'All finished. Do you want a quick cuppa before you go, Eileen?'

'No thanks. I told Billy I'd be back by now.'

They disappeared out of the door, chatting about what Eileen was going to give Billy for his tea. Millie couldn't tell from the conversation whether Billy was her husband, her son or the cat.

'I don't know about you but I fancy something a bit stronger. I'll see if I can find anything suitable.' Naomi began searching the kitchen, looking in cupboards and then she disappeared into the larder.

Helen came back into the kitchen and took her handbag from the table.

'Well, I'll be off now. I think everything went well, don't you?'

'It was super, Helen,' Naomi called from inside the larder. She came out and said, 'Thank you so much for everything. It was a perfect day and Grandma would have thoroughly approved.'

'Bless you,' said Helen and turned to leave with a broad smile on her face.

'I'll see you later, Gran,' shouted Millie after her.

'Yes,' she called back.

'Now, this drink,' and Naomi re-appeared with a bottle of gin in her hand. 'G and T?'

They marched down the garden armed with gin, bottles of tonic, lemon and a jug of ice. Naomi went back for the glasses.

'Is she always as, well like this?' Millie asked Neil as they waited in silence for her return. Both of them were looking back towards the house.

'Oh yes. She's full of life is our Naomi.'

'Have you known her long?'

'Yes. Since she came into my station.'

Millie had forgotten that he was with the police. She had a stereotype view of what policemen should look like.

'Have you been in the police long?' she asked.

'Not by most standards. I came in from university, not one of the lads.'

'Is that difficult then?'

'It's not easy in a place like Halifax,' smiled Neil.

Naomi arrived as he said this and she enquired what was not easy.

'Being a police detective,' he said.

'It sounds like good fun to me, don't you think so Millie? I've always wanted to be a sleuth.' She was busy cutting the lemon and mixing the drinks but she looked straight at Millie as she said this.

'There you go,' as she handed out the glasses and she raised hers. 'To Grandma, bless her! She would have been very happy to see so many friends today. It's a shame you never met her, Neil. She really was an ideal grandmother.'

'She sounds it,' he said. 'I was talking to - who was it? Ian - earlier, and he was obviously very fond of her.'

'Yes. I've known Mr Norwich, Ian, as long as I can remember. I expect he knew me as a baby. His father probably knew Grandma as a baby as well. It's a family business, Norwich, Pearce and Norwich. I think the third one might even be Ian's son. His office is in Skipton. It'll be a nice drive if you want to come Millie.'

'I think I'd better keep Gran company,' said Millie, aware that it was a feeble excuse and she really wanted the opportunity to talk to Andy.

'Well, you're coming Neil. You can do some shopping in the supermarket to pass the time.'

'Thanks a lot. Now I know why you invited me here, to do the housework.'

'Oh no. I have Irene to do that for me.'

'Irene? She sounds exotic. Is she a blonde wench from the village?' asked Neil.

'Not exactly,' she replied, grinning at Millie. 'She's our gardener's daughter and she's in her forties, I should think. Well, you saw her today, she's Tommy's mother.'

'Oh good grief. She's a bit of a battle axe,' he said.

Millie remembered the puzzle over Bert's wife. 'Where was Bert's wife?' she asked. 'I saw her in the church but she wasn't here was she?'

'His wife died years ago. I don't remember her. As far as I was concerned there was only ever Bert and Irene,' Naomi answered. 'Of course then Irene got married and had the kids.'

'So he lives on his own?' asked Millie.

'Not really. Irene's only just down the road at the bottom of the lane. She's in and out all the time. Keeping him in order.'

'Well she certainly keeps the Manor in order,' said Millie. 'It looks very nice and clean and tidy.'

'Odd isn't it? I didn't think she would be in but someone's tidied up. I didn't see her but it must have been her.' Then she turned to Neil, 'Another drink?'

'Not yet,' he answered, 'I'm off to the loo. Back in a jiffy.'

Naomi waited until he was out of earshot and turned to Millie conspiratorially. 'What d'you think? I've had this idea. I thought, why not get Neil down here, like a sniffer dog, see if he thinks there's anything suspicious.'

'Honestly? Do you think it's a good idea?'

'Well it's worth a try, isn't it? Of course I haven't told him anything. I thought it best to see if he picks up any scents.'

Perhaps it was the gin but Naomi sounded quite excited by the prospect of finding clues to the fact that her grandmother's death was not natural. Millie was unsure whether it was healthy for them to pursue this line, after all they may actually find something.

'Where is Neil staying?' asked Millie, to change the subject.

'In a B 'n B in Muker. I think it would have caused too much gossip to give him a room here and Dan would probably have objected.'

'Is Daniel staying?'

'They're off to Edinburgh tonight and coming back with the kids in a fortnight. They're at some summerschool this week.'

'What are they like? The children, I mean?'

'Quite good actually. I suppose they'd have to be wouldn't they? Rod of iron and all that. Sophie's thirteen, or is it fourteen? She's very bright and is bound to go university. She's fond of animals and is mad on riding at the moment. Henry is fifteen or sixteen, I can't remember, and is keen on sports, rugby and cricket. He went on some sort of tour last year with the school rugby team. They're both nice kids. Not the usual delinquents. I don't think they like Scotland much though. They visited me last year and seemed keen to be back in the North of England.'

'Changing the subject, before Neil comes back,' she added, 'I wanted to ask, are you sure you won't come to Skipton? I know Helen's an excuse because I heard her chatting to her chums about going to Richmond tomorrow.'

'Are you sure?'

'Yes. So you can come can't you?'

'I suppose so.' Millie still wanted to talk to Andy and Matt, and it must have shown.

'Millie, what are you up to?'

'I just thought I might have a talk to Andy and Matt tomorrow. I want to find out where Matt has been since Tuesday.'

'Oh I see. I wondered whether it was him when I saw them together. Can't you see them tonight?'

'They might be out.'

'Well, we'll be back in the afternoon, you can see them then.'

'Alright then, if you insist.' She grinned at Naomi.

'I do. I want to show you Wharfedale.'

Neil came strolling down the garden, examining the shrubs.

'I think I ought to go and find this B 'n B soon, Naomi. I don't want to get into their bad books by appearing late.'

'OK. I'll take you down there now if you like.'

'I must be going too,' said Millie, getting up.

'OK, but remember we'll be leaving at, what, nine-thirty at the latest.'

'Right. I'll be up here by about twenty past nine. Bye Neil, nice to meet you.'

She walked round to the front of the house just in time to see a car turning into the drive. It was Daniel and Penny back from delivering the elderly relatives to the station.

'I could murder a cup of tea,' Penny shouted as she climbed out the other side of the car and strode round the side of the house. Daniel slammed the car door and followed her without another word.

Millie walked slowly down the lane and into Laurel Cottage. She was met by Bernie wagging his tail.

'Hello old chap. How are you?' she asked as she tickled his ears and rubbed his head.

There was no sign of Helen but she could hear movements above her head and knew that the boys were in. She wandered through the kitchen and filled the kettle with water.

'Do you want a cup of tea?' she called up the stairs.

'No thanks.' Two male voices responded.

'Coffee?'

'Yes please.'

Bernie followed her round the small kitchen, getting under her feet.

'What do you want, Bernie?' she asked, bending down to tickle him under his chin. 'Do you want a walk?'

He held his head on one side and then on the other, wagging his tail furiously.

'Alright. In a minute.'

Bernie continued to get under her feet while she made the tea and coffee.

'It's ready!' she called.

A door opened upstairs and heavy footsteps sounded on the stairs. The boys had changed into jeans and tee-shirts, and looked their old selves.

'I think I'll get changed,' said Millie. 'Bernie seems keen on a walk. D'you fancy a hike up the hill?'

'Why not? Haven't been up there for a while,' said Andy.

'Yeah, OK.'

She took her tea and went up to her room. She hung the dress carefully on its hanger and found her jeans and a thin sweatshirt. Her boots were downstairs so she brushed her hair quickly and went back down, sipping her tea as she manoeuvred the stairs.

'Where's your lead, Bernie?' she asked, putting her mug down. The dog bounded away to the back door and clawed at it.

'Is it out there? Good boy.' She opened the door and he shot through, jumping and snapping at the leather lead that was hanging from a hook beside the peg basket.

'Come on then, let's go.' He was back inside, claws scrabbling on the lino in the kitchen.

'Are you ready then?' she asked the boys as she passed.

Outside Bernie stood waiting, lifting his paws occasionally, anxious to be off, while they all put their boots on. He pulled Millie up the lane and this time he seemed happy to continue past the Manor and onto the fell.

The afternoon was still warm with a light breeze. The smell of heather wafted across from the fells and the tussocks of grass moved in spasms as the wind caught them. The sheep were sitting comfortably chewing, moving their heads round to watch the party go by. Bernie took no notice of the sheep but pulled on up the path heading towards the Lodge. As she walked along she rehearsed different opening remarks to get Matt talking. The problem was that she didn't know whether they would confide in her or not.

In the end she simply asked, 'So what have you been up to this week, Matt?'

'Earning some money.'

'Easy money if you ask me,' said Andy lightly.

'Well it was. Just a driving job.'

Millie could not see why that would have been such a secret but before she could ask, Matt continued.

'It was a bit odd really. I stayed on at Uni on the Tuesday to see my tutor and Nick phoned. I was due to come back that night but he rang to say he'd got this job if I wanted it, for his uncle. It sounded OK to me, just driving abroad and back by ferry. I needed to get my passport but that was no big deal. He said it was fine but not to let on to anyone where I was going. I told him to let you know,' he nodded towards Andy, 'and he said he would.'

'Well 'e didn't,' said Andy, sharply.

'P'raps he forgot,' replied Matt with a shrug.

'No, because I asked 'im if 'e'd seen you and 'e said no.'

'That's odd,' said Millie. 'So what happened then?'

'I went home by train on Wednesday and saw my folks. I got my passport and came back up on Friday. Nick said that his uncle would meet me at Darlington Station on Friday. I had to be there at five o'clock.'

'What, in the evening?' asked Millie.

'Yeah. I got the train from King's Cross. At about ten to five this Land Rover turns up with a trailer full of sheep.'

'Who was driving it?' asked Millie. She had been listening intently and they had slowed their pace to listen to Matt's story.

'I suppose it was Nick's uncle. He didn't use a name and I never asked. He said he would drive to the ferry and I'd take over then.'

'Where did you go?' Millie was getting very interested.

'To the ferry at Hull and on the boat to Rotterdam.'

'Did you need a green card?' asked Andy.

'I don't know. I didn't think about that.'

Millie had been so engrossed in the story that she hadn't noticed that Bernie had been leading them up the main track to the Lodge. They were nearly level with the old building and she automatically stopped.

Bernie lay down panting and they all found rocks to sit on by the side of the track.

'So where did you go?' Millie prompted.

'I don't really know. I followed Nick's uncle's directions and it was getting dark. We seemed to end up in the country driving up a long drive to a big house. We parked round the back and went into the kitchen. It was a huge place with a cook who made us eggs and toast and stuff. There was a sort of flat over the garages where we could sleep for a while. I don't know what time it was when we left again but it was before the sun came up.'

'Did you bring the trailer back?' asked Millie.

'Yes. I suppose that the uncle was delivering the sheep to a customer. I don't know.'

'Didn't you ask him?' asked Andy.

'Well no. It was a bit cloak and dagger. I didn't want to in case it was bit dodgy.'

They sat in silence while Millie tried to understand what it all meant. It could have been a straightforward business transaction. It sounded as though Nick wanted to keep Andy in the dark but that could just be something personal, perhaps he was jealous of their relationship for some reason. If it was dodgy, as Matt had said, then it must be to do with exporting sheep. She could ask Pete, he would know about export licences. She could go to the auction and find out if necessary.

'Did you get the analyses done alright?' Andy was asking Matt. 'What did old Harris say about the water values, did he think they were worth repeating?'

Millie listened to the two of them discussing their work. She could follow most of it but there were some scientific bits that were above her head. Bernie had got up and was pulling on her arm as he reached the extent of his lead.

'Are you getting bored, Bernie?' she asked.

'Actually we'd better be getting back. 'Elen said she would do tea for six o'clock today,' said Andy.

'Where is she?' Millie realised, with her usual pang of guilt, that she was not spending enough time with her grandmother.

'Went back to the church I think,' said Matt.

As they walked down to the cottage Millie asked the boys to explain in detail what the measurements they made were for and how they did them. As they tried to explain it to her, she was surprised how sophisticated their work was. They were using complicated instrumentation to measure very small amounts of lead, arsenic and other elements that were toxic metals. She would look it up in the library when she got back and make a point of finding out about these environmental problems for herself.

By the time they reached the cottage Helen was preparing dinner. It smelt good and Millie realised how hungry she was. Bernie was also attracted by the prospect of food and lay on the kitchen floor watching them as they moved around above him.

'Have you noticed how well Bernie has settled in now?' asked Helen when they were seated round the table in the sitting room. 'I was wondering if Naomi will want to take him or whether he would be happier staying here?'

'I think that would be a great idea,' agreed Millie. 'He seems so at home now and he's not a lot of trouble is he?'

'No. In fact I think I'd miss his company if he went.' Helen looked pleased with the decision and handed the salad bowl to Millie.

'Well, Matt,' she continued. 'It's nice to have you back with us. I was quite worried about you. Well we all were.' Helen seemed unaware of Matt's discomfort. 'Where did you say you have been?'

'Holland.'

'Holland? Good heavens. Why did you go there?'

'I was doing a job for Nick's uncle.'

'Who? Old Jim Jackson?'

'I don't know his name.'

'Well it's Jim Jackson, Irene's husband. Isn't Irene his aunt?'

'They live down the road at the cottage with a rusty motorbike in the front garden.'

'Yes, that's the Jacksons. An old village family. Apparently they've farmed here for centuries.'

'Which farm do they run?' asked Millie.

'Oh Jim Jackson doesn't have his own farm. Apparently it was sold off a long time ago. He couldn't manage it properly. David's father bought him out and now he works for David.'

Helen picked up the empty plates and carried them out to the kitchen.

'Nick says the aunt's a real dragon,' said Andy in a low voice.

'Yes, I met her today. She's the gardener's daughter, you know, Bert Bartholomew,' said Millie.

Helen came back in and gathered up the rest of the dishes. 'Now, do you boys want any ice-cream?'

'No thanks,' they replied in unison.

'We thought we'd go to the pub,' added Matt. 'I want to have a word with Nick.'

Good, thought Millie. A nice quiet evening in with Gran.

'That's fine then,' said Helen, looking pleased. 'I'm going to play bridge tonight.' Turning to Millie she asked, 'And what are you up to?'

'Oh, I'll be alright,' she said, hiding her disappointment. 'I'll keep Bernie company.' Hearing his name, he lifted his head and wagged his tail.

'Now about tomorrow,' Helen went on, 'I did promise Lillian I would take her into Richmond. Did you want to come, Millie?'

'Actually, Naomi did ask me if I'd like to go to Skipton.'

'Oh you should go Millie. It's a lovely little town and,' she paused significantly, 'it has a supermarket.' She went into the kitchen and came back with a pad and pencil. 'Are you leaving early? I could do a list now. It's just that they do a wonderful selection of bread and pies and the fruit is so fresh, people come from miles to it.'

By the time Helen rushed off to get changed for bridge, Millie had a list of twenty items to be found in Skipton plus requests from Andy and Matt for certain special types of beer only to be found in large supermarkets.

Chapter 11

It was raining hard on the following morning and Helen left the boys with strict instructions to give Bernie a walk when it had stopped. Helen offered to drop Millie at the Manor before picking Lillian up, to save her getting wet.

'You won't forget about the film, will you?' Millie asked as she got out of the car. Her grandmother had suggested that she take her camera if she was going down to Wharfedale but Millie had found that she only had one picture left and used it to take a shot of Bernie. Helen had offered to get the film processed for her while she was in Richmond.

The front door was opened by Neil.

'Good morning,' he said. 'And how are you on this miserable morning?'

'Fine,' answered Millie, stepping into the hall but remaining on the door mat. She had worn her boots because of the bad weather and didn't want to bring mud into the house.

Naomi shouted a greeting and Millie began removing her boots. When she padded into the kitchen she found Naomi eating toast.

'I'm sorry, I'm still eating. Neil's alright, he was given breakfast in Muker but I was a bit late getting up and had to pick him up before I had eaten. Still, I have managed to write a shopping list while I've been getting organised.'

'Gran's done the same,' said Millie, with a grin. 'She sees this as a heaven sent opportunity.'

'Well, we'll get the chores done this morning and take in the scenery later if the weather cheers up. Anyone know what the forecast is?'

'No,' replied Millie and Neil together.

They eventually left the house at just before ten o'clock. Millie insisted on climbing into the back of Naomi's car to give Neil more leg room. He was quite tall, certainly over six foot and even in the front he looked rather uncomfortable with his knees folded up.

Millie had spent her solitary evening looking at maps and reading about some of the villages and towns in Wharfedale. It certainly appeared to be a more popular part of the Dales for tourists and there was a lot more information about places in that area than in Swaledale. She had predicted that they would go via Hawes and so she was not surprised when Naomi headed through Muker and swung the car left up the hill just before Thwaite. It was the same road they had taken the week before when they had visited the estate agent. The weather had been pleasanter then and it was a much wilder scenery that they saw today.

No-one spoke until they were leaving Hawes past the Wensleydale cheese factory. Naomi explained how the factory nearly closed some years before when it was run by a large company but was saved by the enthusiasm of the local shopkeepers and workers themselves. It was now owned as a small business and encouraged holidaymakers to visit the factory to see the cheese being made. Millie was particularly fond of Wensleydale cheese and thought she might return to visit the factory before she went home.

They were climbing a steep hill into the mist that accompanied the driving rain. They passed two cyclists, covered in yellow waterproof capes, pushing their bicycles miserably along the side of the road.

'Rather them than me,' said Neil, looking back at the figures disappearing behind them.

'Nice going down the other side, though,' shouted Naomi above the sound of the windscreen wipers, squeaking at each movement.

'What, in that rain?' said Millie, leaning forward between the two seats to make herself heard.

Once they were travelling downhill the mist disappeared and the rain seemed to lighten a little. They wound slowly down a series of hairpin bends and then began to follow a river that Millie knew must be the Wharfe. It was full and flowed fast.

As if reading her mind, Naomi shouted back to her, 'The Wharfe looks pretty full. Last summer it was as dry as a bone here and they had terrible water shortages.' Millie couldn't imagine this river without water in it.

'What about the animals? Did they suffer?'

'Yes there were some sheep lost but the main problem was the shortage of hay for the winter. They only had one cut and that was poor.'

They were turning over a narrow bridge and into a village called Hubberholme. Millie had read about the church and wished that there was time to look.

'That looks like a good pub, said Neil.'

They passed Buckden and came into Kettlewell. A coach was having difficulty turning round the tight bends and the miserable faces of the passengers peered out from the misted windows, where they had wiped small circles to view the scenery. Naomi looked at her watch and remarked that it would probably be closer to twelve o' clock by the time they reached Skipton. She speeded up outside the village, where the road was wider. Millie saw the signs off to the left to Grassington, not only a picturesque village, according to the books, but also another mining community. If they had had time Millie would have asked to stop. It had been Naomi's fault that they had left late but she didn't appear to be particularly concerned. Millie reflected that doctors were always running late in her experience. She, on the other hand, was constantly watching the clock, time to leave for college, time to be picked up, you couldn't be late home with Dad or Fiona, they worried if you weren't there on time. She wondered if they were missing her now. It was just over a week and she had hardly thought about them. They would probably be on the beach now and she hoped Dad was putting sun cream on to protect his fair skin. She really didn't envy them. She was much happier here, she was enjoying herself thank you. She smiled when she thought about how she had spent the last couple of days: on Monday I went to a funeral, Tuesday I visited a supermarket in the rain, in Skipton, just a couple of hours away.

Naomi shouted something incoherent and Millie nodded. They were passing a large quarry. Neil turned round and shouted, 'One of the less scenic parts but there's a good pub.' Millie smiled back.

It was a short time later that they passed a sign indicating that they were in Skipton. They entered the town by the castle and drove through the main street, busy with shoppers. Although there was a sign for free parking on the left Naomi continued through the town and took a turning into the supermarket car park.

'I'll leave the car here and walk back up to the solicitors' office,' Naomi announced, 'I'll see you back here in an hour.'

'OK,' said Millie. She had spotted a café inside the supermarket and so she did not object to waiting.

'Have you got the list, Naomi?' Neil asked. She handed it to him, together with the car keys and waved as she began to jog towards the town centre. 'Why don't we split up to get the shopping and meet up for a coffee in about half an hour?' suggested Neil.

'Fine,' agreed Millie. She was pleased to be able to wander round at her own pace. They each took a trolley at the entrance and set off in opposite directions. Millie headed for the bakery counter, selecting a fruit pie from the display.

'Is that all, love, or d'you want something else?' The woman behind the counter smiled and Millie was struck by how friendly she was.

'Can I just have a look for a minute?'

'Course you can, dear. Just you take your time, love.'

Well that was different from her own local supermarket. There was a wide choice of everything she had on her list, in contrast to the small village shops she had been using this last week. Millie picked up quite a few extra things that she could use in pasta dishes and a variety of pulses that would be useful for the vegetarian meals. She also remembered to buy more films for her camera and the beer for Andy and Matt. As she queued she could see Neil a couple of checkouts away. From her position behind the sweet racks she could watch him.

She still found it difficult to think of him as a policeman.

Millie put her carrier bags back into the trolley and wheeled it out to the entrance, where Neil was waiting for her.

'Shall we put these in the car?' she asked.

They took their loaded trolleys out to the car park, where the sun was beginning to break through and it was warming up. Neil packed the bags in the tiny boot but there was not sufficient space and Millie put two of her bags onto the back seat. She was looking forward to a well-earned break and took one of the films with her to put in the empty camera while she drank her coffee.

'What time was it when Naomi went off?' Neil asked.

'Just before twelve.'

'So we've got about twenty minutes, if she's back on time. Which I doubt,' he said, looking at his watch.

They went back into the café. Millie found a table and Neil came back with coffee and doughnuts. They ate in silence each coping in a different way with the oozing jam.

Neil finished first. 'Is this your first visit to the Dales?' he asked.

She nodded, her mouth still full. 'And is it yours?' she asked.

'No, actually I used to come here quite a lot with my Dad. He was a keen walker. Fitness mad. Walking, cycling, swimming. Bit ironic really, he died of a heart attack five years ago.'

'I'm sorry.'

'Oh it's OK. I know this part better than Swaledale. We never went up there, too far. Mainly

Linton and Grassington, the well-known parts. I remember visiting Skipton Castle as a kid.'

'Halifax must be very different.'

'Yeah. Still I wouldn't want to live out here. Not all the time.' Neil's eyes were drawn to the entrance and when Millie turned she saw Naomi standing at the door looking round for them. She came over looking rather serious.

'Sorry it took so long,' she said.

'Do you want a drink?' Neil asked. 'They do good doughnuts.'

'Yes I do,' she said 'But not coffee. Let's find a pub.'

She didn't say anything else and they followed her out in silence. The car was warm and smelled of fresh baked bread.

'Where shall we go?' asked Neil.

'I don't know,' Naomi replied without feeling, as she started the engine. She muttered at the cars in front as they waited to get out of the car park. She drove back through Skipton but instead of following the road towards Grassington, Naomi turned right onto the road signposted to Harrogate.

'Was it bad news?' ventured Neil once they were driving along the main road.

'No, I'm sorry. It was exactly what I expected. I suppose it hits you when you hear it though. Dan gets the house and the land associated with it. I get some money and Ivy Cottage. I shouldn't be unhappy with that should I? My own holiday cottage, as long as he doesn't sell the rest off.'

'Do you think he might?' asked Millie.

'He certainly won't live there.'

'Could you buy it from him?' asked Neil.

'No way! I've got money but not that much.'

Naomi swung the car off the road in front of a pub. There were very few cars and Millie wondered if Naomi knew the place or had stopped at the first pub she had come to.

'We'd better stop or it will be closing time,' she said. As they walked to the door she added, 'I hope they do food.'

'The chicken pie is finished and there's no vegetarian curry,' she said, pretending to be the landlady. 'And can you hurry up and decide because Trevor wants to get off early.'

When she returned from ordering the food Naomi suggested that they change the subject and decided how they should spend the afternoon.

'If we turn a bit further, are we on the Burnsall road?' asked Neil.

'Yes,' said Naomi.

'In that case,' he went on, 'we could stop at the Strid. I used to go there with my Dad a lot.'

Millie had read about the Strid, the section of the Wharfe that flowed through a narrow valley above Bolton Abbey.

'Right then,' said Naomi. 'By the way, Millie, did you manage to have a word with your student friends.'

'Oh yes. I saw them last night, so there's no need to rush back.' She wasn't going to report what they had said in front of Neil.

They started out at the Cavendish Pavilion, where Millie picked up a leaflet describing a number of nature trails along that stretch of river. Naomi wanted to go as far as Barden Tower because it had a tea-rooms and so they crossed the bridge to walk up on the opposite bank. It was a fresh afternoon and although it was damp underfoot the air was clear and the sun was shining intermittently. Millie, who was pleased that she had her walking boots, noticed that Naomi was wearing rather stylish suede fell boots, while Neil was in trainers. They were the only walkers in sight except for two elderly couples walking their dogs.

'We should have brought Bernie,' Millie commented. 'You know Gran's getting quite fond of him now.' She wanted to know what Naomi planned to do about him.

'Is she?' she asked. 'I suppose he's a lot of work though.'

'Who's going to have him when everything's sorted out?' asked Neil innocently.

'I don't know,' said Naomi. 'It's a problem. He's so happy here, it seems a shame to have to take him to Halifax. I would love to have him but it seems unfair on him.'

'What if Gran was willing to keep him?' Millie asked.

'That would be wonderful but I doubt...'

'She would you know.'

'D'you think so, really?' Naomi looked pleased.

'I think if you asked her, she would be very happy to keep him.'

The footpath was going downhill towards the river and at the bottom of the path they emerged into an area of flat brown rocks, shiny with rain. Shallow hollows in the rocks were full of water. The river rushed loudly through the narrow gap between them. The white foam frothed and bubbled.

'Shall I jump across?' asked Neil as Millie held her camera, ready to take a picture of them.

Naomi looked alarmed. 'No you mustn't do that. It's impossible and people have drowned here!'

'Only kidding,' said Neil holding up his hands and grinning. Naomi's reaction was to give him a shove and he slipped backwards, landing in one of the shallow pools.

'I'm sorry. Are you very wet? Oh dear, rather a damp bum I'm afraid.' Naomi giggled.

Neil did not seem over concerned, 'It'll dry.'

Millie had been studying her leaflet. 'It says here that anything that goes into the Strid rarely surfaces for several days.'

The three of them stood looking solemnly at the racing water. 'There's a legend about Alice de Romilly. Her son was supposed to have drowned here and that's why she founded the first priory which became Bolton Priory.' Millie was reading from the leaflet again.

They continued silently along the river path in single file, watching the water for signs of fish and birds. Neil said that they might see a kingfisher but they didn't. There were sand martins and dippers and occasionally they heard the splash of a fish jumping. Millie had to walk quickly to keep up with the other two. It was getting hot and she carried her jacket over her arm, wishing that she'd put a tee-shirt under her sweater. Eventually she fell behind and they waited by the next stile for her to catch up.

'Do you always walk so fast?' she asked, trying not to sound as if she was complaining.

'Yes, when there's tea and cakes at the other end,' answered Naomi.

'Of course you know that she jogs for at least four miles a day?' asked Neil.

'Really?' Millie was impressed.

'Well, Neil runs for the police, you know,' countered Naomi. 'He's much fitter than me.'

'And I'm the original couch potato,' grinned Millie. 'So you'll have to slow down for me.'

'Come now, that's not true. What about all your hikes to Gunnerside Gill with the students?' asked Naomi. 'You've done quite a lot of walking up here.'

'That's true,' answered Millie.

'Students?' asked Neil.

'The boys who were staying with Grandma. They board with Helen,' explained Naomi.

'What are they doing in the Dales?'

'They're studying the effects of lead mining on the environment,' Millie replied, keen to expand on the subject.

'Sounds like a good excuse for a holiday,' said Neil.

'It's not,' objected Millie. 'It's very interesting, arsenic and lead in soil and grass.'

'Why? Is it poisoning the sheep?' Neil's voice was slightly mocking as he set off over the stile.

'A case for Sherlock Holmes, eh Chief Inspector Clark?' laughed Naomi, following.

Millie ignored them. At least Pete had been as excited by the crushing mill as she had and he hadn't thought her odd.

Naomi, letting Neil march on, had hung back to meet her. 'By the way, Millie, did you manage to find out about the student's mysterious disappearance?'

'Yes, actually. He's been doing a job for Jim Jackson. Do you know him?'

'Yes, he works for David Price.'

'That's right. He'd been delivering some sheep for him.'

'Where did he go?'

'Holland.'

'I didn't know that David exported his animals but he certainly is into everything. I bet he'll be on to Daniel soon to buy some of the land. He's always been keen to let Grandma know he's in the market to expand.'

'Do you know David well?' Millie asked.

'Quite well. We've grown up together really with our land being adjacent. We were at school together until he went as a boarder but we'd meet in the holidays. He has always been ambitious though and wouldn't let anything stand in his way. I feel quite sorry for Jean sometimes.'

'Jean?' Millie lowered her voice, although Neil was nearly out of sight.

'Yes, he can be quite a miserable sod when he wants to be.'

Naomi stopped on the path and looked down, poking at a root with her foot. 'I just hope that he's not got anything to do with the threats to Grandma,' she said slowly, aware of the impact that her words would have.

'What d'you mean?' asked Millie.

'She'd had phone calls and letters. Someone wanted to buy the Lodge and they were using threats to persuade her.'

'Who?'

'They didn't know, the solicitors I mean. They just had this phone call from her a couple of weeks ago. I think that's why Ian Norwich wanted to see me personally. He said that she rang him saying that someone was trying to persuade her to sell the Lodge. He told her not to worry, no-one could force her to but she said that she had had phone calls and letters telling her that it would be in her best interest. That worried him and he told her to tell the police but she said she would rather talk to him first. She had arranged to see him this week.' Naomi had been looking down all the time, playing with the dust on the path with the toe of her boot. She wiped at her face and Millie knew she was crying. Neil was coming back down the path.

'Come on you guys, it's ten past three, at this rate the teashop will be closed.'

'Righto,' said Naomi and they walked on together. Millie was trying to assimilate what Naomi had told her. There was nothing that she could put her finger on but it could make sense of what had happened to Bernie. Suppose someone took him and tied him up as a threat. Letting Lizzie know that they were serious. Perhaps someone was supposed to find him and bring him back, to show her that they meant business, only it was too late.

They walked in single file for the rest of the way to Barden Bridge. Here they crossed the river and climbed up a road winding in a steep curve for about a hundred metres. Before they reached the top they saw the picturesque ruins of Barden Tower and climbed over a stile into the grounds of the teashop.

The room was quite full and there were two large groups of middle-aged friends making most of the noise. They ordered tea and cakes, and Neil also had scones, jam and cream. He was obviously determined to cheer them up and began describing some of his adventures in the Dales with his father. He soon had them in fits of laughter and the rest of the customers were looking towards their table to see what all the noise was about.

The walk back seemed much shorter to Millie. This time they did not cross back over the river. There was more shade and in the late afternoon it felt a lot cooler. Naomi seemed more relaxed and to Millie's surprise began to talk about her grandmother's phone call to Ian Norwich in front of Neil.

'She was being threatened by someone who wanted her to sell him the old shooting Lodge.'

'Who?' Neil looked concerned.

'We don't know. She didn't tell the solicitors.'

'Did she know who it was?'

'I don't know.'

'But surely,' said Millie. 'Lizzie must have known who was threatening her?'

'Not necessarily,' said Neil. 'Clever people wouldn't give away their identity, would they?'

Millie had a thought. 'Whoever it is will be bound to ask your uncle to sell won't they? You just have to wait and see'

'Clearly your grandmother didn't want to sell this Lodge. So surely your uncle won't do so now, will he?' asked Neil.

'Difficult to tell isn't it?' said Naomi shrugging her shoulders. 'Ian Norwich promised to let Dan know what was happening and ask him not to sell. I thought that would make it more official but I don't suppose there's anything legal that can be done,' she said looking at Neil quizzically.

'Nope. But if you knew who had been threatening her then they could be prosecuted.'

Millie wanted to share her idea about Bernie. 'I was thinking that this might explain why Bernie was tied up. Another threat do you think?'

'Of course!' exclaimed Naomi. 'It's obvious. Why didn't I think of that.' She went on to explain to Neil about how Millie had found Bernie. Millie provided the details, blushing slightly when she referred to Pete. Neil nodded and looked pensive.

Eventually he said, 'Well, it's certainly a bit of a mystery. What we need is more information about these threats. I wonder if she ever phoned the mystery person, we could check that from phone bills. Did she mention it to anyone else, Helen for example?'

It was nearly five o'clock when they got back to the car park.

'I hope the shopping's alright,' said Naomi as they climbed into the car. There was a strong smell of fruit in addition to the bread now. 'It would have been nice to stop on the way but I'm beginning to worry about the food.'

It was a long ride back and Millie was hot. She found that she could hardly keep her eyes open and she dozed until they reached Kettlewell, waking with a start when Naomi stopped for petrol. Once they set off again her eyelids began to drop and she struggled against sleep. Next time she woke as they swung across the bridge at Hubberholme and she heard Neil regretting that he couldn't stop for a drink. She could see the church, tombstones, centuries old, generations of families buried in every one. Lizzie in Muker church, the church where her own grandmother had been hit over the head. Something about that was important. She dozed again and woke to find herself outside Laurel Cottage. Neil was already unloading carrier bags from the boot.

'I'll give you a ring tomorrow,' Naomi shouted as she drove off up the lane.

Helen came out and helped carry the bags inside. She unpacked the groceries excitedly and expressed pleasure at the additional items that Millie had brought for her. Millie described her walk along the river and Helen was astonished that they had gone so far in an afternoon.

'They both walk so fast,' said Millie. 'I'm shattered.'

'That Neil seems a nice boy,' said Helen. 'He looks like a pop star with that pony tail. I can't remember the name of the group but I quite like one of their songs.'

Matt and Andy arrived a little later. They had been up Gunnerside Gill and Bernie was with them.

'Was he alright?' asked Helen, giving the dog a pat while he wagged his tail and licked her hand.

'Absolutely fine,' said Matt.

'By the way,' said Millie, suddenly remembering her conversation with Naomi about Bernie. 'I think if you would like to keep Bernie, Naomi would be very pleased.'

'Really? That would be lovely wouldn't it Bernie?' and Helen tickled his ears until he rolled over and wriggled on the floor with delight. 'Oh by the way Millie, Pete rang to suggest that the vet should see Bernie, just to make sure everything is OK. I said that we'd take him into the surgery tomorrow morning.'

'Fine.' Millie wondered whether it was only the dog he was interested in.

Chapter 12

The air felt chilly as Millie and Helen coaxed Bernie into the car. Eventually Millie offered to sit in the back with him, hanging onto his collar to prevent him from fighting his way to the front.

'I think he's used to travelling in the front seat,' said Helen, as they set off down the lane.

They had got up early at Helen's suggestion. The surgery opened at nine o'clock and there was no appointment system. The boys had been about at breakfast and Millie was pleasantly surprised when they asked her to go up the gill with her.

'We're going to do some soil sampling today and we thought you might be interested,' Andy had said.

'And you could carry some bags,' added Matt with a grin.

They had agreed that she would catch up with them in the afternoon and they showed her their planned route on the map.

'I think Bernie's totally recovered now,' said Helen. He was lying down next to Millie and she stroked his head.

'Yes. I thought I'd ask whether I could take him for a good long walk tomorrow. I might ask Naomi if she'd like to come.'

'That's a good idea, Millie. We can ask Mr Evans, if it's alright to do that when we see him.'

'It's still odd, isn't it? What happened to Bernie. Do you think someone did it to frighten Lizzie?' Millie was looking for an opening to ask her grandmother whether she knew anything about the threats that Lizzie had been receiving.

'Oh I shouldn't think so dear. No-one would want to hurt her, of all people.'

'I just wondered. Wasn't she frightened of anything?' They were passing through Gunnerside and her grandmother paused while she waited for a van to cross the narrow bridge.

'I've never known her worry about anything, except that time I had the bang on the head. She made a terrible fuss about that.'

'Oh yes?'

'Yes. Everyone else said it was unfortunate, you know, bad luck. It wasn't me particularly, I just happened to be there. But Lizzie was much more concerned. She even said to me that it might not have happened at all if she hadn't lent me her car. Can you imagine?'

'Why did she say that?'

'I don't know. I can't see how borrowing her car made any difference, although I suppose if I hadn't I wouldn't have been there at all, perhaps. Anyway,' continued Helen, 'you could say that borrowing her car helped me. If Bert Bartholomew hadn't seen it he wouldn't have come in and found me. I might have laid there for hours.'

'That's true.'

'Well, here we are,' said Helen cheerfully, as they drew up at the vet's.

Once out of the car, Bernie pulled to get into the surgery. He was a well behaved dog and sat patiently in the waiting room for twenty minutes before it was his turn to go in. Pete came out and smiled at them.

'Hello Mrs Johnson. Hello Millie.' He looked tall and competent in his green medical smock. When he smiled at Millie she felt that she could trust him totally. Bernie obviously felt the same.

The vet was in the surgery waiting for them. 'Hello Bernie, old chap. And how are you?'

The collie wagged his tail excitedly and almost leapt onto the table without assistance. Millie watched him gently examine Bernie's legs and back.

'Yes he's fine. Is he eating alright?'

'Oh yes,' laughed Helen.

'Well I think he has recovered very well. All due to your good care, Mrs Johnson, of course.' He smiled at Helen, and she beamed back, blushing slightly.

'I wondered,' said Millie, 'I wondered if it would be alright to take Bernie for a long walk now. You know, on the hills, for a day?'

'Yes, I think that's a good idea.' He smiled at her again. 'Where were you thinking of going?'

Millie hadn't thought at all but, not wanting him to think her woolly and indecisive, she said, 'Keld,' and saw her grandmother look towards her.

'That sounds like fun. When are you going?' asked Pete.

'Tomorrow.'

'That's my day off!' he grinned. 'Can I come too?' She could tell that he was not joking.

'Well, er... Naomi is coming,' she blurted out and then added, 'But of course that would be fine.' She was bright red.

'Down you get Bernie,' he said as he lifted the dog down. His tail flicked Pete's hair and left him looking dishevelled.

'Good, I'll come over about ten then, shall I?' he asked, smoothing down his fringe.

'Yes,' nodded Millie, distractedly. She was busy planning how to persuade Naomi to come too.

'Thank you so much for everything you've done,' said Helen to the vet, adding 'for Bernie,'as if to clarify the statement.

'See you all tomorrow then,' shouted Pete after them.

Millie nodded and rushed off with Bernie dragging her through the waiting room and into the car park.

'Well,' said Helen, once they were back in the car and on their way home. 'He really is a nice young man, isn't he?'

'Not so young, Grandma,' she said.

'Well everyone seems young when you're my age, Millie.'

'Really?'

'No, I suppose not everyone. But quite a lot of people.'

'But you keep very active Gran. You're not old yet'.

'You're only in your teens. You've got your whole life in front of you. You must think about what you want to do with it.' Helen sounded serious.

'You're right. I'll think about it after the holiday.' She knew that it was no answer but for now she wanted to concentrate on more important issues, like ensuring that Naomi was free to come to Keld tomorrow.

As soon as they were in the house, she called the Manor. The phone rang and rang but Millie was not going to hang up readily. Eventually a breathless voice said, 'Hello!'

'It's only me Naomi, Millie.'

'Oh, hi.'

'How are you?'

'Oh fine. I've just literally got back from picking Neil up.'

'I've been to the vet's with Bernie,' said Millie casually.

'Is he alright?' she sounded concerned.

'Yes, he's fine, just a check-up. In fact he said that it would be OK for him to have a good long walk.'

'That's good.'

'Yes. I thought I might go to Keld tomorrow. Would you like to come?'

'Well, yes. Let's think. No, that's fine. I've got to run Neil back to Halifax sometime but we can go this evening.'

'Well, if it's not convenient...' In fact she was quite pleased to hear that Neil was going back that night. It meant that they wouldn't end up as a 'foursome.'

'No, it's OK. Don't want you having to go alone.'

'Well actually there will be someone else.'

'Oh yes? Who's that?'

'Pete, the vet's assistant.'

Naomi paused.

'Oh yes?' She sounded amused.

'He invited himself, if you must know.'

'Did he?' she continued to sound highly amused. 'Are you sure you want me to come with you?'

'Yes. That's why I want you to come. Will you come? Please?'

'OK, but you owe me! Now listen, I rang Dan this morning, first thing. He said that he has already contacted David about selling some land. Can you believe it? I told him not to but he won't listen. I told him that he was not to do anything without telling me but I don't think he will.'

'What is he trying to sell David?'

'Whatever he wants by the sound of it. The trouble is that I don't know what he does want. What if he wants the Lodge? Is it him that's been threatening Grandma do you think?'

Millie felt that it was time to tell Naomi what she knew about the Dutchman. She lowered her voice.

'Look, I think there is someone else interested in the Lodge. A Dutchman. A company that rents it for shooting. I remember Lizzie mentioning it when I met her.'

'What's the name?' asked Naomi.

'I don't know but he rented the Lodge for the grouse shooting. The whole season, she said. The estate agent told her.'

'I could ask them. If I knew the name I could ask Neil to run a check on him. If he rented the Lodge they must have the details. Name, address, phone number.'

'Right.'

'D'you want to come into Hawes with us?'

Millie was tempted but she wanted to go up to join the boys at the gill.

'No, you go. I've got to help the boys sample this afternoon.' It made her feel quite important when she said it.

'In that case we'd better meet up again when we get back. Why don't we have a drink? Back here? About seven?'

'Yes, that's fine.'

'Good. Bye for now then.'

When Millie had put the phone down she went to find a large scale map of the area, one that showed Keld. It was not a long walk, about six miles altogether. The route followed the river Swale right up the valley and on the way was Swinner Gill, the site of an old smelting mill. At that point the path was part of the Coast to Coast Walk and the Pennine Way went through Keld itself. A great cross roads where the two tracks, one travelling South to North and one West to East, meet for a moment in Keld. It was possible to do a circular route from Mossy Bank along the Coast to Coast to Keld and down the Swale to Muker and back.

Millie began to look forward to the day as she planned the route, deciding where they should stop and eat their picnic lunch. It was only when she remembered that there would be three of them sitting by the river eating that she once again felt anxious about it all. Funny how they would be visiting yet another smelt mill, she thought. Picking up a guide to Swaledale she read 'A short diversion should be made to the smelt mill remains and the awesome view down the gill.' It sounded impressive.

'Millie, d'you want an early lunch if you're going out this afternoon?'

Her grandmother prepared some salad, while Millie kept her company in the kitchen.

'You seem to have been up here for weeks now,' said Helen

'Yes. I feel quite at home.'

'Well, you seem to have made lots of friends already.'

Millie agreed.

'I was talking to Lillian yesterday. She asked how long you were staying and I couldn't believe you're only here for another week.'

'Ten days.' Millie had been counting.

'I wonder how your Dad's getting on?' said Helen.

'D'you know, I've hardly thought about them,' Millie admitted.

'Out of sight, out of mind!' laughed Helen, carrying the plates through to the other room.

'I really haven't thought about them at all. Isn't that bad?'

'No, I don't think so.'

Millie was surprised.

'You've been through a lot,' went on Helen, 'and it's time to think about yourself for a change. Enjoy yourself. It won't last!'

'You're right there,' agreed Millie.

'What about your spare time. What do you do?'

'Nothing much,' admitted Millie. 'I tend to slump in front of the TV once I've finished my coursework.'

'There you are then. You should have your own interests.'

'What? Like basket making?' Millie was joking but she could feel herself slipping into the petulant granddaughter role.

'No, seriously, Millie. Make some time for yourself. Do something *you* want to do. It's important.'

'OK. I'll try.'

As soon as lunch was over, Millie put on her boots and packed her waterproof jacket in the rucksack. Putting Bernie on his lead, she set off for Gunnerside Gill. It was not as chilly as it had been earlier and the sun warmed her as she strode up the lane. She saw that Naomi's car was gone from the Manor and she guessed that she and Neil were in Hawes. Feeling good out in the air again, Millie realised that she actually felt more independent and capable when she was walking alone in the open hills. Sheep wandered aimlessly plucking at the grass and staring at her as she went past, their jaws working steadily. Occasionally there was a single bleat for no apparent reason and a second would reply, as if the sheep needed the reassurance that another was nearby.

She knew the route well now, where each smaller path went off, to the right or to the left. She was passing the fork where the larger track continued up to the Lodge. It was marked by a small pile of rocks, a cairn that was hardly big enough to be called one. Here the bracken gave way to the heather and the sound of buzzing prevailed. Millie could see that the bees came from over the stone wall that marked the edge of the land around the Manor and she wondered if Bert Bartholomew had any bee-hives down there.

The boys had planned to collect their soils and sediments in the same places as the water samples they had taken the week before. Turning right Millie made her way down the path, following the gill. Bernie was thoroughly enjoying himself off the lead, running backwards and forwards along the track. It was quite steep at this point and the path dropped away out of view below her. Bernie suddenly pricked up his ears, raced way and disappeared. Thinking that he had seen a rabbit she expected him to reappear quite quickly and she walked on for short time but there was no sign of him. She ran down the path, calling him and shouting angrily for him to come back at once. Turning a bend in the track she saw someone waving and there, down by the gill, were Matt and Andy, making a big fuss of Bernie. They were pleased to see her and explained what progress they had made with their collecting. They were sampling from the side of the gill and also taking sediments from the bottom of the stream where possible.

'Where possible is about right.' complained Andy.

The water was clear and he pointed out the large smooth rocks that formed the stream-bed.

'Never mind,' said Matt, 'we'll do what we can.'

They showed her how they used an auger, a special device which looked like a giant corkscrew, for taking samples of soil. Millie was able to help by noting down the places where they took their samples and the time passed very quickly.

'What do you do with them once they're all collected?' she asked, referring to the soils.

'We've got to take 'em back to the lab, dry 'em, grind them up, and do extractions on 'em,' explained Andy.

'Extractions?'

'Different chemicals to take out different elements. It tells us about their bioavailability,' he replied.

Matt tried to explain more clearly. 'Take arsenic. Even if it's in the soil, it might not be in a form that's available for plants or it may not come out into the water.'

'I see,' Millie thought that she understood. 'And is it bio...er...available? The arsenic?'

'We don't know yet,' answered Andy.

'We don't even know if there's any in the soil.' added Matt.

They stopped to have a drink of tea from the thermos provided by Helen accompanied by slabs of home-made cake and then continued with the last three sites. By five o'clock they were on their way back to Mossy Bank.

'I've been thinking about that trip you made to Holland,' began Millie.

'Yes?' said Matt.

'Do you think you might go again?'

'He didn't say so,' Matt answered.

'Oh.' Millie tried not to sound disappointed.

'Why, did you want some duty free?' asked Matt laughing.

'No. I just thought we might find out what they're up to, that's all.' Millie waited for their response.

'D'*you* think it's dodgy then?' Andy sounded worried.

'It is odd,' she said.

'Just a bit,' agreed Matt.

'Best keep out of it,' said Andy.

'No, not necessarily. It might be something worth sorting out,' said Matt, seriously. 'To be honest I wasn't entirely happy taking a load of sheep to be slaughtered in Holland.' He seemed to have been quite worried by the whole experience.

'Oh yes.' Millie had forgotten that he was a vegetarian and saw how this might be the lever she needed.

'Perhaps they *are* exporting the sheep illegally,' she suggested.

He took the bait. 'That's true. Maybe they don't have a licence or aren't. We should investigate it.'

'What I thought,' Millie said, slowly, 'was that you could see if you can do the trip again.'

'I could ask Nick, I suppose,' said Matt, looking at Andy.

Andy nodded. 'We could see him tonight at the pub.'

'Hello.' Millie heard a man's voice behind her and looking up she saw Neil following her up the drive to the Manor. He was wearing jeans, a tee-shirt with the name of a band on and large white trainers. He was carrying a holdall.

'Hello. Where's Naomi?' she asked.

'Indoors, she dropped me off in Muker, so I could pack. I'm off back to the big city tonight.'

'Yes, Naomi said. Did you find out anything interesting in Hawes?'

'Yes and no. Yes, interesting really. Let's go in.'

They walked round to the back door of the Manor.

'Did you find out the Dutchman's name?' Millie asked.

'Well, we got the name of this Dutch company that rents the Lodge.'

'But they must have had to give a contact name?'

'Yes, they did.'

'And?'

'D. Price.'

'David?'

'Yep.'

Millie thought about this piece of news.

'He did say that he helped organise beaters for them.'

'Did he?' Neil asked, obviously surprised.

'Yes. He said so. When I went to dinner, last week.'

Neil held the door open to allow Millie into the kitchen.

'What is this David Price like? Is he the sort of bloke to threaten old ladies?'

'No.' she said immediately, and then added, 'Not really. I'm sure he wouldn't.'

'Sure?'

'Well, he is very ambitious. His wife said so. She said that he wants to expand and that he'd been keen to go to Holland. Yes, she said that! Do you think he's involved then?'

'I don't know. To be honest it's a bit of a long shot all round, isn't it? And what does it mean anyway? Actually it's all a bit irrelevant now that Naomi's grandmother's dead.'

'I don't think Naomi would say that.' Millie was disappointed that Neil was not more concerned but she didn't really want to believe that David was the villain.

'Would you be able to find out anything about this company, Neil?'

'Oh yes. If they're registered we can trace them.'

'And will you?'

'Yeah, for Naomi.' He smiled at her.

Millie wanted to ask about his relationship with Naomi but she couldn't ask him such a personal question.

'Have you known her long?' she asked casually.

'Not such a long time. Not long enough for her, I think.'

'Why?' Millie felt emboldened by his confiding in her.

'I think she needs to know someone a long time before she trusts them.'

'I see,' Millie didn't really understand.

'What about you?' Neil asked bluntly.

'I'm sorry?' Millie was taken aback.

'Do you have a boyfriend?'

'Oh no,' she said, blushing.

Neil turned and began examining the contents of the refrigerator as Naomi burst into the kitchen.

'Sorry I was in the garden – look at these courgettes! Have you been here long?'

'Stir fry or risotto?' Neil asked, throwing vegetables onto the table.

'Whatever.' Naomi replied. 'Have you told Millie about our trip?'

'More or less.' Neil was cutting up vegetables, occasionally offering them a piece of carrot.

'What d'you think? It's that damn David Price behind it all! I thought it was but this proves it.'

'Are you sure?' asked Millie. 'I told Neil, he organises beaters when they're shooting. Maybe he organises the bookings too.'

'Maybe he organises the threats as well. Frightening old ladies, a speciality.' Naomi looked excited, her eyes were wide and she had a half-smile on her face.

Millie said nothing.

'Look, I'll run a check on this Dutch company,' said Neil, putting his hand on hers. 'I can find out who owns it, what they do and where they're based. That's the first thing. Don't jump to conclusions.'

Naomi pulled her hand away. 'I know. Be rational. Well I am and I don't like what I see.' Then she added, 'I'd like risotto, thank you.'

'Millie?' Neil looked at her enquiringly.

'Oh, not for me thanks, I'll eat later, at home.'
While Neil was cooking, Naomi continued her tirade against David.

Finally he said, 'There's nothing you can do at the moment is there?'

'There is. I can go and sort him out. Ask him!'

'Not 'til we've got the facts. Agreed?' he looked at her seriously.

'Why?' she sounded like a petulant child.

'Because it would be daft.' He paused. 'After all, if he has been a naughty boy, we don't want to give him any warning that we know, do we?'

'That's true. We've got to catch him red-handed.' Naomi had lost her initial excitement.

'So hold on 'til we know what we're dealing with. OK?'

'I suppose so.'

When the food was ready Neil ate in silence while the two women discussed their plans for the following day. Naomi did not refer to the fact that Pete was to accompany them on their walk and Millie was relieved.

'We'd better be off then,' said Neil when they had finished eating.

'Would you like us to stay a bit longer?' asked Naomi, glancing at Neil.

'No, no, you've got to get going.' Millie was conscious that they were only driving back to Halifax that night so that Naomi could accompany her on her walk.

'If you're sure? We had better go, hadn't we Neil?'

'Yep.' He picked up his holdall and smiled at Millie. 'Cheers Millie. Nice meeting you.'

'Won't you be back before I leave?' She had assumed that he would.

'I doubt it,' he said, glancing at Naomi. 'We'll see.'

Naomi leant across the table and squeezed Millie's arm. 'Bye Millie. When will I see you tomorrow?'

'About ten? We'll call for you on the way.'

'We?' asked Neil and Millie blushed.

'Ah. It's a long story. I'll tell you on the way,' said Naomi and with a grin back at Millie she led the way to the door.

'I didn't know whether you wanted something to eat?'

'No, it's alright Gran.'

'So I made a lasagne,' she went on.

'Wonderful.'

They sat together enjoying their quiet meal while Millie described her route for the next day.

'You seem to be having such a busy time with your new friends, it's especially nice that you get on so well with Naomi.'

'Yes.' Of course her grandmother had no idea of all the activity she had been involved with since her arrival. To her, she had been going off to visit Hawes and Skipton with Naomi as a sightseeing expedition.

'Is Naomi bringing that nice young man tomorrow?' Helen asked.

'Who? Neil? No, she's taking him back to Halifax tonight.'

'To Halifax? Good heavens! You young folk.'

Millie laughed. 'Have you seen Andy or Matt since they went to Reeth?'

'No dear.'

After they had washed up, Millie took the map and studied the route again. She found a book that described the villages and spent the evening reading about Upper Swaledale, while her grandmother read a novel. Millie waited for the boys, expecting them to appear at any moment.

After eleven o'clock they burst in, obviously having had a few drinks.

'Hello Mills, we went to see Nick. At the pub,' said Matt.

'We've had a drink,' explained Matt, with a grin.

'Well two or three, actually,' added Andy, laughing.

'What took you so long?' asked Millie, crossly, ushering them through to the kitchen so they could talk.

'We had a drink,' repeated Matt in a whisper, who was also laughing.

'Well, two or three actually,' added Andy, who was by now in hysterics at the joke.

'What did Nick say?' asked Millie, she couldn't help smiling at their antics.

'He'll let us know,' said Matt, looking suddenly serious again. 'He'll tell us tomorrow down at his Aunt's house. Ten o'clock.'

Chapter 13

Millie was lacing up her boots when she heard Pete's car coming up the lane. She looked sideways to check it was him and then continued to tie them up. It was only five to ten but she had been awake since seven. Her first action had been to check the weather. It was dull but dry. She had wandered downstairs and made some tea, taking it back to bed with her, sipping it while she thought about the day ahead. Now she and Bernie were ready to go and she would have given anything to avoid meeting Pete again.

'Good morning!' he shouted, cheerfully, as he pushed open the little gate.

'Hi.'

'I brought the dogs. I should think Bernie will get on with them. Won't you old chap?'

'Oh yes. No problem,' said Millie. There was a pause. 'Did you want some coffee or something?'

'No thanks,' he said, looking at her boots.

'Right then, we'll go and get Naomi.'

Millie went to the front door and shouted to Helen that she was off. Then, before her grandmother could appear, she slammed the door and walked quickly down the path and out of the gate. Pete was letting his dogs out of the car and pulling on his rucksack. Bernie made a fuss of them and all three raced up the lane. Millie followed quickly and Pete only caught her up as they reached the entrance to the Manor. Neither spoke as they walked up the drive. Bernie was dancing around on the front lawn with his new friends and Millie was reminded of her first visit to the Manor. It was the first and last time she had seen Lizzie, alive.

They had to ring several times before Naomi opened the door. She wasn't ready and left them outside while she got organised.

'How long have you known Naomi?' asked Pete.

'Not long. Only since...,' she paused, 'Only since her grandmother died, actually.'

'How exactly did she die?'

Millie felt uncomfortable answering his questions. She looked behind her, into the hall. 'A heart attack.'

'She seemed so active.'

'I thought so.' She changed the subject by pointing at Bernie, who had a stick in his mouth and was being chased by the other two dogs.

'They all seem to be getting on well,' he said.

Not like us, thought Millie.

Soon Naomi hauled a large rucksack through the doorway. Millie noticed she had a very professional looking jacket and was wearing her suede fell boots.

'I'm sorry you had to wait,' she said. 'I was up rather late this morning.'

Pete flashed a broad smile and introduced himself. Millie had forgotten that they hadn't met and muttered an apology.

Pete called his dogs and Bernie followed, falling on Naomi when he realised she was there.

'What a fuss!' she said and Millie could see she was pleased.

Finally the group started out towards the fells. It was still dull and they spent several minutes discussing the outlook. After that the conversation waned, until Naomi asked Pete about his veterinary course. Once he discovered that she was studying medicine they were chatting like old friends and

Millie was happy to walk along in front, listening to them and keeping an eye on the dogs. At the fork in the track Bernie turned right down the smaller path towards Gunnerside Gill. She called him back and they continued up the main track. Ahead, on the grass past the Lodge, she could see a Land Rover parked.

'I wonder who that is?' Naomi exclaimed.

'Just the local farmer, I expect,' answered Pete, cheerfully.

Millie looked at Naomi. Her mouth had tightened and she was screwing up her eyes to see.

'Well that would be David Price, wouldn't it?' she said slowly, emphasising the name.

'Yes, of course,' said Pete. 'Perhaps we'll meet him up there.'

I hope not, thought Millie.

They walked in silence until they came level with the Lodge.

'Lovely old building.' Pete stopped to admire it. 'I wouldn't mind a place like this, up in the middle of nowhere.'

'Wouldn't you?' asked Naomi sharply. 'Well it's not for sale!'

'Oh. Is it part of your estate?' Pete sounded surprised and apologetic.

'Yes. That is, it belongs to my uncle now.' She was looking at the ground.

Millie was embarrassed by the exchange and looked about for a distraction. Unfortunately it came in the form of David Price, striding down the track towards them. Pete followed her gaze.

'David! Hi! What are you doing up here?' he called.

'Just looking for sheep,' he called back.

Millie sensed Naomi stiffen and turned to say something, anything, to avoid a scene. Naomi had gone quite red and shouted, 'What the hell are *you* doing here?'

'What d'you mean?' David had stopped suddenly, genuinely startled by her outburst. Millie and Pete were caught between them and stood speechless.

'I said, what the hell are you doing here?' she repeated slowly, emphasising each word.

'Just looking for sheep,' he repeated with a shrug.

'Well kindly remove yourself and your vehicle from my property!' Naomi was bright red and Millie could see that she was shaking.

'What d'you mean, *your* property?' he asked nastily. 'I thought it belonged to Daniel now?'

That was it. Oh please go away David, thought Millie.

'Well it doesn't belong to *you* David Price, so just get off or I'll, I'll call the police!'

'Don't be a stupid bitch, Naomi Banford. This is a public right of way.'

Millie could see that she was close to tears.

'You bastard! I know what you've been up to. I'll prove it, don't you worry and I'll bloody well make sure that everyone knows it too!' She turned and ran off down the hill.

'Naomi!' Millie called after her and started to follow, Bernie at her heels. She couldn't keep up the pace and after only a few yards she gave up. Almost in tears herself, her legs were shaking and she flopped down on a rock, watching Naomi as she continued to run towards the Manor. She felt Bernie's wet nose on her hand as the tears rolled down her face. Looking back up towards the Lodge, she could see Pete standing watching David climbing into his Land Rover. She heard the roar of the engine as it came down the track towards her. As he passed she could see his face set in a hard stare. His dogs were barking and jumping about in the back. What would happen when he reached Naomi? She watched as the gap closed between them but the Land Rover sped past and left Naomi standing staring after him.

'What do we do now?' Pete was walking slowly back down to where she sat.

'I don't know,' she said, wiping her face with the back of her sleeve. Pete sat down beside her.

'What was that all about?'

'I'd better go back and see if she's alright.'

'Why did she blow up that like?'

'I don't know,' she lied.

'What's he done to her?'

'She's upset.'

'You can say that again. The way she jumped down my throat about the Lodge.'

'Well it's the same thing really. She thinks that David wants it.'

Millie watched Naomi's figure still making her way steadily down the track. 'Perhaps I'd better go back and see she's OK.'

'It may be that she needs time to herself. She's clearly upset over her grandmother's death. It's understandable.'

'David wasn't very understanding,' Millie sniffed.

'No, but your friend was being rather aggressive, wasn't she?'

'I suppose so.'

She imagined how it would be if she did go back to the Manor now. What if Naomi was so upset that she didn't let her in? What if she did do something silly like calling the police? She'd call Neil, wouldn't she? He'd calm her down. She would drop in when she got back. It would be unfair to leave Pete on his own. She sat weighing it up. Then she got up slowly.

'OK. Let's go,' she said, unenthusiastically.

For a while they walked in silence.

'What *has* he done to her?' Pete asked

'He's being awkward, that's all,' she lied again.

'I actually find David rather difficult myself. He can be very touchy over quite small things.'

'Jean told me that he is quite ambitious.' Millie ventured.

'Oh yes, he knows what he wants and he doesn't like anyone trying to stop him.'

'Do you think he might want some of this land?'

'I can see that it would make sense to expand up here.'

'Jean said he wanted to.'

'Well then.'

'What if Naomi tried to stop him?'

'He'd probably try to get his way, one way or another.'

'He wouldn't get violent though?' Millie was not thinking of Naomi now but Lizzie.

'No! Well not with a woman, anyway. But she should find out her legal position. He's bound to be on to that already if he does want to buy. Probably phoning his solicitor at this moment, knowing David.'

'I wonder if I should have a word with Jean. See if she knows what he's up to?'

'Might be a good idea.'

Millie was tempted to tell him about why Naomi had reacted to David in the way that she did but she was still unsure whether she could totally trust him.

After all, he had been talking to the Dutchman at the auction last week.

The track had levelled out and they walked steadily, watching the dogs jumping through the heather further up the fell. Occasionally a grouse would flap up in front of them, objecting loudly, but they hardly seemed to notice in their enjoyment of each other's company. Millie was also feeling more comfortable with Pete than she had done earlier that morning. A group of backpackers called cheery greetings as they marched passed them in single file.

'They must have come from Keld, doing the Coast to Coast,' she said, checking her map.

'That's right. We'll probably pass more of them. By the way, did you notice that we'll be passing a smelting mill on our walk?'

'Yes. The guide book says 'awesome views'.'

They had left the sheltered valley above Mossy Bank and moved round and down towards Swaledale. Her eyes followed the track as it gradually descended the fell and disappeared into the next valley. Examining the map, she could see that they would soon reach the old smelting mill at Swinner Gill. Recalling the visit to Grinton, she remembered how interested Pete had been in the history of lead mining. This time he had brought a book with a large section on the area and when they had climbed down to the ruins of the mill they spent a long time exploring the remains.

It was past noon before they thought about moving on and they agreed to have lunch with the 'awesome' view of Swaledale at their feet.

'I've just realised,' said Millie, searching through her rucksack, 'Naomi's got the sandwiches!'

'Don't worry; I've brought loads, if you don't mind sharing?'

She reddened. 'Of course not.'

Millie couldn't remember a time before when she had been so completely alone with someone. She felt an inexplicable awkwardness, that she hadn't felt when she was out on the fells with Matt and Andy. Pete, on the other hand seemed perfectly at ease. She ate in silence and looked at the view. A small patch of blue sky was appearing through the clouds and when the sun did appear momentarily, it was very warm in the shelter of their stone wall.

Pete entertained her with descriptions of the small patients at the surgery, the rabbits and the hamsters, until she suggested that they should move on. Retracing their steps, they crossed the small stream and continued down towards the Swale. Their path joined a larger track that followed the course of the river upstream to Keld. It was steep and Millie began to tire. She dawdled, frequently stopping to admire the view and occasionally to take photographs. The clouds were clearing and it turned into a warm afternoon.

Millie was disappointed when they reached Keld. The waterfall was swarming with visitors and when they crossed the bridge and climbed the steep path to reach the village itself, she found that it contained only a few buildings. She did, however, take advantage of the public conveniences and when she returned Pete was reading his book on lead mining.

'Imagine that. The population here was over 1,000 in the 1890s. And what are there now? About fifty?'

'Amazing.' Millie was tired and wanted to leave the crowds behind. 'Which way do we go now?'

'Back along the same path.' He indicated the track, signposted Muker.

They made slow progress following the footpath sign, indicating the Pennine Way. She felt a thrill to think that she was actually walking along the famous route that extended so far up the backbone of England.

'Have you ever walked the Pennine Way or the Coast to Coast?' she asked Pete.

'No. I want to but I've never found the right time, or company. And you?'

'Oh no.' She was surprised that he thought she might have done.

'No? What about the Three Peaks?'

'What's that?'

'It's a challenge walk, here in the Dales. You have to walk Pen y ghent, Whernside and Ingleborough in twelve hours.'

'How far is it?

'About twenty-two miles but it's up and down!'

'I couldn't do that.'

'Why not? I've done it, although I might need a bit of training now.'

The way back led them down from the Pennine Way out across open fields. Yellow spots, painted on stiles and barn walls, marked the route. The dogs scampered across the soft grass and Millie noted again on how unperturbed the sheep were.

'They're pretty hardy, the fell sheep.'

'I like the very woolly sheep I saw at the auction. I think they were Teesdales.'

'Teeswaters,' he corrected her. 'What about the Wensleydales? They're similar.'

'Will you be working at the auction this week?' Millie suddenly asked.

She had been thinking about how things might work out on Friday if Matt did get another driving job from Nick's uncle. It would be helpful to have Pete around. Perhaps he could introduce her to the mysterious Dutchman.

He hesitated. 'It isn't my turn. But if you want to go I can easily be there.'

She hadn't meant it to sound like that.

'I didn't mean... I just thought...'

'It's no trouble.' He smiled at her.

Oh dear, she thought.

'Are there any special licences or certificates that you have to have to export sheep abroad?' she asked.

'Yes. There are loads of regulations now.'

'Does the vet have to inspect anything, when he's on duty?'

'Only if he's asked to.'

'What if you thought there was something wrong with an animal? Can you inspect it then?'

'Well, the auctioneers ask us to be around in case there are any queries.'

Millie took a deep breath. 'It's just that Matt thinks there may be something fishy about some sheep he might be driving to Holland.'

'To Holland? Well, if he does, let me know. We can always have a look at them. Who is buying them?'

'I'm not sure.'

'There's a guy I know by sight from Holland. I could ask *him*.'

'Oh no!' said Millie quickly. 'Please don't do that. It could be, well, embarrassing.'

'OK. I'll be diplomatic.'

Eventually the path took them right into the bottom of the valley, beside the river. Millie envied the dogs; they were splashing about in the cool water.

'Come on you lot,' Pete shouted. 'We want some tea!'

'Can we go into Muker?' Millie asked.

'That's the general idea.'

They put the dogs on their leads to take them through the hay fields. The grass hadn't been cut and a narrow path led directly across the middle from stile to stile. Millie hadn't seen these traditional gate stiles that were no more than narrow slits between two wooden boards, with a small gate boasting a very strong spring that slammed back into position. Although she was not fat, she found the gaps difficult to get through. They were designed by men, for men with long legs not for short women with ample thighs and bottoms.

They sat outside the teashop at a wrought iron table, the dogs tied to the heavy chairs. Muker was alive with visitors wandering up and down the street. Millie had finally relaxed and enjoyed Pete's easy conversation. He was recollecting a particular visit to an elderly farmer in the vicinity who was prone to calling the vet out on a wild goose chase. When he'd finished, he suggested that they should be heading back.

'Isn't there a bus?' she asked, half joking.

'Bus? You must be joking. There's only one this afternoon and it's already gone.'

'Well, I suppose we'll *have* to walk then.'

They disentangled the dogs and set off back up the hill past the church. Millie would have liked to stop and wander round the churchyard but they retraced their steps across the meadows and through the stiles until they reached the river. Here they released the dogs and crossed a narrow foot-bridge, taking a right turn sign-posted to Gunnerside.

'Are you serious about going to Leyburn tomorrow?' Pete asked when they turned up the lane into Mossy Bank.

'Yes, I'd like to go again.'

'Can I pick you up then?'

'Yes, of course.'

Millie was pleased when he declined her offer of tea. He had to get back, he said.

'Thank you for the day,' Millie said, politely. 'I did enjoy it.'

'So did I.' Then he added, with a smile, 'I'll see you tomorrow then, about ten?'

'Right.' She went straight into the tiny front garden and busied herself taking off her boots, while he put the dogs in the car and climbed into the driver's seat. But when he started the engine and turned the car round, she stood up and waved, watching him disappear down the road. Then she quickly tied Bernie up to the gate and ran inside to telephone Naomi.

Chapter 14

'Yes dear, I'll have a word with her and get her to give you a ring shall I?'

'Is that Naomi?' Millie almost wrestled the receiver out of her grandmother's hand.

'No!' hissed Helen, pulling away and holding up her free hand. 'Right Jean, yes dear, I will. Goodbye dear.' She put the receiver down thoughtfully. 'Well, really, I don't know what that was all about I'm sure.' She looked quite worried.

'Can I just call Naomi?' Millie guessed it was about the events of the morning and she wasn't keen to start a discussion just now.

'Yes, of course dear but I thought she was with you?'

'I'll explain later,' she promised. She let the phone ring for a long time but there was no answer. She called again but there was still no reply. 'Damn,' she muttered.

'Now please explain what Jean was on about, Millie.' Helen was standing waiting for her to finish. 'She was in a flap over Naomi. I said she was with you, wasn't she?'

'No, I think I'd better see where she is.' Millie went straight off to the Manor, taking Bernie with her and leaving her grandmother's questions unanswered.

She rang the bell and knocked on the door but there was still no answer. Naomi's car was in the drive and, refusing to give up, Millie called Bernie and went through the side gate into the garden. The dog bounded off and she heard Naomi's voice greeting him.

'Are you there, Naomi?' Millie called.

'Over here!' She found her under the tree where Bert Bartholomew had sat on the day of the funeral. Naomi was sitting alone with Bernie at her feet.

'Hello,' she said, looking sheepish.

'How are you? I was worried about you.'

'Oh, I'm alright. I'm sorry about this morning. It's not like me really.'

'I know. Pete said he thought it was probably the reaction to your grandmother's death catching up with you.' She sat down beside her.

'Yes, you're probably right. I felt such an idiot as soon as I got back and spoke to Neil.'

'I thought you'd probably ring him. That's why I didn't come down, well one reason.'

'Pete must think I'm awful.'

'Not really, he's alright.'

'Did you have a good day?'

'Yes, I quite enjoyed it in the end actually.'

'I've been out here nearly all day. It's so peaceful.'

'It still looks lovely. The roses are wonderful.'

'Well you know that old Bert still comes in to do it all?'

'Really? Did your uncle ask him to stay on?'

'No, he doesn't think there's any point but Bert still comes. I explained that we wouldn't be paying him but he says he owes it to Grandma. She only left him a few pounds though.'

'Well he certainly keeps it nice. Perhaps *he* finds it quiet in here as well.'

'Away from his bossy daughter d'you think?'

Millie wondered whether she should tell Naomi about Jean ringing Helen.

'What did you think about David's behaviour this morning?' she asked.

Naomi laughed. 'I think it was a perfectly reasonable reaction to a stroppy woman screaming abuse at him. Don't you?'

'You were a bit, well, over the top.' Millie giggled.

'I really ought to apologise. I can't go round accusing people of goodness knows what.'

'Is that what Neil said?'

'Not quite his words but he did point out that there are ways of doing things and outright accusations are generally the least effective.'

They sat in silence for a few minutes.

'By the way,' said Naomi. 'Neil has run that Dutch company name through the police records and he's come up with three addresses. That's all the information he could get and he says that they may be totally unrelated to our people. Actually he said it would have been a lot better if I hadn't shouted at David 'cause I could have asked him for details on some pretext or other. I can't really now.'

'I wonder if there's another way we can get it from him anyway?' Millie wanted to tell Naomi about the plan for Matt to drive to Holland again but she didn't want Neil to know. Anyway she still wasn't sure that Matt's Dutchman was anything to do with the Dutchman at the Lodge or at the auction. She had told no-one about her visit to the Lodge and couldn't explain it now, not to Naomi.

'Millie, what if we had a look in David's house? I could go round to apologise and somehow have a look through his papers. He's bound to have something about the Dutch company, letters and stuff. I could pretend to go to the loo and …'

'I don't think that's a good idea, Naomi.'

'What about baby-sitting? You do that don't you? What if you offer to baby-sit?'

'Justin is about twelve, he'd be around most of the evening I should think.'

'Alright then, I'll invite them to dinner!'

'They'd think that very odd. They might be busy.' Millie didn't like the idea of snooping round their house with Justin there.'

'You're right. I'll invite them for a quick drink.'

'Look, there must be an easier way. What if I invite them round to Gran's. It wouldn't seem so odd.' In fact, although she couldn't say so to Naomi, it would be the answer to the phone call from Jean. 'I owe them a meal anyway.'

'Shall I make some tea?' Naomi asked quite suddenly and disappeared indoors without any further comment, Bernie close at her heels.

Millie sat in the shade of the tree, her head swimming with plans. None of them made sense and she decided it was best to forget the whole idea. When Naomi came back carrying a tray slowly down the path, she looked triumphant.

'I've got it! You invite David and Jean to lunch with the kids. I'll get in while they're out and take a look around.'

'How will you get in?'

'I just rang Neil,' she said with a broad smile, 'and he's coming down for the weekend. He can help me.'

'Are you sure?' Millie doubted that Neil would want to be involved in anything so shady but Naomi knew better.

'Yes. It's settled. You just have to issue the invitation.'

'That bit's simple.' She then confessed that Jean had been on the phone to Helen and that the first thing she was going to do when she got back was to explain to her grandmother exactly what had been going on earlier that day. It would be quite easy to arrange a lunch-time meeting over the weekend.

She left Naomi at about seven. Bernie had been ferreting around his old garden and was not keen to go back with her.

'Let him stay. I'll bring him over later.'

Millie found Helen in the back garden weeding the small flower bed. Standing over her, she described the events that had taken place that day, from the scene with David at the Lodge to tea at Muker.

'Well that explains Jean's call,' she said when Millie had finished. 'We must let her know that Naomi is sorry.'

'I thought it might be better if I let Jean know how upset Naomi has been, over her grandmother. She's bound to understand. In fact, I thought it might be nice to invite her over.'

'Mm.' Helen was carefully extracting a daisy,

'How about lunch on Sunday.'

'Lunch would be nice. She could bring the baby.'

'Right I'll give her a ring. What's the number?'

Fortunately Jean answered.

'Oh Millie, I'm so glad you rang. I told David it was probably all a mistake but he's steaming. What on earth happened?' She sounded close to tears. 'I rang Pete and he said it was probably nothing but David's been to the solicitor's. He said there's a letter going. I've never seen him so angry.'

Millie tried to calm her down and explained that Naomi had over-reacted. She suggested that they all came to lunch on Sunday and Jean leapt at the invitation.

'I know it sounds silly but could it be sooner?'

Millie suggested Saturday, looking at her grandmother, who nodded.

'No problem. I'll tell Gran, she'll be really pleased.'

Helen was relieved that it had been settled so easily and proceeded to concentrate on what shopping she would need the following day.

Matt and Andy didn't appear until nearly eight o'clock and they had only just finished eating when Naomi arrived with Bernie. They all talked enthusiastically about any topic that was raised and Millie sensed a false sense of light heartedness that hid the underlying threads of intrigue that were beginning to gather them in. Matt and Andy were only aware of the impending trip to Holland, with whatever that held in store. Naomi knew only that someone had been threatening her grandmother before she died and that it may involve a Dutchman and worse, David Price. Millie felt that she had more bits of the puzzle than anyone else but there were still large sections missing. As the night drew in Helen chattered away unaware of the subplots that were uppermost in the others' minds.

At just before ten, Matt got up and said that he and Andy would go and see if Nick was making a trip to Lancaster the next day. He looked at Millie as he left and raised his eyebrows. The conversation then moved to the boys and Naomi chatted with Helen about her studies as Millie tried to imagine what was happening down the lane.

'You're very quiet, Millie.' Helen was smiling at her. 'I think that walk has tired you out as much as it did Bernie.'

The dog was lying flat out with his nose resting on the hearth.

'Yes it was quite a good stretch.'

'I should have come with you,' Naomi offered, looking across at Helen but she was not drawn to discuss what had happened.

Eventually Helen said that she would like to go to bed. It was awkward because she was sleeping on the sofa and Millie insisted that she used her bed so that she and Naomi could stay up and chat. When Helen had gone up, Naomi said that the boys should come back to the Manor. Clearly she could not offer space in the house itself, now that Daniel owned it, but Ivy Cottage was hers and it was not booked for the next couple of weeks anyway. Millie pointed out that she was only going to be with her grandmother for one more week anyway and so that would be fine.

Millie told Naomi that the plan to invite Jean and David had worked better than expected and they were coming on Saturday.

'That's great. I'm picking Neil up early on Saturday morning.'

As time went on Millie began to feel anxious about what was happening to Matt and Andy. In the end she decided to tell Naomi about the trip to Holland. She had to start at the very beginning and explain about Matt's first trip. She described how Nick had asked him and explained that it was the reason he had disappeared at the time of Lizzie's death. She told her about the secrecy and the fact that it seemed as if it might be something illegal. She particularly asked her not to tell Neil, in case it was. She didn't want Matt to get into trouble.

When she had finished, Naomi asked, 'What do *you* think it is that they're up to, these people?'

'We don't know. We think it's something to do with exporting sheep. I've asked Pete about it.'

Naomi frowned at her.

'No, it's alright. I haven't said anything at all, just general chat about the auction. Oh and I'm going there tomorrow, he's taking me.'

'Is he alright? This Pete? He seemed a bit too matey with David for my liking.'

Millie told her what Pete said about David.

'I'm convinced he's got no particular friendship with him, quite the opposite in fact.'

They sat in silence waiting for the boys until Naomi asked,

'Do you think the Dutchman who buys sheep is the same man who rents the Lodge?'

This was difficult for Millie. She had met the Dutchman and his two English friends in the Lodge. She had seen them at the auction and she was sure they were the same. She couldn't tell anyone about her visit to the Lodge that day, she was too embarrassed.

'I think so but I can't be sure.'

'Even if they're not the same, they could work for the same company.'

Millie agreed.

'But your student could get the address if he goes again and we can check that with Neil's information?' suggested Naomi.

'Yes.'

'Brilliant. All we need now then is to prove the connection between David and this Dutch company.'

'Why?' asked Millie.

'Don't you see? It's obvious. If the Dutchman rents the Lodge and David is something to do with him, then it could have been him threatening Grandma.'

Naomi was still there when Matt and Andy finally appeared at ten to twelve.

'Where have you been?' Millie asked.

'In Muker.' Matt looked tired.

'Nick took us down to the pub, to meet his uncle,' Andy explained.

'Why there?'

They glanced at Naomi and back to Millie. 'It's alright,' she said, 'she knows about it.' They looked at each other and Matt nodded. The movement was almost imperceptible.

'OK, well - it's on!' Matt looked pleased, although Andy remained solemn.

'Just Matt,' he said, 'I can't see why.'

'Same trip as before. Exactly the same, they said.'

'So where do you meet? At Darlington again?' Millie wanted to know the plan in detail.

'No. That *is* different. They said to meet them up at the Lodge.'

'At midnight, they said,' added Andy, 'I think it's bloody odd.'

'It's OK,' said Matt, calmly, 'not far to go.'

'Well I'm going to get my passport anyway.' Andy looked at him sulkily, 'Just in case.'

Matt shrugged.

'Who will be going with you? Nick's uncle again?' asked Millie.

'Yep. He was at the pub. He organised it all.'

'Who is this uncle of Nick's?' Naomi spoke for the first time.

'It's Jim Jackson, according to Gran,' Millie answered.

'Jim Jackson? Are you sure? He works for David!' Naomi leaned forward in her chair. 'If he's involved, David must be behind it all!'

Matt and Andy looked startled by her outburst and Millie tried to calm her.

'Well if it's David's sheep, maybe he helps transport them.'

Naomi expressed her scepticism with a grunt. 'So what are we going to do when Matt drives to Holland?'

'Matt should make a note of where he goes,' replied Millie. 'That's all we can do at this stage.'

Andy and Naomi were all for following the trailer to Holland but Millie insisted that it was not practical.

'All we need to know is where it goes,' she said, firmly. She surprised herself with her air of authority. 'Neil can look up the address on his police files. OK?'

The others reluctantly agreed and Naomi left. When she had gone Andy continued to express his concerns about the trip.

'He's got this theory,' explained Matt, raising his eyebrows.

'What's that?' she asked.

'It's about the sheep, right?' began Andy. 'Why should these people be worried about transporting sheep?'

'I don't know.' Millie was waiting.

'It's illegal, right? It must be. Why should it be illegal to move 'em? Because they're nicked? They aren't. They must 'ave something wrong with 'em.'

Millie sat patiently while Andy pointed at each of the fingers on his right hand in turn as he checked off the reasons. She wished that he would get to the point.

'What could be wrong with 'em?' he paused, significantly, 'They could 'ave 'igh levels of toxic metals in 'em, like lead or arsenic, couldn't they?' He looked at her triumphantly, waiting for her reaction.

'I don't think so,' said Matt.

'Well I do. Round 'ere there's loads of lead and Nick's uncle works for a local farmer. Anyway the Dutch 'ave loads of regulations about pollution. Maybe their laws are stricter than ours.' Andy looked pleased with himself.

'So why transport them to Holland then?' asked Millie.

'They're smuggling the sheep to avoid the regulations!' Andy was triumphant.

Millie couldn't decide if he was talking nonsense or not but Pete would know. She told Andy that she would talk to the student vet.

'Great.' He beamed at her and Matt laughed, shaking his head.

'I thought I'd go to the auction tomorrow,' Millie said, reddening. 'Pete'll be there. I can keep an eye open for what sheep are sold and who to.'

'I'm going back to get my passport,' Andy said, 'so we'll be in Lancaster tomorrow. We'll see you back 'ere tomorrow night.'

Millie slept badly that night. She tossed and turned on the sofa, waking early. Her watch showed seven fifteen when she crept upstairs to the bathroom and by eight, she was eating breakfast with Helen. It was a dull day and, although it was no longer raining, the ground was wet. Pete arrived early.

'Hi,' he said as Millie sat down beside him in the passenger seat. 'How are you?'

'I'm fine.'

'Not too tired after yesterday?'

'No.'

The journey was more pleasant than it had been with David the week before and she admitted to herself that she really did not like him very much. She did not dislike him in the way Naomi did, however, and she could not share her suspicions about him being responsible for the threats to Lizzie. Millie was still sure that the Dutchman was the culprit.

Leyburn was already busy and Pete had difficulty finding a space in the large car park next to the auction mart. As Millie climbed the steps to the auction buildings she could see the Land Rovers and trailers queuing to unload sheep and cattle. She didn't recognise anyone and was glad that she hadn't to meet David again.

'So. What do you want to do?'

'Just watch. I'm interested in how it all works.' A thought occurred to her. 'Andy was saying that there are regulations about the animals. Like the levels of things like lead. For export I mean.'

He looked puzzled. 'I don't know about those regulations,' he said. 'Not in this country. If levels in the blood were too high the animal might get sick.'

'How?'

'Let's see. I think too much copper causes the staggers or is that a deficiency?. Lead and arsenic? I'm not sure. I'd have to look it up.'

'Do you have books?'

'Yes, there are some at the surgery.'

The ring was filling up. A farmer sat down next to Pete and they began discussing a problem he was having with a ewe. Millie listened while she watched farmers come and go, standing in groups or walking from one group to another.

At eleven o'clock the auction began. Pete went to join the vet at the pens and Millie sat, as fascinated by the proceedings as she had been the week before.

It was twelve thirty before she saw the Dutchman. He was dressed in his casual but smart style and stood out against the farmers. Millie couldn't tell if he was bidding but he stood close to the ring side and spoke to no-one. Soon after that six sheep were herded into the ring and then duly sold, although Millie could not detect who was bidding. Almost immediately the Dutchman left.

Millie jumped up and went after him but by the time she'd got outside he had disappeared. She looked round for Pete and found him outside leaning against a Land Rover, talking to the driver. To her embarrassment he glanced round and saw her, waving her to go over.

'Let me introduce you to Ken,' he said with a broad grin. 'Ken's our area officer.' Ken poked his head out of the window. 'Hello.'

'Ken's responsible for food safety, indirectly. He knows everything there is to know about nutrients and trace elements. I was asking him about lead.'

'Ah'

'Never seen owt up 'ere suffering from lead poisoning.' The man shook his head. 'Nowt.'

'Ah,' she repeated.

'Anyway, must be off now. See yer.' He drove off without another word.

'Bit shy is our Ken. But he doesn't see any problems with lead or arsenic round here. So there you are.'

'Thanks.' It wasn't quite so simple to Millie. After all, lead poisoning might be different to just having unusually high levels of lead in the blood or meat, couldn't it? She would have to look it up. She had another question for him.

'Pete, would you be able to find out who's just bought some sheep and who they belong to?'

He looked at her, thoughtfully. 'I shouldn't really but I could.'

'Would you? It's just that it's interesting,' she lied.

He looked puzzled but said, 'I don't see what harm it would do. Which sheep are they?'

She described the group of six sheep that had been sold when the Dutchman was at the auction. He told her to stay there and disappeared into the building. After about five minutes he came out looking worried.

'Why did you ask about those sheep particularly?'

'I just wondered if a particular person had bought them.'

'A Dutchman by any chance?'

'Yes. And did they belong to David Price?' Her hunch had been right then.

'Yes. How did you know?'

'I just guessed.'

'Is this something to do with your questions about poisoning?'

'Ah, yes.' She decided to stick to Andy's story. 'Andy thinks that they might be ill.'

Pete looked even more concerned.

'Is there any way we could test them?' she asked.

'You could take blood samples and get them analysed but not without permission. We'd need David's permission first.'

'No you wouldn't,' she corrected him, 'They belong to the Dutchman now.'

'That's true. I'd need his permission though.'

'Do you need permission if you think there's something fishy? Perhaps you'd better do it anyway?'

Millie could tell that he was concerned but that he didn't want to be drawn into anything clandestine, particularly where David was concerned. Without another word Pete strode back into the building and came back a few minutes later with another man, who he introduced as a member of the auction office staff. He told the man that Millie was a member of an animal rights organisation and that she wanted to see that the animals were being handled properly. He seemed happy enough. Millie was impressed when Pete continued.

'She represents a Dutch group and so she would like to see the animals that are going to Holland.'

The official said that he would arrange it if they could return at two o'clock. Pete accompanied the man back inside and Millie watched as they talked with a lot of shrugging and arm waving. Millie could hardly keep a straight face as she waited for Pete to return. He had lied through his teeth for her and had completely changed her impression of him. He returned looking a little worried.

'I'm not sure I should have done that.'

'No? It was great.'

'But what if the buyer is there?'

'That's alright, just tell him the truth.'

'What if the seller is there?'

'Ah.'

They were lucky, there was no sign of David. At two precisely the auction official escorted them to an old trailer. No-one else was there and the official opened it for them. The sheep were already inside. Pete made a pretence of looking at each animal in turn, their eyes, their feet, and then he took a sample of blood from each. Millie watched, making a mental note of the number plate of the trailer. The sheep looked perfectly normal and she could see nothing odd about them at all. When Pete was finished the man closed the door and followed them back to the building.

'Thanks a lot John.' Pete waited until he had disappeared and then said, 'I don't know how long it will take to get these analysed.' He held the vials up to the light, looking rather stressed.

'I'm sorry,' she said.

'Oh don't worry,' he said, 'I rather enjoyed it. But I don't think we'll find anything.'

'Let's hope not.' There was nothing more to do there and she told Pete that she had to get back. On the way she told him that Jean and David were coming to lunch the next day and asked if he could come too. To her disappointment he explained that he was working, so she promised to spend Sunday with him.

Chapter 15

Millie asked Pete to drop her off outside Mossy Bank Manor. To her surprise Bernie came racing to meet her as she climbed out of the car and Naomi was leaning out of an upstairs window at Ivy Cottage.

'Hello Millie, we're tidying up the cottage for the boys!' She disappeared inside and Millie went in with Bernie at her heels. Her grandmother was in the kitchen washing up some dishes and Naomi came thundering down the stairs to join them.

'It was Naomi's idea, for the boys,' explained Helen, pulling off her rubber gloves. 'She thought it would give us more space, just for this week.'

'It was was nice of you to help, Helen.' Naomi took the gloves from her.

'Well, I'm only sorry I can't stay longer but I must go and get sorted out. I'll just pop into Muker.'

'D'you want me to look after Bernie?'

'Oh yes, that would be helpful. He seems happier here anyway, don't you think?'

Millie did, but she didn't say so.

'So, how did you get on?' asked Naomi, as they watched Helen go.

Millie described what had happened, particularly how Pete had taken the blood samples from the sheep.

'Really?' Naomi was shrieking with delight as she related how Pete had pretended that she was an animal rights activist. 'Well, well,' she said, 'he sounds more interesting, your Pete.'

'Not *my* Pete,' objected Millie.

'Well, whatever. Helen is quite excited about lunch tomorrow, by the way. She actually asked if I would like to come!'

'What did you say?'

'I told her I thought it was more tactful if I didn't. She knows that David and I don't get on.'

'It would defeat the whole purpose of inviting them.'

'Exactly. Neil is coming over tomorrow. So now we're in business.'

'I suppose so.' Millie didn't share her friend's obvious excitement.

'What about the plans for tonight?' Naomi continued.

'I don't know. I'm not sure what's best. I'm just hoping that Andy doesn't do anything silly.'

'And I told Neil about what was happening,' Naomi declared, looking at Millie anxiously.

'Did you?' She was disappointed. 'You know I didn't want to get Matt into trouble. '

'It's OK. I was hoping he would get here tonight and that he could help. He said we should tell Matt not to go, to postpone it somehow.'

'Oh no!'

'Don't worry, I don't think we should. There's no problem is there? He's done it before hasn't he?'

'Yes. Just the same as last time, they said.'

'Well, that's OK then. We can follow him until he gets on the ferry.'

'Andy wants to follow him across to Holland. I think it would be difficult and it's not really necessary is it? After all, we only want to find out the address this time, don't we?' It seemed to Millie that it was beginning to get out of hand.

'You're right. He can keep in touch by mobile while he's over there.' Naomi's matter of fact tone reassured Millie. She continued, 'I wouldn't mind having a look at the Lodge before tonight. Just to have a wander up the track to see if there's anyone there. If they're leaving from there tonight, there ought to be some activity beforehand.'

'Yes. When should we go?'

'After lunch? Why don't we finish off in here and then I'll make a snack. We can spend the afternoon up there.'

They ate in the garden while Bernie ferreted about in the flower beds. Millie could see Bert Bartholomew working on the vegetable garden. He was using a hoe and every now and then he disappeared as he bent down to pick up weeds.

'I see you've still got your gardener,' she remarked.

'Oh my God, I forgot.' Naomi leapt up and shouted across the garden. 'Would you like something to eat Mr Bartholomew?'

He straightened up and turned round. His face was red with his exertions and he mopped it with a handkerchief. 'What's that?'

'Would you like a sandwich or a cup of tea?'

'Just a mug o' tea.' He returned to his hoe.

By the time Naomi returned with his tea, Bert had appeared at the side gate and stood wiping his forehead with his handkerchief.

'It's hot work,' said Millie.

'Ay.'

'Is that alright?' Naomi asked as she handed him the tea.

He took a large gulp and nodded. 'Not bad.'

'Are you sure you don't want anything to eat?'

'No. I always said to Mrs Banford, a mug o' tea's reet welcome but I gets fed at 'ome. No need to bother. Mind, she made a good bit o' parkin did yer grandmother.' He began to look a little unsteady and Naomi pulled a chair out and indicated that he should sit down.

Millie watched him as he sat with his tea. His hands were like gnarled twigs and his face had deep lines in his weathered brown skin. She wondered how old he was. 'Have you always lived in Mossy Bank?' she asked, hoping for a clue.

'Mostly. Apart from t'war years like. When I were a lad I went t' Leeds for work but it didn't suit. I were soon back.'

'You preferred gardening.'

'Oh ay. It's been me life.' His eyes looked watery and he used his handkerchief to wipe his face. He turned to Naomi and pushed his face nearer to her, 'Your grandmother were such a fine woman. It should never 'ave 'appened, yer know.'

Naomi looked at Millie and back to Bert. 'What do you mean?' she asked.

'It weren't right, what 'appened. That's all I'm saying and I know the truth of it. It weren't right.' There was silence as Millie tried to find the right words to ask him to explain what he was getting at.

'Mr Bartholomew,' Naomi began. 'Bert, are you saying that you know something about my grandmother's ...' she hesitated.

There was a sudden shout from Bert and he jumped up. 'That dog! He's in me vegetables!' and he ran, shouting, as he disappeared back through the gate. They could still hear him yell, back in the vegetable garden, when Bernie appeared wandering nonchalantly through the side gate as if nothing had happened.

'Well I don't know,' said Millie. 'I think he must have imagined it.'

'Very convenient. Do you think he was trying to tell us about Grandma's death?' Naomi looked distressed. 'I think he knows something and is trying to let us know.'

'Perhaps we should ask him straight out?'

'No. He'll do it his own way, I suppose. But I'd like to know what it is.' She stood up and picked up the tray. 'Let's get moving. It's time we went up the road.'

They left Bernie in the house and locked the back door. There was no-one out on the fells and no sign of any vehicles or people around the Lodge. They took the path directly to the building and Naomi peered through the windows.

'No-one here,' she shouted to Millie, who was hanging back.

'Where shall we go?' asked Millie, looking round. She wanted to get out of sight as soon as possible, in case someone did appear. 'What about up behind the Lodge?'

'No. We won't be able to see the door,' replied Naomi.

'Where then?'

'Over there,' she pointed past the Lodge, further up the track. Above, in the bracken, was a large boulder. Millie followed her behind it. 'If we hear a car we can look round,' said Naomi confidently.

'Are you sure we can't be seen?' Millie felt anxious.

'No problem. I used to do this all the time in the Girl Guides. It's fine.'

They made themselves comfortable, leaning their backs against the rock, with the sun in their faces. There was a light breeze that occasionally moved the bracken gently. Naomi entertained Millie with stories of guide camp holidays she had spent, campfire songs, collapsing tents and kit inspection.

Millie looked at her watch. It was just after three. 'How long will we stay here?'

'A bit longer, what do you think?'

'We ought to be back later for Matt and Andy. We need to sort out what we're doing.'

'OK. We'll stay 'til six.'

'Six?' It was not unpleasant sitting in the sunshine but Millie felt ill at ease, not knowing what might happen. 'What if someone does come? They'll see us if we go back down the track.'

'I hadn't thought of that,' Naomi agreed. 'P'raps we'd better move.'

'What if someone comes?'

'We'll go up to the back of the house, then even if someone comes now they won't see us.'

Millie kept an eye on the track as they walked behind the Lodge. There were nettles and thistles growing there and they made slow progress. As they reached the end of the building the track came into view again and Naomi grabbed Millie's arm, 'Someone's coming!'

Below them a Land Rover was moving up the lane and onto the track to the Lodge.

'Quick further up the hill!' Millie tugged at Naomi and they scrambled up to the cover of some bracken.

'Damn,' whispered Naomi. 'Now we can't see the front.'

Millie was feeling quite shaky and she tried to breathe slowly before she spoke. 'Never mind. We must just keep calm.'

As the Land Rover came closer, Millie tried to make out how many people were in it but the sun shone directly on the windscreen. She moved lower into the bracken and waited. She could hear the engine clearly just before it disappeared in front of the building. The engine died and doors slammed. No voices.

'Damn, damn, damn,' Naomi cursed softly. 'I can't see a damn thing.'

They sat in silence for a while, scratching their arms where the bracken tickled and flicking flies from their faces. Millie checked her watch. Three-twenty.

'It's no good,' hissed Naomi. 'I can't sit here doing nothing. I'm going to talk to them.'

'What?' Millie was horrified. 'You can't!'

'I can. Look I practically own the Lodge. I'm entitled to go and say hello.'

'No!' Millie couldn't shout and before she could stop her physically, Naomi had stood up and was quickly moving down the hill. She disappeared round to the front of the house and Millie could hear her banging on the door. It was quiet and Millie found that she was shaking. Several times she imagined that she could hear the door open. She strained her ears for the sound of voices but nothing was happening. Eventually a door slammed and she expected Naomi to re-appear, but no, there was no sign of her. She sat, following the second hand on her watch, wondering what to do.

The sound of the door opening made her jump. She felt relief until she heard an engine starting up and watched the Land Rover setting off down the track. She couldn't see who was in it. It drove quite normally, not too fast, not too slowly, down the hill and onto the lane but instead of continuing through the village it turned into the Manor. Had they given Naomi a lift back? Why would she ask for a lift? Don't be silly, she told herself, Naomi could hardly have said that her friend was hiding at the back of the house! With a feeling of relief she stood up. It was wonderful to stretch her legs. She waited for the Land Rover to reappear but after several minutes she sat down again, they were taking a long time, what were they doing? Now she wanted to get down to the Manor and make sure that Naomi was alright. When the Land Rover finally turned out into the lane and disappeared through the village, she jumped up and, ran round to the front of the Lodge. To her surprise the front door swung open sharply.

'Oh no!' She shouted, stepping back as she came face to face with 'the Dutchman'. He was holding Naomi roughly by the arm.

'Naomi!'

'I'm OK,' shouted Naomi angrily. 'If this idiot would let go!'

Millie lunged at him and pulled his left arm, trying to free Naomi. With that the man simply waved the shotgun in his right hand.

'I suggest you remain calm, both of you or someone will get hurt,' he said slowly, his strong accent making him sound even more menacing.

He pointed with the shotgun in the direction of the house.

'Get in there.' He pushed Naomi roughly into the sitting room and onto an old sofa, Millie sat down quickly beside her. They automatically clutched at each other.

'So what are you really doing here?' The Dutchman asked Naomi waving the shotgun in her face.

'I told you, I'm the owner of this Lodge,' said Naomi with exaggerated dignity.

'Ah – in that case we should chat about coming to an agreement for selling it,' he replied smiling unpleasantly

'It was you that tried to persuade my grandmother to sell, wasn't it? Well I have no intention of letting you have it.'

The Dutchman's expression changed to one of distaste.

'You should reconsider very carefully, young lady.'

'I have friends in the police force you know.'

The Dutchman laughed. 'I am sure that you will not be so silly.'

'I know you were bullying my grandmother.'

'Ha! You have no proof. You can prove nothing.' He waved his gun towards the hall. 'Get out both of you, you are ridiculous!'

Naomi stood up and hesitated, she looked as if she was going to speak. Millie grabbed her arm and pulled her towards the door.

'Naomi! Now!' and she dragged her out of the house and down the track.

Millie could hardly walk, her legs were shaking so much but Naomi seemed angry as she strode purposefully down the track.

'Well Bert Bartholomew knows something and I'll find out in the end,' she said fiercely.

They had almost reached the Manor and Naomi was obviously recovering from her ordeal. Millie was beginning to wonder what the Land Rover had been doing there if Naomi was in the Lodge all the time.

'Naomi, someone drove down here when he left the Lodge. He was here for about ten minutes.'

'What was he doing?'

'I don't know. I thought he was dropping you off.'

'What the hell was he up to?'

They looked round the outside of the house but there was nothing disturbed. They went in and Bernie seemed pleased to see them but was not at all upset or agitated. When they let him out he sniffed round the garden and ran around the vegetable garden but there seemed to be nothing wrong anywhere.

'Look, it's nearly six. Why don't I clean up and come over. Maybe Helen will give us tea. I'm starving.' Naomi was obviously feeling better.

Millie was shaken by the events of the afternoon and she insisted on waiting for Naomi before they walked together back to Laurel Cottage with Bernie. She was relieved to be in the comforting atmosphere of her grandmother's house.

'No sign of the boys yet?' Naomi asked Helen as soon as they arrived.

'No. They said they might be late today. Matt's got some work to do later, he said,' she replied.

'Yes.' Millie wondered if she might be able to tell her grandmother the reason for all their comings and goings but it was difficult to see where she could start. The boys were moving to Ivy Cottage so it would be easier to cover their activities but she wasn't sure about her own.

'I'll make some tea for *us*, anyway. You'll stay won't you dear?' she asked Naomi, who smiled sweetly and nodded. 'I thought I'd do it early because it's Friday and I usually play bridge tonight. That's if you don't mind, Millie?'

'No, of course not Gran.' She smiled at Naomi, who winked back. 'And we'll give the boys something when they arrive.'

When Helen had gone, Millie went upstairs to fetch the photographs she had taken at the auction in the previous week. She wanted to check that the Dutchman she had seen buying sheep was the man who had just threatened them. Using the technique she had seen on television, she gave them to Naomi and asked, 'Do you recognise anyone in these photographs?'

Naomi flicked through, pointing out people she recognised, including David's son, Justin. She stopped at one and exclaimed, 'That's him, that's the Dutchman.' She pointed at the man that Millie referred to as the Dutchman, accompanied by the tall, thin man with the Yorkshire accent.

'Well that must be Nick's uncle, Jim Jackson, then.' Millie said, pleased with herself.

'No, that's not Jim. I don't know who he is.' Naomi looked puzzled.

'Did you let Neil know what's happened?' Millie asked .

'I tried ringing him at home but he didn't answer. I didn't expect him to, he's got some job on tonight. Surveillance or something like that.'

'Well it makes a difference doesn't it?'

'It certainly does. We know who we're dealing with now. That Dutchman is the madman that killed my grandmother. That's for sure and we'll know tomorrow whether David's involved.'

'But I meant about tonight. Surely Matt shouldn't work for him if he's dangerous.'

'But that means telling him that we know.'

'So?' Millie couldn't see the problem.

'I don't know. I'm not sure. Suppose he's in on it?'

'What?' Millie was upset by her friend's innuendo.

'But how do we know he isn't?'

'But he can't be.' Millie felt sure he wasn't.

'We don't know do we?'

'Who can we trust if you say that?'

'We must be careful, mustn't we? There's Nick's uncle, there's Nick, he's a friend of theirs. They could both be in it.' Naomi seemed to distrust everyone, perhaps even her.

'So what do we do?' Millie was tired and confused by all the discussion.

'Let's carry on as if nothing's happened. It's better for everyone if they don't know.'

'Right but I'm getting worried about it now. It could be dangerous couldn't it?'

'It'll be OK once Neil's here, he'll sort it out.'

'I hope you're right.'

Matt and Andy didn't arrive until nearly eight o' clock. They seemed strained and had obviously been arguing. Eventually Andy announced that he'd brought his passport, in a tone that sounded as if he were issuing a challenge. Wishing to avoid an argument, Millie remained silent, but Naomi said, 'Do you think it's wise to follow them, Andy?'

'Oh, he's not going to follow,' said Matt, bad temperedly, 'He wants to come along!'

'But I thought...' Naomi was cut off by Andy. 'They said I wasn't to come but I thought they might change their minds if I just turned up.'

'I don't think that's a good idea, Andy,' said Millie, and thinking quickly, added, 'We'll need your help to follow them to Hull.'

'If I came with you I could get on the ferry and go as far as Rotterdam with 'em.'

Naomi looked at Millie and raised her eyebrows, indicating that it might be a possibility. Millie thought about it. 'We wouldn't wait for you to come back,' she warned.

'That's OK.' Andy had cheered up. 'I can 'itch, no problem. Great.'

Matt didn't argue so Millie assumed he thought it a reasonable compromise.

While the boys were upstairs changing, Naomi went off to get her car. By the time everyone was back in the tiny sitting room, Millie had made some coffee and sandwiches. It was only half past nine. No-one spoke much. Once or twice Millie thought of telling Matt and Andy about their visit to the Lodge but she guessed that Naomi would have told them if she felt that they should know. Did she really distrust Matt? Could he possibly be part of the Dutchman's group?

Naomi suddenly said, 'By the way. I had a look when I went home and there's no-one at the Lodge yet.' Millie stared out of the window, searching for the headlights of a Land Rover. Instead she saw the reflection of four anxious faces, all looking directly back at her.

'I've been thinking,' said Matt, 'that I might go up early and wait.'

Millie looked at Naomi and Andy. 'I think we should keep a look out here and only go up when they're up there.'

No-one disagreed with her and she nodded. 'Right that's settled.' She deliberately switched off the overhead light, leaving a single lamp on in the corner and moved her chair so she could look down the road. It was dark except for the lights from the cottages down the lane. She noticed two figures at the door of Bert Bartholomew's cottage One was the stout figure of his daughter, the other had his back to her but she could not mistake the old Morris Minor parked outside, belonging to Dr Mellor.

'Looks as though Bert's not well. Isn't that Dr Mellor?' she said, turning to the others.

Naomi came to the window and stood beside her. 'It is. Oh dear, I wonder if I should go and see.' She looked at her watch. 'I'll pop down. See if he's OK.'

Millie watched her walk purposefully down the lane and cross to Bert's cottage. Dr Mellor and Bert's daughter were standing by the old car. She watched the three figures in deep discussion and saw the doctor put his arm round the older woman's shoulder. She appeared to be crying. Millie assumed that Naomi would be going in to see Bert but she remained in the group, listening with her head on one side. Eventually the doctor climbed into his car and Naomi disappeared down the road with the daughter, back to her own cottage.

Half an hour went by while they waited for Naomi but no vehicles went up or down the lane. Lights were being put out in the cottages and it was so dark outside that they could only see their own reflections in the window. They jumped when there was a knock on the door.

'I'll go,' said Andy, clearly glad of something to do.

Bernie ran to welcome Naomi as she came in. She was pale and looked anxiously round to find Millie.

'It's Bert,' she said. 'He's dead.'

Chapter 16

Naomi had not been able to get much information from Dr Mellor or Bert's daughter. They had found him lying on his bed, fully dressed. The doctor would not be drawn to give any further details and Irene was too upset to make much sense but merely said that he must have overdone it. Naomi had insisted that there should be a post mortem and this time Dr Mellor had not disagreed.

'He seemed fine this morning, didn't he Naomi?' Millie said.

'He certainly was. He was chasing Bernie round the garden.'

The boys smiled and looked at the dog, wagging his tail when his name was mentioned. The sound of a car drawing up outside made Naomi rush to the window and Millie switched off the lamp so they could see better. It was only when she heard the key in the front door that she realised that her grandmother was back from bridge already.

'Will someone tell me what's going on?' Helen asked as she came through the door. 'I couldn't see to get the key in the lock.'

'Sorry, Gran, we thought it might be...,' Millie stopped.

'Someone else about Bert,' offered Matt, quickly.

'There's been people at his cottage,' added Millie

'Why?' Helen looked puzzled.

'Bert is dead, Mrs Johnson,' said Naomi solemnly. 'I'm sorry.'

'Oh, my.' Helen sat down. 'Oh dear. How?'

'They don't know. They'll be a PM, a post mortem,' explained Naomi.

'I wonder if I should… ,' Helen got up again.

'No, it's OK. I took Irene home and she'll be fine. Her husband's there to look after her.' She looked at Millie as she said this. Millie did not miss the significance of it. If Nick's uncle was at home, he was not driving to Holland.

Andy made some tea and they sat talking about Bert. It seemed to help and after a while Helen was suggesting that she would go to bed.

'Oh, don't forget to tell Helen about the arrangements for tonight, Millie.' Naomi nudged her.

Millie stared at her blankly.

'You know. The boys are in Ivy cottage and I asked if you would mind staying with me tonight, remember?'

'Oh yes.'

'Of course dear,' said Helen. 'There's so much room over there isn't there? I'll see you tomorrow then. Goodnight to all of you.' She shut Bernie in the kitchen and went upstairs.

Millie looked at Naomi, who whispered, 'Well, how else are you going to explain us all disappearing off now?'

Millie had almost forgotten that the evening had not yet begun. Matt looked at his watch. 'We'd better get going or I'll be late,' he said.

As they drove up to the Manor in Naomi's car, they could see lights on in the Lodge.

'How the 'ell did they get up there without us knowing?' exploded Andy.

'Must've missed them,' said Matt. 'Unless they came up the other way, from Muker.'

'Can they do that?' asked Millie.

'Yes. It's a bit steep but passable,' said Naomi.

'Let's go and have a look at them,' said Andy, getting out of the car as soon as it stopped in the drive.

'Why? We know what they look like!' laughed Matt.

Naomi was unlocking the front door. 'What does Nick's uncle look like?' she asked, casually. 'I thought I knew but the man I saw tonight with Nick's aunt was not the same man.'

''E's tall and thin, with a weasel face,' said Andy.

'Not short and fat with a red face?'

Millie understood what she meant. The man that Naomi had pointed out in the photograph was the tall one. If Nick's uncle was the short fat one, he wasn't the man involved in the job tonight.

'I really think I ought to be going,' said Matt, apologetically. 'It'll be nearly twelve by the time I get up there.' He produced a large flashlight and switched it on.

'Well, be careful, Matt.'

'Right then, cheers Naomi. I'll try to ring but it might not be easy. I don't know when I'll get back but I'll call as soon as I'm on my own again. Bye mate,' he turned to Andy.

'Yeah.' Andy looked at the ground.

'Bye Matt and good luck.' Millie smiled at him. 'Don't forget we'll be following you as far as Hull.'

'And I'll be on the boat,' added Andy.

'Right then, I'm off.'

They walked with him down the drive and stood watching the flashlight disappearing up the track. A large moon had appeared, the sky was clear and it was bright now. They could easily distinguish the outline of the Land Rover now and the trailer Millie had seen at the auction.

'I hope it's going to be alright,' Millie found herself saying aloud. She immediately wished that she had kept quiet for Andy's sake.

'Of course it is,' said Naomi, cheerfully. 'We'd better get ready to follow. It'll be too obvious if we appear from here. Perhaps we should go down the road a bit.'

'Yes. Why not park down past the junction, they're bound to take a left for Hull,' Andy suggested.

'I'm not sure,' said Naomi. 'They fooled us getting to the Lodge. I think I'd rather be within sight of the track. We'll stop down the lane a bit.'

Naomi cut the engine as they turned back into the village and let the car roll gently into position in front of Helen's car, so they were hidden from anyone coming down the lane. They seemed to sit in silence for hours before Andy suddenly let out a yell from the back, 'Headlights!'

The lights were moving slowly down the track, winding round and getting larger as they got nearer. Millie held her breath and they all automatically lowered themselves down in their seats as the Land Rover and trailer went by. From her position in the front passenger seat, Millie could see two figures and she guessed that it was Matt driving. The trailer was dark but the number plate was lit up and she recognised the registration from the auction. It turned left at the end of the lane and Naomi sat waiting a few seconds before switching on the engine.

'Well, here we go,' said Naomi, excitedly.

Andy said nothing but Millie could sense him leaning forward behind her, breathing on the back of her neck. The cottages were in darkness and, as they moved off, Millie felt a surge of anticipation tighten in her stomach.

The journey was not difficult. Naomi drove steadily, keeping well back in those areas where the route was obvious. In towns it was not difficult to keep a little closer and Millie noticed that only Matt had a wing mirror, on the driver's side. If they kept well back, with dipped headlights, the passenger would not be aware of them at all. It certainly seemed to work well and Millie sensed that Andy too had relaxed back as time went on. The journey through the dark roads was hypnotic and Millie began to wonder if the whole thing was a weird dream. Was it all a huge mistake? Had they been drawn into imagining that an innocent journey to deliver some sheep was a dramatic crime. Had the whole thing become totally out of proportion?

When they arrived at Hull the town was quiet.

'I'm going to assume that he's heading for the ferry,' said Naomi. 'I daren't stick to them now or they'll get suspicious.' She pulled over and they sat watching the back of the trailer disappear from view.

'What time is the ferry, I wonder?' asked Millie.

'Five o'clock,' replied Andy.

'How d'you know that?' asked Naomi sharply.

'They told Matt.'

'Fine. Let's try to have a rest 'til about four and then join them. Are you hungry?' asked Naomi.

'I'm starving,' said Andy, dejectedly.

Naomi climbed out of the car and opened the boot. She brought a rucksack into the car and took out a thermos and a packet of biscuits.

'I thought we might need provisions,' she said.

'Thanks.' Millie was grateful for the coffee although she couldn't eat anything. They were all noticeably more cheerful afterwards.

'We'll have to be careful when we get to the ferry,' said Naomi. 'The guy with Matt has seen us all before and might suspect something.'

They sat at the roadside and listened to the time moving slowly past by the sound of a church clock chiming the quarter hours. There were few cars on the road except the occasional taxi and once a police car cruised by, slowing down as it passed. Millie held her breath until it disappeared from sight and remained anxiously watching for it to return.

'It's OK, Millie,' said Naomi, sensing her concern. 'We're only passing the time until the ferry is due, aren't we?'

She needn't have worried. The queue for the early morning ferry was building up, mainly with long distance lorry drivers but the car park just before the entrance was nearly empty. No-one would notice them.

'There they are!' exclaimed Andy, leaning forward. 'Near the front of the queue.' Sure enough, the small Land Rover and trailer were dwarfed by the container lorries behind them.

Naomi was able to park the car in a spot where they could watch the trailer's progress until it disappeared into the car deck. Andy made for the door. 'Right,' he said. 'I'm off.'

'You will be careful, Andy,' Millie said.

'Come straight back on the next ferry,' warned Naomi. 'Remember we need you to tell us what's happening.'

'Yes, yes, OK. See you tomorrow, I mean today.'

They watched him making his way towards the ship until the lorries rolled forward and he disappeared from sight.

'I hope he's doing the right thing,' said Naomi, yawning. 'I feel so helpless now. We can't do anything until they come back. I feel shattered.'

They waited until the ferry left and then set off back to the Dales. By the time they reached Mossy Bank the day had begun and as they sat eating toast and drinking coffee, Millie thought Naomi looked awful. Neil was due to arrive any time and she didn't want to know how they planned to raid the Price's house. She decided to leave before he arrived and go to help her grandmother prepare for the lunch.

'Don't let Neil do anything to endanger Matt, will you?' she pleaded as she left.

Naomi smiled. 'Of course not, Millie. I'll let it take its own course. There's no need for him to worry about Matt. The more I think about it, the more convinced I am that the sheep are a red herring.' She laughed at her own pun. 'What I really want is to sort out whether David is involved with the Dutchman and his attack on Grandma.'

'Right.' Millie was inclined to believe that the red herring was the threat to Lizzie and as she walked down the lane she began to reflect again whether these were all the activities of perfectly innocent people. Last night it had seemed so mysterious and suspicious but in the morning sunshine, with a fresh breeze blowing and the birds singing, it all had a simple explanation. Even the departure at midnight that had seemed so undercover, so criminal, was explained in the light of the ferry departure time.

Laurel Cottage contributed to the air of normality as Helen busied herself in the kitchen. It was hot with the oven on and Millie told her grandmother that she would sit down in the garden for a minute. She had been awake all night and it had begun to catch up with her. If she shut her eyes for a minute or two...

'They're here!' Helen's voice startled her. It was mid-day and she wasn't even changed. She rushed upstairs and in less than five minutes was down in a more respectable pair of jeans and a tee-shirt. Jean and Helen were chatting in the kitchen and again Millie felt out of place beside Jean who was wearing a simple navy dress and had her hair swept up in a smart French pleat.

'Hello Jean,' she said awkwardly. Justin was in the garden playing with Bernie. There was a pushchair outside in the shade and she guessed that the baby was asleep. There was no sign of David. 'Where's David?' she asked.

'I was just telling Helen, he had to call out the vet. Mr Evan's going to be there in about half an hour. One of the cows has a touch of mastitis and David's getting in a stress, as Justin would say.'

'Oh dear.' Millie was wondering how to contact Naomi.

'Oh, it's quite common. It just needs antibiotics,' said Jean brightly.

'Right.' She should warn Naomi. 'I won't be a minute. Phone call.' Her grandmother looked puzzled.

She rang Naomi's number and waited impatiently for her to answer. Eventually she heard her voice.

'Hi, it's me.'

'Millie?'

'Yes. Just calling to say that I'm having lunch with Jean today.'

'I know that, you dope.'

'No. Not David. He's got a problem with a cow.'

'What?'

'He's had to get the vet.' Millie stressed the word vet.

There was silence at the other end. Eventually she said, 'Where is he?'

'Don't know. At the farm I expect.'

'Damn.'

'I'll see you later then?'

'Yes. I'll think of something. Don't worry.'

As she put the phone down Millie felt a sense of relief. At least it meant that Naomi and Neil could not attempt to break in, and also David would not be at lunch. She went through to the garden where Helen was admiring the baby. She had woken up and Jean was feeding her. Justin looked bored. Bernie, tiring of their game, was lying down while Justin tried to enthuse him by bouncing a ball gently off his nose.

'Do you like dogs?' Millie asked him.

'Yes. Dad won't let me have one. He says all dogs should work.'

'Would you like to give him a brush?' she asked, reaching for the box of Bernie's belongings and pulling out a brush and comb.

'Can I?' Justin sounded pleased. She showed him how to be careful not to pull his tangles but tease them out from the end. He was totally absorbed and Bernie was thoroughly enjoying the attention. When lunch was ready Justin had to be persuaded to come inside and leave the dog.

'Wash your hands, Justin,' his mother instructed as they went to sit down.

Helen and Jean chatted about village groups and various activities due to take place in the next few weeks. Millie let the conversation flow over her and was relieved that there was no mention of the bad feeling between David and Naomi. After lunch, when Justin had retreated to the garden with Bernie, the subject of Bert's death was raised.

'Do you know what happened?' Jean asked Helen.

'Not really. It was Millie who told me.'

'Well, I heard that he'd collapsed,' said Jean.

'In fact Jim Jackson told David that he'd collapsed at the Manor, working in the garden.'

'Really, dear? Did you know that, Millie?'

'No. I wonder who brought him home then?'

No-one expressed any further curiosity but the conversation turned to what arrangements there might be for the funeral.

'I believe there's going to be an inquest,' said Helen.

'Just a post mortem,' Millie corrected her.

'That takes ages,' said Jean. 'I remember when David's father died. It held up the funeral for days. Very distressing for Irene and the family.'

It wasn't until Jean was getting the baby organised to leave that Helen ventured to ask whether David had calmed down.

'A bit.' Jean smiled wanly. 'He seems rather pre-occupied at present, to be honest. I keep meaning to ring Naomi but somehow I haven't got round to it. I don't want her to take David's reaction the wrong way.'

When Jean announced that they were going, Justin, who had resumed Bernie's grooming, said that he wanted to stay to finish the dog's ears. Jean seemed pleased that he was so well employed and Millie suggested that she could walk him back to the farm with Bernie later on. She had an ulterior motive because she rather hoped that Pete would still be there with the vet. A little later, a very smart dog walked jauntily down the lane with Millie and Justin.

'Why's Bert's curtains closed?' Justin asked as they passed the cottage.

'Er, didn't you know that he died yesterday?' Helen and Jean had been discussing it earlier, hadn't they? Justin, of course, wasn't there.

'No.'

Millie explained that Bert had collapsed.

'Where?' asked the boy.

'At home, in bed. It was very peaceful.'

'He must've been ill before that.'

'Not necessarily, Justin.'

'Yes he was.'

'What do you mean?'

'There were two men. They were looking after him.'

Millie's heart thumped. 'Really? When? Yesterday?'

'Yesterday, after dinner. Dad sent me up with a message for Jim Jackson. He thought he'd be at home but he wasn't. But his Land Rover was outside Bert's so I thought Jim might be with him. But these two men came out and said Bert weren't well, so I put the note through Jim's door and came home.'

'So Jim Jackson wasn't one of the men.'

'Course not.'

They were turning down the farm track and Millie took Bernie off his lead. As they reached the bend in the track she saw Naomi's car coming towards them.

'Hello Millie!' she called cheerfully as she slowed down. There was no sign of Neil.

'I just popped down to see David and guess what? Pete was there so I made them some coffee.' She grinned like a Cheshire cat. To Millie's horror she saw a large beige folder on the back seat.

'See you later then.' She waved cheerfully and drove off.

Millie reached the farm in time to see David and Jean saying goodbye to Mr Evans. Pete waited until the vet had left and then offered her a lift. When she hesitated he insisted, opening the back and putting Bernie in with his own dogs. She understood why when they were out of earshot.

'What the hell is your friend up to now?' he asked, angrily.

'What d'you mean?' Millie was defensive.

'She was very, very odd. All over David, friendly as pie. In and out with coffee and biscuits, while we looked at his herd.'

'Perhaps she feels she owes him an apology.'

'Oh, come on! She was up to something. It was obvious.'

'Did David think so?' Millie was alarmed.

'Of course not. He's arrogant enough to think that she does want to apologise!'

'That's alright, then.' Millie was relieved.

'Are you going to tell me?' He had stopped the car at the end of the farm track. He looked at her and she knew that she could not leave him in the dark if she was to need his help again.

'Well, actually.' Her voice sounded small. 'She wanted to have a look at his papers to see if he does work with the Dutchman.'

'My God. She *is* mad.'

'You being there,' she went on, 'was quite useful, it was a diversion.'

'I'm not sure I like being a diversion,' he said grimly. 'It sounds more like collusion to me. What happens now?'

'I don't know. I need to go and see what she's found out.'

'Well, keep me posted.' He gave her a resigned smile. 'I've got to go back to the surgery now but I'll come over about ten tomorrow. OK?'

'Yes that's fine.' She smiled and he took hold of her arm. 'You will be careful won't you. This is beginning to sound like a cops and robbers movie.'

'Yes.' She was bright red. 'I'll walk from here I think.' She climbed out of the car to cover her embarrassment and got Bernie out of the back, setting off up the road without looking back. A few moments later she heard his car coming along behind her and turned round. When he drew level Pete leaned across and said. 'By the way, those blood samples. I can't get them done 'til next week. Is that alright?'

'No!' shouted Millie. 'That's too late.' She would be back in the south of England by then. 'Have you sent them off?'

'No.'

'Well hang on to them then. I'll think of something.'

'You're the boss,' he said with a grin and drove away.

Walking straight up to the Manor to see what Naomi had found at the farm, Millie passed a police car outside Bert's cottage. Naomi and Neil were in the kitchen.

'There's a police car outside Bert's cottage. What's going on?'

'Just routine,' said Naomi. 'They've been up here, checking on Bert's movements yesterday.'

Millie looked at her.

'I told them that he was here yesterday afternoon when we went out and gone by the time we got back.'

'Not much help really,' added Neil.

'Did they tell you what happened?' asked Millie.

'Not really. Must have gone to bed feeling unwell and died during the evening,' Naomi replied with a shrug.

'Do they know what caused it?' Millie wondered if she knew more than the police, but didn't want to talk in front of Neil. She deliberately refrained from telling them about what Justin had seen yesterday.

'No. They're doing the PM now.'

Neil was turning pages in the large beige folder that Millie had seen in the back of Naomi's car.

'Is that it?' she asked, changing the subject with a glance at Naomi to see if it was alright to talk freely.

'Yep,' said Neil. 'Nothing at all. Clean as a whistle.'

'Well what is it?'

'It's a file called 'shoots'. It's got all David's letters relating to the shooting season for the last three years,' explained Naomi. 'Letters to the Dutchman, details of the shooting parties they booked, lists of beaters, payments and so on. There's nothing dodgy at all.'

'In fact,' said Neil waving the folder open at a hand written page, 'quite the reverse, Naomi. There's a letter here from the Dutch guy suggesting that if David owned the Lodge himself he could give him a long term contract or even purchase it under very favourable conditions. This letter from David explains why he can't. It says "I understand your interest in a package deal for your shooting parties but the Lodge is owned by Mrs Banford, a good neighbour of mine, who wishes to keep the property in her family. You might want to approach her directly but if she asked my advice I would certainly tell her to maintain ownership of such a potentially valuable property." So there you are.'

'What did the Dutchman say to that?' asked Naomi, moving closer.

Neil turned the page. 'Dear Blah, blah...Thank you, blah... with respect to your comments regarding the Lodge, I am most disappointed with your attitude. We may have to reconsider our source of beaters when we plan our future visits, in the light of your comments. Please reconsider our request.'

'When were those letters written?' asked Millie.

'Last October and November,' said Neil, turning the pages.

'Does David reply to the last one?' asked Naomi.

'No. There's nothing until March when they ask for costs for beaters this year.'

'So are there any bookings for this year?' asked Millie.

Naomi took the folder and turned the pages. 'No.'

'I wonder if that's why he's a bit preoccupied, as Jean put it,' said Millie. 'Perhaps he depended on that work.'

'Could be,' said Naomi. 'It's difficult surviving on farming alone in the Dales.'

'It would certainly put the pressure on him,' suggested Millie.

'It puts him in a different light though, doesn't it?' said Neil. 'I think you owe him an apology, Naomi.'

She blushed. 'Well I can hardly take this back and say I'm sorry, can I?' She waved the folder at him.

'No, we'll have to drop it in somehow. He may miss it soon,' he replied.

'Pete might be able to,' volunteered Millie and everyone looked at her. 'I had to tell him, he was *very* suspicious you know.'

'Well, if he can that would be brilliant.' Naomi thrust the folder at her. 'I'd better get you to Muker and see if the good folks at the B and B can find space for you,' she said to Neil.

Millie said that it was time she got back to her grandmother's.

'Just a second.' Naomi caught her as Neil disappeared. She seemed to change. She almost stammered as she said, 'What's this about Bert? What's happening? What do they mean?'

'What did Neil think?' asked Millie.

'Oh, he said it was probably old age. But why do they think he collapsed here?'

'I don't know but Justin saw two men outside his house, *with a Land Rover*. Either they were visiting him or they brought him home. It was the men from the Lodge, I'm certain. They went into your drive and stayed there for some time. Enough time to get Bert and take him to his cottage!'

'Oh no! It couldn't have been the Dutchman. How can we tell the police? Should we tell them? How did they kill him? Was he injured?'

'Calm down, Naomi. You're the doctor. What will they look for in a post mortem? Injuries? Drowning? Poisoning? What?' Millie asked.

'Anything. Everything. Unless they have a clear idea. If they think it's heart, then they'll check for that. If it is, they may not look any further. I think we should tell them.'

'Tell who what?'

'The police. That Grandma was killed.' Naomi's voice was getting louder.

'We can't prove that, Naomi.'

'That the Dutchman threatened us with a shotgun.' She was shouting at Millie.

'His word against ours. We didn't report it.'

'That Bert was murdered! To shut him up. He was trying to tell us about Grandma's death and...,' she stopped and continued slowly, 'and I told the Dutchman in the Lodge that he knew and I said that he would tell the truth about them.' She put her head in her hands.

Millie talked slowly and deliberately. 'We have to tell Neil everything, Naomi. I mean everything. When I was in the Lodge before...' Naomi looked puzzled. 'Yes, I haven't told you about that. We need to put everything together and then we might be able to work out why Matt is in Holland with someone who might have already murdered two people.'

Chapter 17

'Lovely flowers,' Millie called from the kitchen.

'They're for the church,' replied Helen from the next room. 'It was Lizzie's turn on the rota. I'll be going down to do them soon. Would you like to keep me company?'

'Yes, of course.'

She examined the flowers while she waited for the kettle to boil. They lay on several sheets of newspaper. Flowers from the garden. Roses, aquilegia, carnations. An earwig scuttled across the photograph of a page three model. Not her grandmother's sort of newspaper.

'Did they come from your garden?'

'No, from Naomi's actually.' Helen stood in the doorway, smiling at the arrangement on the kitchen surface. 'It was funny really. I felt a bit awkward about it to be honest. Lizzie always got Bert to pick some flowers for the church when it was our turn on the rota. She knew I didn't have a big stock of flowers in my tiny garden. When she died I thought he wouldn't remember and with him being taken ill I really didn't expect him to have done it. But I thought I'd go over to the greenhouse, just in case, and there they were, laid out ready on the paper.'

'That's nice.'

'Yes. I was quite touched really. Then I wasn't sure whether they were meant for the church. But he'd written on the newspaper, you know, her name, so I knew they were for me.' She moved the flowers to one side and pointed to the writing. It was in a large scrawl and looked as if he had used a very blunt pencil. He had written 'Mrs Banford'. Underneath Millie made out another name 'Roy' something.

'What's this bit?' Millie asked.

'I don't know what that means,' said Helen. 'It looks like 'Roy's Lad'. Probably the name of a horse he had a bet on. Sad to think that was probably the last thing he did before he died.'

Millie stared at the writing. 'Roy's Lad'. She resolved to check the sports pages of the paper when she came back from church.

Muker was quiet. It was the time of day when walkers had returned to their hotels and rented cottages to enjoy a hot bath before re-appearing in the pubs for a pint of dark beer and a substantial meal. As they walked up to the church, Millie could feel a cool breeze in the air.

'I suppose Bert will be buried here?' Millie asked as they entered the neat churchyard. She could see the flowers on Lizzie's grave, still fresh from the funeral.

'Yes, I imagine so. Although, he wasn't a great church-goer. He was usually only part of the congregation at Easter and Christmas, and at funerals of course,' she added.

The church was empty and still very light for the time of day. Millie sat in a pew and watched her grandmother bending down near the alter to arrange the greenery. In the winter it would have been nearly dark by five, no wonder Helen hadn't noticed her assailant. The carpeted floor would have muffled any footsteps. She shivered. She supposed it had been the Dutchman or one of his accomplices who was responsible for that attack on her grandmother. The first of the series of incidents that had led to two deaths. She wished Helen would hurry up so they could get back. She pondered the message in the newspaper. 'Mrs Banford. Roy's Lad.' Her grandmother had proposed a simple explanation for the message but if they really were the last words that Bert wrote maybe they had a greater significance. Some sort of message. Perhaps he had seen his attackers coming and tried to leave a clue.

'There! What d'you think?'

'They're lovely, Gran.' She jumped up, anxious to be off, and was holding the door open before Helen had gathered up the cuttings. She was about to screw up the newspaper when Millie stopped her.

'Keep the paper. It might be useful.' She nearly added, as evidence, but stopped short.

Helen shrugged. 'If you like but I've got plenty at home.'

Back at Laurel Cottage, Millie took the sheet of newspaper that Bert had written on and carefully folded it. She noticed that it was Thursday's date, so it was not an old message. She would show it to the others the next day.

There was no sign of Andy, and Millie wondered whether she should contact Naomi. There seemed to be little that they could do until Matt phoned or Andy arrived back and she decided to stay close to the phone that evening.

'The time has gone so quickly,' announced Helen at dinner. 'I wonder how your Dad and Fiona have been getting on?'

'I expect they're enjoying themselves,' said Millie. She felt a pang of guilt over how little she had thought of them. Out of sight, out of mind.

'It seems amazing that you're only here for one more week. Of course you've been very busy.' Helen paused, as if she was expecting Millie to tell her what she had been doing.

'Yes. I've seen quite a lot of the area with Naomi, and Pete,' she said. 'He's coming over tomorrow actually.'

'That's nice dear. He strikes me as a very pleasant young man. I'm glad you've made some friends of your own age up here.'

Millie laughed.

'What I meant was, it's time you had some fun. You're growing up and you should think about your future.'

Millie nodded. She was unsure what her grandmother was driving at but she didn't want to spoil the moment by disagreeing. She yawned.

'I think I'll head for bed.' She was irritated by the lack of contact from Matt and was beginning to worry. She felt a headache coming on and just wanted to go to sleep.

Next morning her head was worse. When she looked out it was dull and the trees dripped although it appeared to have stopped raining. She delayed getting up until nearly nine o' clock and was surprised to find Andy downstairs eating a large breakfast.

'You see, he hasn't really moved out at all!' joked Helen.

'You look very wet, Andy,' Millie remarked.

'Only from moving my stuff over to the cottage. 'Elen told me to 'ave breakfast 'ere.'

'What time did you get back?'

''Bout six.'

'Is everything alright?'

'Yeah fine.' He smiled and she assumed that his part of the journey had gone smoothly. She would have to wait until they were alone before she could find out the details.

She nibbled some toast and took some paracetemol with her tea. The headache was an excuse to stay at home and Helen set off to church alone, but not before she had made Millie promise to invite Pete to eat with them.

'Have you 'eard from Matt?' Andy asked as soon as the door slammed.

'No, not yet. How was the trip on the ferry?'

'OK. Luckily it was a smooth crossing. I kept my 'ead down but I could see Matt and the tall skinny guy in the bar.'

'Not drinking and driving I hope,' said Millie.

'Matt wasn't. No. The other guy was knocking it back the whole trip.'

'Did you get off the boat?'

'Yep. I watched 'em get off and then turned straight round. Just glad the sea was OK both ways.' Andy looked pleased with himself but his faced changed as he added, 'I 'ope 'e rings soon though.'

'Well I stayed in all last night, in case.'

'I can stay 'ere today.'

'Good idea.' Millie thought that he looked as though he could do with a rest anyway.

Pete arrived at ten thirty, and apologised for being late. He had left his dogs at home and so Millie did not suggest taking Bernie. He was comfortable enough sitting with Andy, who was on the sofa next to the phone. As they left she passed on Helen's invitation to eat with them.

'In that case I'll take you out for coffee,' he smiled. 'I know just the place.'

Millie was still tired and her headache had not completely gone. She was happy to climb into the old car and be driven in silence over Grinton Moor. At first she thought they were heading for the mill again but to her relief they passed the parking spot and continued over the top and down the other side. The sign said Redmire. A few moments later they were entering another village.

'Castle Bolton!' announced Pete. 'And this is Bolton Castle.'

In front of them was a medieval castle. It was perfect, not a ruin but with much of it intact.

'Can we go in?' she asked.

'Go in? Of course. This is our coffee shop.'

Millie was pleased. Pete was full of nice surprises like this and it made going out, being shown round by him, fun. They wandered round the large rooms and he told her about Mary Queen of Scots and Lady Anne Clifford's connections with the castle. Finally they entered a large hall where they found mugs of coffee and slabs of chocolate cake.

'This is perfect,' she said aloud and Pete laughed at her.

'Don't you get coffee castles in Surbiton?' he asked, with a grin.

'Sutton, but you're right, we don't.'

The hall was empty and they sat alone making small talk for a minute or two. Soon, however, Pete looked serious and asked. 'Did you find out what your friend was up to yesterday at David's?'

Millie blushed. She remembered that she still had the folder and had promised to ask Pete to return it.

'She found a file which proved that David hadn't been helping the Dutchman.'

'Thank God for that! Did she really think he was?'

'Possibly. Anyway, he clearly hasn't. Now all that's needed is to get it back again.'

'What? The file?' He looked puzzled.

'Yes.' Millie looked down at the tablecloth and back up. 'I wondered...'

'Oh no! Don't look at me. I'm not getting involved. I'm not breaking into people's houses.'

'It won't be breaking in. Just return it next time you visit him. Pop it in his office.'

'I'll think about it,' he said seriously. 'Now what else has been going on?'

'Nothing much. Did you know that Bert Bartholomew has died?'

'Who?'

'The gardener. He worked for Lizzie Banford. He was still doing the garden. Found dead on his bed.'

'Is that suspicious?'

'Not necessarily but we think he was last seen with the Dutchman and his side-kick.'

'We?'

'Naomi and I. We were up at the Lodge... '

'The Lodge? Why the Lodge?' Pete looked alarmed.

Millie realised that there was a lot of information that Pete didn't know about and she wasn't sure whether to tell him. What had she said to Naomi? That she should tell Neil the whole story. Perhaps she should tell Pete too. She trusted him and he had helped her at the auction.

'If I tell you everything that I know, perhaps you'll be able to make some sense of it all.' She took a deep breath. 'First there are the threats to Lizzie. You know that Naomi thought someone was trying to frighten her. Well, we think it was the Dutchman. He uses the Lodge for shooting parties and wanted to buy it. In fact David's file proved that. We don't know why but it might be because he's exporting sheep with lead in their blood.'

'By the way,' interrupted Pete, 'how are you going to get those samples tested?'

'I thought Andy might know someone at the university who could do them.'

'Have you asked him?'

She shook her head.

'Ask him when we get back then. Go on then,' continued Pete, nodding encouragingly.

'Well Matt had another job, going to Holland, driving the sheep back for the Dutchman. He had to be at the Lodge on Friday night so Naomi and I thought we would go up and look at the Lodge earlier in the day.'

'Did you?'

'Yes. Naomi went and knocked on the door and, well, to cut a long story short the Dutchman threatened us with a gun...'

'What? Did you call the police?' He looked almost angry.

'No.' Millie was regretting her decision to discuss it with him.

'Why on earth not?' She realised he wasn't angry, he was concerned.

'There was no proof. And we're so close to getting them now.'

He was serious, leaning back in his chair and staring at her. 'So what happened?'

'Well we got out and came back.' Millie felt rather silly now. 'But while I was waiting for her I saw his accomplices go into the Manor.'

'The Manor?'

'Yes. Then later Bert was found dead.' She looked round to see if anyone was listening. The place was still empty. 'We think that they killed him.'

'Have you told the police anything at all?'

'Not yet.'

'So what are you waiting for?'

'For Matt to get back from Holland. We don't want to do anything until we know he's safe. He's going to phone as soon as he can, to let us know what's going on and where he made the delivery.'

'What will you do then?'

'Once we know what's happened, what amounts of lead are in the sheep, we can tell the police.'

Pete looked unconvinced. 'We'd better get these samples analysed as soon as possible.'

'Yes I suppose we should.' Millie felt so much better now Pete was helping.

He still looked anxious. 'Have you really thought about how dangerous this is, Millie? It's not a game you know.'

'I know.' She felt hot. If he was going to behave like an older brother she would tell him where to go.

'I only mean, it could be dangerous for you and your friends.'

'So what would *you* do?' She knew that she sounded like a sulky child.

'Well Neil's the police, isn't he? He's the best person to advise us, isn't he?'

'Yes, I suppose so.'

'Right then. I think it's time to get back - the roast potatoes are calling!' He tried to lighten his tone and she smiled back.

The sun was out when they left the castle. Her head felt better and she was sure it was right to confide in Pete.

The smell of lunch filled the cottage and they sat with Andy while Helen finished off the preparations. Bernie had moved from beside Andy to sit at Pete's feet and they talked about how much better the dog was.

'Is there any news?' Millie finally asked Andy.

'Nothing. Not a sausage.' Andy looked dejected.

'Perhaps the mobile doesn't work in Holland. I hadn't thought of that,' said Millie.

'You could ask Andy about the blood, Millie,' Pete prompted.

'Blood?' Andy looked up sharply.

'The sheep's blood,' explained Millie. 'We've got samples from the animals that Matt took to Holland. Pete can get them tested for lead and arsenic…'

'Brilliant!' exclaimed Andy.

'…but not yet,' she continued. 'We wondered if you would be able to do it instead?'

He looked pensive. 'It's not like doing water or soil but I know someone who might be able to do it for us. Sam. She's a PhD student. She's a chemist. She might know how to do it. I'll ask her tomorrow if you like.'

'Are you going back there?'

'I can. If I get a lift.' He looked at her questioningly. Pete spoke first.

'I can drive us all over tomorrow if you like. I'd be interested in seeing how it's done.'

'Are you sure?' Millie was surprised at his offer.

'Certainly. it will be a learning experience.'

'What's that then?' asked Helen as she came in carrying a vegetable dish.

'Learning how to test blood, Mrs Johnson. Andy's going to show us how to do it.'

'At the university? That will be interesting, won't it Millie?'

'Yes Gran.'

'You should talk to the professors over there, see if there's a degree you could do with your exams.'

'Gran!' Although she blushed and raised her eyebrows at the others, she thought it was not a bad idea.

After lunch Pete suggested a walk. Millie asked Andy if he wanted to come but he was determined to stay by the phone until Matt called.

'Where shall we go?' she asked as they left the cottage with Bernie.

'I've got an idea.' Pete smiled and opened the car door.

As they approached Reeth, Pete turned to her with a grin, 'Don't worry,' he said, 'we're not stopping for long. I'll just pick up Jess and Blackie.'

Back in the car, he said, 'I thought we'd park in Healaugh and go for a good walk across the moors to Langthwaite. Do you know it?'

Millie admitted that she did not.

'Well, it's quite a nice stroll.'

They parked in the village and set off, apparently up the drive of a big country house. She was relieved to see a public footpath sign as they left the track and climbed the stile into a field. The sun had dried the grass and they disturbed some rabbits that were taking advantage of the heat to catch up on their feeding. Bernie and the other dogs were off, scattering them to the four corners of the field. Soon they were out on open moorland and Millie felt once more the sense of release that she now expected when she was on the fells. There was no clear path but Pete seemed to know the way as he guided them through the heather. He pointed out a bird of prey hovering in the distance and they stood shading their eyes to watch as it soared away. Pete talked about the birds he had seen on his visit to the Pyrenees the previous year. She learnt that he was a keen walker and had travelled as far as Thailand on walking and climbing trips.

'This is Reeth Low Moor,' announced Pete, after they had been walking for a while. He was keeping up a brisk pace and Millie was getting quite tired with the speed of the walk.

'Do you mind if we slow down a bit?' she asked.

He stopped. 'I'm sorry. I forget. I usually walk on my own, well with the dogs. D'you want to stop for a minute?' Without waiting for an answer he pulled off his jacket and spread it on the short tufty grass. Millie noticed that he had not cleared the grass of sheep droppings first.

There was not a lot of space on the jacket and she had to sit close to him. The dogs came racing back and sat, waiting to see what would happen next. There was now a good view down to the road, winding away up the next valley.

'That's Arkengarthdale. There's the top road. You can get right back round to Keld that way, past Tan Hill - the highest pub in England. We could go there one evening,' he looked round at her and said, uncertainly, 'that's if you wanted to, of course.'

'Of course.' She blushed. He must think I'm really stupid, she thought. She really didn't know how to behave. He must find me immature. Bernie began pawing her hand and she was relieved to have her attention distracted.

'Alright, Bernie, we're coming.' She jumped up rather too enthusiastically and once more wondered if she had acted incorrectly. She wanted Pete to like her but just at the moment there were such important things to worry about.

It was downhill now and soon they reached the tarmac road to Langthwaite. There was a surprising amount of traffic. The improvement in the weather had clearly brought out the trippers, thought Millie, who no longer considered herself a visitor to the Dales. They had to walk down the road to the village itself and Millie was not disappointed when Pete suggested a drink in the pub by the bridge. Afterwards they bought an ice-cream and wandered along the riverbank while Bernie cooled himself down.

'We can go back this way,' said Pete, pointing further on down stream.

It grew quieter as they went over the river on a small footbridge, following a narrow track that was enclosed on both sides with a dry stone wall. Millie proudly indicated to Pete that they were travelling up an old 'green lane'. He turned and pointed to the steep hill which rose up on the opposite side of the river.

'There are lead mines up there. I expect the men used this track to come over from Swaledale.'

Millie could hear the sound of the boots and their voices as they marched across down the lane. She imagined them at night, or was it early morning? It was dark and their lanterns were swinging as they made their way up the hill. Further on, in front of them, she could see shooting butts on the hillside.

'Do they shoot up there?'

'Only grouse,' joked Pete.

'Why is it so important?' Millie muttered. She was wondering why someone would be so determined to be able to continue to hold shooting parties that they would frighten an old lady into parting with a dilapidated Lodge. 'Why would that old building be important for shooting?' she asked aloud.

'What, at the gill? It isn't important,' Pete replied. It's not used by the guests. It's not used for entertaining. Perhaps they keep the guns there?'

'Where do the guests stay then?'

'Up at a big farmhouse near Thwaite.'

'How d'you know that?'

'My boss's aunt does the catering,' Pete answered simply.

Millie considered whether the Dutchman kept his guns at the Lodge. There hadn't been any sign of them when she was there, although it was a good isolated spot if you wanted to be sure no-one would interfere with them. Not very secure though. Perhaps it was the isolation that was important. No-one to see any illegal activities that they were involved with. It was quiet and, as they had already found out, it could be approached from either of two directions. A sudden sound brought her back from her thoughts. Bernie had disturbed a grouse and it made a chattering ascent from the heather. She looked at her watch; it was getting on for five o'clock.

'Hungry?' asked Pete, noticing.

'No. I was wondering how late it was.'

'We'll soon be back in Healaugh. Do you want to get back to see if Matt has phoned?'

She was surprised that he was thinking of that. 'I suppose so.' She knew that she sounded rather depressed and she didn't want Pete to think that she hadn't enjoyed herself. She did her best to chat on the rest of the walk. Somehow she found herself discussing music and found that they liked the same bands. They were interrupted by insistent barking in the distance.

'Quick!' shouted Pete and grabbing her hand he pulled her down the track towards the noise. The three dogs were leaping about barking loudly and gingerly pawing the ground. Millie was out of breath and stood gasping for air as she put Bernie's lead on him and pulled him away. Pete had ordered his dogs off and was examining the ground. He pushed some tall grass out of the way and exposed a large hedgehog that had formed a tight ball to protect itself from the attack.

'Come on, let's find the car!' Millie let Pete take her hand again and they made their way down the track into the village. She wasn't sure what holding hands signified and decided that it didn't necessarily mean a lot. After all, they were good friends weren't they?

Back home Andy was in a miserable state. He had been waiting by the phone all day and there had been no call from Matt. He was obviously getting himself in a state and Millie tried to persuade him to have a break, go out for a drink or something. After a while Pete said that he had to go and Millie saw him to his car.

'I'll be round as soon as possible tomorrow, certainly no later than nine,' he promised. 'It'll help Andy to have a day off too.' He leant over and gave her a kiss on the cheek. She blushed, muttering a goodbye as he climbed into the car and drove off.

She wanted to ring Naomi and see what she and Neil had been doing but Andy wouldn't let her use the phone unless it was an emergency.

'OK, I'll go up and see if she's there.'

Naomi was pleased to see her and ushered her into the kitchen, where Neil was washing up.

'Has she told you her latest scheme, Millie?' said Neil, nodding in Naomi's direction.

'No.'

'She wants to go and tackle this Nick character, the one that works in the pub at Reeth.'

'Irene's nephew,' explained Naomi. 'He'll be able to tell us what's going on.'

'I said wait.' Neil was drying his hands. 'Have you heard from Matt yet?'

'Nothing,' replied Millie. 'Andy's glued to the phone.'

'Poor lad,' said Naomi. 'He would be useful when we go to visit Nick.'

'Well he won't come until he gets the phone call, that's for sure.' Millie shrugged shoulders. 'Anyway we're going to Lancaster tomorrow to look at these blood samples that Pete took from the sheep.'

'Right!' Neil sounded impressed.

'There was something I wanted to talk about,' added Millie, and she told them about the newspaper and Roy's Lad. She wished that she had brought it with her but promised to show it to them next day.

'What d'you think it is?' asked Naomi. 'It sounds like a horse, doesn't it?'

'Was he a betting man?' asked Neil.

'I don't know really, but I expect he would have been, don't you?'

'Is there any way we can find out?' asked Millie.

'We could ask his daughter, Irene,' said Naomi. 'I wanted to have a chat with her anyway.'

'We could check the racing papers for horses or dogs. What about pigeons?'

Millie wasn't sure if Neil was joking. 'Pigeons?'

'Yes, very popular up here. Maybe he was a pigeon fancier.'

'Surely he wouldn't be betting on them would he?' Naomi was laughing.

'Well, horses would be more likely. I'll find out,' agreed Neil.

Naomi said that she and Neil would pay a call on Irene to see how she was and try to find out about Bert's gambling interests.

'Did you ask Pete about returning the file to David?' Naomi reminded Millie as she was leaving.

'I asked but I'll mention it again tomorrow. I think he'll do it.' Somehow she felt more certain now.

When she got back to Laurel Cottage, the front door swung open and the light from inside threw a yellow oblong along the path.

'Matt's on the phone, now. Quick!' Andy was hopping from one foot to the other. 'E wants to speak to you, now!'

Chapter 18

'Did 'e say what time 'e'd be arriving?' Andy asked, when Millie put down the receiver. Matt had sounded fine but relieved to be coming back. It was the first chance that he'd had to make a call out of earshot of Nick's uncle. He just wanted them to know that he was safe and would be travelling back on Tuesday.

'No,' replied Millie. 'But there's probably only one ferry in the afternoon or evening. We can find out and follow them back here.' Millie was puzzled that Matt had given them no other information and went on, 'Did Matt tell you what has been happening?'

'Nope. 'E's been stuck there waiting for instructions. The same place as before. They said there was a delay but 'e couldn't find out what it was.'

'Does he know where the house is?'

'Not really. 'E couldn't keep track of it once they were in 'Olland.'

Millie dialled Naomi's number, to give her the news.

'Thank God he's OK,' Naomi yelled down the phone. 'Now, that means we can go and see our friend Nick, see if he can tell us what's going on. Are you coming?'

Millie hesitated. She wasn't keen on the confrontation and decided that her grandmother would prefer her to spend the evening at home.

'No, but what about Andy? He knows Nick and it might seem less, well you know, less important if you go along as his friend.' She covered the mouthpiece and asked Andy if he fancied going to Reeth for a drink. He nodded enthusiastically.

'Right. Andy said yes.'

'Fine. We'll be round in a minute.'

Millie quickly explained to Andy about Naomi's idea of talking to Nick. He wasn't keen but agreed that he should go along to make it seem like a casual visit. By the time he had fetched his jacket, Naomi and Neil were knocking on the door. Bernie was pleased to see them and Naomi was down on the floor playing with him when Helen asked them to stay for a drink.

'Sorry, we'd love to but we're taking Andy out to Reeth.' Naomi was apologetic.

'Oh dear,' said Helen. 'I was hoping that you'd be able to tell me what is happening about poor Bert. Have you seen Irene since the other night, dear? I thought she looked awful when I saw her at church yesterday.'

'No, I haven't.' Naomi looked thoughtful. 'Although it could be a good idea.' Millie thought she knew what she was thinking.

'Why don't you and I pop down to see her?' asked Millie, 'Neil and Andy can go for a drink, can't you?'

The two men agreed in unison.

'Oh Naomi, are you sure? I didn't mean... Well... ' Helen was clearly embarrassed.

'No, you're right Helen. Millie and I will go and have a chat with her. Make sure she's alright.'

Millie was amused by the way Naomi always managed to appear to be concerned over others when she was doing exactly as she wanted.

The four parted at the gate. Neil and Andy climbed into Naomi's car while the two girls walked slowly down the lane.

'What are you going to do?' Millie was beginning to get nervous about the visit. She knew how hotheaded Naomi could be and didn't want her getting carried away.

'I thought we'd see how Irene is. Find out if there's any news about the post mortem, the cause of death and so on. Maybe find out if Bert liked a little flutter.'

'Do be careful.'

'Aren't I always?'

They had reached the Jackson's cottage. There were on lights inside and a short fat man soon answered their knock.

'Yes?' he asked peering out at them. 'Oh! Miss Naomi! And... well, ay.' He obviously didn't recognise Millie. 'Come in. 'Ave you come to see missus?' and he called out 'Irene! It's young Miss Naomi and 'er friend for yer.'

He led them into a small sitting room. The heat hit Millie like a furnace. There was a fire burning in the hearth, almost hidden by the clothes hanging round it.

'Oh Jim!' exclaimed the large woman jumping up and snatching wildly at the clothes. She was folding the clothes horse, still clutching the bundle of washing in her arms.

'I seem to be at sixes and sevens. Normal times these would be ironed and aired by now.'

'I'm sorry Mrs Jackson,' began Naomi. 'We didn't mean to intrude. We just wondered how you were.'

'Sit down, sit down,' urged the woman, pointing to the old sofa in front of the fire. Millie was glad to sit; she was already feeling overpowered by the heat of the tiny room.

'Tea? Would you like some tea? I'll put kettle on.' She seemed flustered.

'No, please, it's alright. We're fine. Honestly.' Millie silently agreed with Naomi. She did not want hot tea but ice cold water would have been nice. She wished that she hadn't agreed to come. They were intruding on the couple in their grief. She felt like a tabloid journalist. Jim Jackson disappeared and Irene sat down with a crumpled shirt in her lap.

'Well,' she said at last. It was not so much a question as a statement.

'I wondered,' began Naomi, 'purely in a professional capacity, of course.'

'Of course,' repeated Irene Jackson, looking alert and serious.

'Whether you had received any further information concerning your father's,' she paused, 'your father's death.'

Irene gave a sigh. 'Oh yes.' The woman looked exhausted. There were bags under her eyes and she stared vacantly at the fire, clutching the shirt to her ample bosom. 'The doctor says it's heart failure but we've got to wait for the post mortem. The funeral's supposed to be on Thursday.'

'Poor Bert,' said Naomi. 'He was such a lovely man.'

'Like your poor grandmother,' cried Irene, suddenly. She dabbed her eyes with the shirt. 'Like your poor grandmother. She was a lovely lady.'

Millie's head was beginning to throb and her mouth felt dry.

'She loved the garden, you know,' said Naomi. 'Bert kept it so nice. He spent so much time on it.' After a short pause, she added, pointedly, 'I don't suppose he had time for much else.'

Oh dear, here we go, thought Millie. The heat was unbearable. She just wanted to get outside again.

'Not rightly. 'E liked 'is garden but it were very small. 'E liked his pint with his mates, as well.'

'Did he go out much?'

'No.' She dabbed her eyes again and absently folded the shirt. 'Sometimes 'e could be a stubborn old man. I told 'im to get out more.'

Millie began to feel nauseous and wanted to speed Naomi up. 'My grandad used to enjoy horse-racing. He had a bet on the National and the Derby.'

Naomi frowned at her.

'Not Dad!' answered Irene. 'A mean old man 'e were over some things. Never once bought a lottery ticket; said 'e didn't want to be a millionaire. Daft sod.'

She could see that Naomi was going to pursue the topic. Surely she wasn't going to start on greyhounds or pigeons.

'Perhaps we should be going, Naomi.' Millie deliberately stood up, pulling at her friend's arm. 'I'm sorry Mrs Jackson but we should be off.'

'Well, thank you for coming. You'll be at the funeral, won't you?'

'Yes, of course.' Naomi answered for them both, as Millie made for the door. She took deep breaths of fresh air as she stood on the path, waiting for Naomi to appear. Her head was pounding.

Naomi was excited. 'Did you hear that? Not a betting man! I reckon that message is a clue about the killer.'

Millie didn't answer. She grunted quietly. She didn't have the energy to disagree but found it difficult to contemplate old Bert leaving clues in newspapers. After all, how did he know anyone would find it?

'We've got to find out about Roy's Lad. Is it a person? Someone he knows?'

'Probably a climbing rose.' Millie felt exhausted.

'Should I go back and ask Irene?' Millie surprised herself when she shouted 'No!' and marched into Laurel Cottage holding her forehead. 'Let's wait until tomorrow. Maybe Neil and Andy will find out something.'

Millie had not expected to see Neil and Andy for the rest of the evening and when Helen suggested that the three of them had dinner, she excused herself, took some paracetemol and went to bed. She knew that her grandmother would be happily occupied chatting to Naomi and didn't feel at all guilty about retiring early. Her head pounded and she felt quite sick. She woke when the door slammed later but she didn't have the energy to find out if it was Andy returning or Naomi leaving.

Millie crawled out of bed slowly the next morning, despite the fact that Pete would be there in fifteen minutes. She dressed and brushed her hair, staring at her face in the mirror. She looked awful.

Andy was downstairs. 'Your Gran said sorry but she's gone to Richmond. She didn't want to wake you.'

'Oh.'

'I came over to see 'ow you got on with Nick's aunt?' announced Andy, briskly. Clearly the previous evening had not exhausted *him*.

'Nothing, really. Apparently Bert wasn't a gambler.'

'What?'

'No horses, no dogs and no pigeons.'

'Sorry?' he said shovelling a spoonful of cornflakes into his mouth. 'You've lost me there.'

She realised that Andy knew nothing about the message on the paper and had to explain it to him. He was not able to make any clever suggestions regarding the meaning of the words 'Roy's Lad' either.

'What about your chat with Nick?' she asked, hoping that she could sit quietly and drink her tea while he told her.

'Wasn't there.'

'What?'

'It wasn't 'is night on. 'e wasn't there.'

'So what did you do?'

'We 'ad a drink and came back. Well, a few drinks really. Neil's a nice bloke. Not like a copper at all really.'

'Didn't you look for him anywhere else?'

'The only other place was 'is aunt's and you were there, we thought it might look a bit odd if we turned up as well. 'E's working tomorrow night so Neil said we'd go then.'

'It sounds like a good excuse for a drink to me,' laughed Millie.

The letter box rattled and Bernie went racing out of the kitchen.

'Post,' said Andy, jumping up and racing after him.

He came back with a postcard in his hand.

'Not from Matt, surely?' said Millie.

'No, it's for you.' He handed her the card, smiling.

'Who's that from?' she asked.

'Your Dad?' he suggested, handing it to her, picture side up.

There was a colour photograph of a crowded beach. That was Dad's choice, Millie thought as she turned it over. *Dear Millie, the weather is hot and I have got sunburn so has Fiona. The food is good but not the beer. Fiona fell over on a rock and hurt her toe but it's better now. love to Helen from Dad.* Millie read it to Andy.

'Well, it sounds as though they're enjoying themselves. I 'ope the sunburn isn't too serious,' Andy commented.

'It didn't sound as though it was worrying them too much,' Millie replied, thinking how she had told them to be sure to put cream on. Typical of Dad to forget. She left the card on the table in the sitting room so that her grandmother would see it later.

'Are you ready for the trip to Lancaster?' she asked Andy.

'Yep.'

'Well, Pete should be here soon.'

It was nearly nine thirty when Pete's car pulled up outside the cottage. He was very apologetic. He had arranged to leave his dogs at the surgery and the vet had delayed him discussing the case of a cat with a broken leg.

The weather was dull but not actually raining and there were views across the Dales as they climbed from one valley into the next. They spent the journey getting Pete up to date with what had been happening since the previous day. When the conversation petered out, Millie was content to watch the scenery. Moving further away from Mossy Bank, the focus of all the drama over the last two weeks, moving from the centre of the mystery, she could look at it more clearly.

'Does Neil know that we're going to check the blood today?' she asked Andy, turning to look at him in the back of the car.

'Yep. I told him. 'E said 'e'd see us tonight. 'E's got to go into Halifax and Naomi's taking 'im. They'll come over when we get back.'

At least she'll be out of trouble until tonight then, thought Millie.

Pete had chosen the quickest route to Lancaster, which took them to Kirkby Stephen and then to the motorway. It seemed very strange to be travelling so fast in three lanes of traffic after two weeks of being on narrow country roads.

The university was not far from the motorway and soon Andy was directing them to his department. It was all much bigger than Millie had imagined it. Andy proudly showed them up the stairs and along a corridor, greeting people as he went. Several of them asked where Matt was, but he just shrugged his shoulders. They passed doors on both sides and where they were open Millie could see into offices and laboratories. There didn't seem to be many people about but, as Andy explained, it was the summer vacation and only postgraduate students were around. Pushing through some swing doors he pointed to his left. 'That's the lab. I'll take you in and find a lab coat for you. They might be a bit big, though,' he said looking at Millie.

They followed him into a large laboratory full of complicated looking instruments. A girl with long fair curly hair was sitting in front of a computer screen, while a machine beside her moved round and round, pumping liquid into a large metal box.

'Hi Andy.' She smiled, looking up at them.

'Sam. These are the people I told you about. This is Sam.' He beamed at them. She continued to smile and blushed slightly.

'Have you brought the samples?' she asked and Pete reached into his pocket. Millie listened while she asked him about them, when they were taken and whether he had added anything to them. 'It'll take several hours,' she warned as she shook each vial, peered at it and put it into a rack. Then she started to write out labels for them.

'Can we watch how you do it?' Millie asked.

The girl seemed surprised and pleased. 'Of course. Look, I'll start the prep off and then I can talk you through the instrument and how it works.'

'I've got some things to do,' Andy said apologetically. 'Can I come back later?'

'That's fine, Andy,' Sam replied with a smile. 'You know where to find us.'

The girl turned out to be an excellent teacher. First she showed them how she prepared the blood samples. She used a microwave, which looked to Millie just like her own at home but Sam told her it had cost thousands of pounds and was very high tech. When the samples were dissolved in acid, Sam said that she would put them into a large machine that had a very powerful flame. She could understand how it all worked when Sam explained it but she knew that she wouldn't remember the details. They had been watching her and listening to her explanations for several hours. Millie envied her, she was young, she clearly enjoyed her work and was very clever.

'Do you have any books or leaflets about how it all works?' she asked, as they sat watching the solution disappearing into the metal box.

'I can give you a paper which describes the theory and how the instrument works,' offered Sam. 'I think we should go and get something to eat before that. I'll take you to where I usually go.'

Millie looked at her watch and realised that it was after two o' clock. Sam led the way along corridors and down stairs until they were finally out through a door, into the fresh air. It was nice to be out in the open for a short time before she led them into another building and through double doors into what could only be a student cafeteria. It was still apparently open, although it was very quiet. They chose sandwiches, crisps and some chocolate biscuits. Pete paid for them all and they allowed Sam to lead them to the smoking section and watched her light a cigarette. Sam asked Pete about veterinary school and quizzed him on the samples she was analysing. She told them that she'd actually done some work measuring arsenic in the wool from sheep and joked that next time he could snip some wool for analysis too.

Millie was anxious to get back and see what the samples would show and as soon as they had eaten she suggested that they carried on. Sam stubbed out her cigarette and got up.

'First we must run some standards to calibrate the instrument.'

Millie looked at the samples now they were dissolved in acid. They didn't look like blood but had formed a clear solution. She handed each sample to Sam as she needed it and they sat watching it being sucked into the machine. The signals showed up on the computer screen.

'Doesn't look like anything much.' Sam pointed out the places where she expected to see the traces for lead and arsenic. She pressed a button and the trace got bigger as she expanded it, but there was nothing there. 'Perhaps the next one,' she said.

Each time they introduced a sample they went through the same ritual, looking for something to show up on the screen. Nothing appeared. Finally, as the last sample finished, she said. 'I'll print it out but I don't think there's anything there of interest.' The printer chattered and page after page of type appeared. Sam peered through it all.

'Well, there's something.' Both Millie and Pete sat up. 'But nothing abnormal. Do you know what normal levels are in sheep?' she asked Pete.

'No,' he said, 'I don't.'

'Well, these samples are well below normal for humans or animals, as far as I can see,' she said, shrugging her shoulders. 'I'm sorry.'

'It's not your fault,' said Millie, not wanting to sound ungrateful, 'It's a good thing really, isn't it Pete?'

'Well, yes, I suppose so.' He was thoughtful and Millie decided that he was probably thinking about the lengths that he'd gone to get the samples. 'Would you definitely see anything abnormal?'

'Oh yes, it's very sensitive to small amounts of lead and arsenic. I can see it there but it's so low it isn't unusual at all.'

They stood up and Millie tried not to look as disappointed as she felt. She told Sam how grateful they were and Pete thanked her again.

'I'll go and find Andy, he's probably next door,' said Sam and she went off.

'Well, I guess we should be relieved really,' said Pete, putting his arm round her shoulders. His action made Millie want to cry but she swallowed hard and smiled.

'I suppose so, although it means our theory was wrong. It's not a case of poisoning after all.'

'Sam told me,' shouted Andy as he came into the laboratory. He was alone. 'Can't understand it but if Sam says nothing, then it's nothing. She's the expert.'

Pete looked at his watch. 'Are you ready to go Andy? I've got be back for surgery at six tonight. I might just make it if we go now.'

'Fine. I'll get my bag.' He disappeared and they went into the corridor to wait for him. Sam came along and gave Millie a small document. 'This is the paper I told you about. I hope you can understand the jargon.'

'I'll try, and thanks Sam. I know it was a lot of your time.'

'That's OK. If you'd found something it could have made an interesting study. Will you be doing any more?' she asked.

'Oh I don't think so!' Pete was smiling but he was looking Millie directly in the eye when he said it and she knew that he had no intention of repeating his performance.

Andy re-appeared and they were soon back on the motorway. Millie began to feel angry with disappointment. 'Well, that's put us back where we started. Now we've no reason at all for the Dutchman to want to get rid of anyone!'

'If it's not poisoned sheep, perhaps it's something else,' said Andy. 'Could still be in some dodgy racket. Contravening import licences or something.'

'What, like guns?' asked Pete.

Of course, thought Millie. They had talked about storing guns at the Lodge the night before. 'Maybe he's smuggling guns into the country?' she suggested aloud.

Pete sighed. 'Perhaps he just wants a holiday cottage. It's a nice spot. Perhaps he just wants it for himself.'

The voice of common sense, thought Millie. Poor Pete. She was worried that he had found it a waste of time, their wild goose chase. She looked across at him and he smiled.

'It was a nice day out, anyway,' he said, perhaps sensing the atmosphere and her embarrassment. 'I've always wanted to know how a 'whatever it is' works.'

Millie laughed. 'It's an atomic absorption spectrometer,' corrected Andy from the back.

'Well, whatever. I must say I prefer working with animals to all those instruments, myself.' He was turning off the M6 and now they were heading back to Kirkby Stephen. It was a pleasant evening and she was glad to see the hills and the sheep again. Andy asked Pete about his work and Millie simply sat and listened as they chatted, while her thoughts drifted to the postcard from her Dad. Gran will have seen it. She must have dozed because when she looked up they were turning into Mossy Bank. Pete had to rush back to the surgery and so he dropped them off, promising to get in touch that night.

'I saw the postcard, Millie,' the first words Helen said when they went in. 'Sounds as if they're having a nice time.'

'Yes, I think they are,' she agreed.

'By the way. I saw Jean today. She popped round to invite you and Pete to dinner before you go. Maybe Thursday she said. She says that Pete doesn't usually do surgery that evening.'

'That's nice.' Millie immediately thought that it would be a good opportunity to return the file that Naomi had taken.

'And Naomi rang. She said she might pop in later. She's gone with Neil to Halifax but they'll be back tonight because Neil wants to go out for a drink with Andy. Is that right?'

Millie silently hoped that Naomi wouldn't pop in. She didn't want to break the news that the blood was normal.

'Oh, and she left a ferry timetable of all things. Did you ask her for one?'

'Oh that's for me,' said Andy quickly. 'I've got to meet Matt.'

Helen fetched it from the kitchen and Andy rifled through it. Eventually he said casually, 'The sailings come back into 'Ull at six in the evening.'

Neil arrived during the evening and to Millie's relief, Naomi was not with him. She wanted to go and see Nick with them but Neil wanted to make it appear to be an official police visit and it was best that only Andy went. Millie sat impatiently with her grandmother waiting for their return. If they could get some information out of Nick it would make up for a very disappointing day in Lancaster.

Helen was repairing an old blanket that Bernie used as a bed and he lay at her feet, sleeping. Millie was flicking through a guide book. She was not reading but looked at the glossy photographs, thinking about the conversation that might be taking place at the pub in Reeth.

'Did you see any of the professors at the university today?' Helen asked, as she snapped the cotton thread with her teeth.

'No,' she replied. 'We were too busy really.'

'What exactly were you doing, dear?'

'Just getting some analyses done.' She felt rather guilty as she fabricated a story about the blood and how Pete was searching for the cause of an obscure illness in some sheep.

'It's fascinating, isn't it? I always wished that I'd become a vet.'

There was no answer to that and Millie continued by describing Sam and what she was doing at the university. It surprised her when her grandmother asked whether she would like to do research.

'Yes I would, but I don't think I'd be able to.'

'Why not?' Helen asked. 'I've always thought you undersold yourself. I always said to your mother that she should have encouraged you more in your school work.'

They chatted about her college and the time went more quickly than she had expected. By ten thirty Neil had dropped Andy back and Millie could tell from his face that something had happened. They had to wait until Helen had gone to bed before she could find out the cause of his excitement.

'Brilliant. Neil was brilliant.' His eyes were shining, excitedly. 'Of course, 'e's a copper so he knows all the stuff but we had it sorted before we got there. 'E made out that 'e'd got me under suspicion. Clever, eh? I 'ad to be surly like, you know, pretend

I didn't like 'im. 'E asked Nick what Matt was up to, made out 'e didn't believe me. I just kept saying that it was nothing.'

'Did Nick say anything about where Matt was?'

'Not at first. 'E just played it cool. But Neil, 'e was quite 'eavy really. Told 'im it meant mighty 'eavy trouble if 'e didn't co-operate. Then Nick said that it was nothing to do with 'im – 'e just organised the driver.'

'Did he ask him about the address?'

'Yeah. But 'e said 'e didn't know. Anyway, in the end, just as 'e's turning to leave, 'e goes back, Neil. 'E gets hold of him and says, real mean like, "We know you're involved in the death of Mrs Banford and if you don't talk it'll be real bad for you." He stopped and looked at her.

Millie put on a suitably impressed expression. 'And?'

'And 'e said rubbish, or words to that effect. But then Neil said someone had seen 'im and then 'e panicked a bit. 'E said 'e'd only taken the dog, that was all. 'Is uncle had told 'im to. Told 'im to kill it - to put the frighteners on 'er but 'e said 'e couldn't so 'e left it up the gill.'

'Good grief.' She was thinking about Nick, pushing Bernie down the tunnel. He had a gold ring in one ear, just like Andy. What had Pete said about Bernie being aggressive to Andy? That it might be his red hair? It wasn't, it was the earring! The dog had seen Andy's earring and associated it with Nick abandoning him in the tunnel. Bernie had stopped barking at Andy when he removed it for the funeral!

Millie looked at Andy, who was clearly enjoying the excitement of it all and decided it was best not to mention it.

'What happened then?'

'Neil told 'im to keep quiet. That 'e'd be alright if 'e didn't say anything to anyone. Told 'im they 'ad this system that would see 'im alright if 'e grassed on the others. 'E said if 'e breathed a word to 'is uncle or anyone 'e'd be picked up by the boys in blue straight away.'

'Do you think he believed him?'

Andy laughed. 'Yeah. Never seen anyone so shit-scared as 'e was!'

Chapter 19

Naomi was at the cottage just after eight. She was very excited by the confession that Nick had made. Andy and Neil were at the Manor and she insisted that Millie dressed and came back with her immediately.

'You can have breakfast over there,' Naomi said impatiently.

'I'm sorry Gran but Naomi wants me to give her a hand.' Helen seemed to be used to her absenting herself with the minimum of excuse and merely asked her if she wanted anything from Reeth.

'No thanks,' she called back as Naomi led the way.

It was a warm morning, despite the fact that it was early. A faint breeze came from the fells and Millie could detect the scent of heather. Naomi gave her the details of the interview that Neil had related to her.

'I knew he was at the bottom of it. I wish I'd been there, I'd have given him a piece of my mind.'

Millie was secretly thankful that she hadn't been. She just hoped that the lad was sufficiently scared to keep quiet about the visit and would not tell the uncle or the Dutchman before Matt got back safely. Everything seemed to hinge on Matt's return now. He was the only one who could tell them what it was all about; what the Dutchman was up to and why it was so important to buy the Lodge.

Neil and Andy sat at the kitchen table clutching mugs of coffee. Naomi fetched one for Millie while Neil went through, yet again, what had happened last night.

'I reckon he'll keep quiet,' said Neil. 'I put the fear of God into him.'

'Let's hope so,' said Naomi, 'What do we do now, though?'

'Surely we shouldn't do anything 'til Matt gets back?' pleaded Millie. She was really concerned about what would happen next.

'That's right,' agreed Neil. 'We must make damn sure that we pick up the trailer at Hull and follow it back here.'

'Or wherever it goes,' added Andy. 'We don't know exactly what will 'appen, do we?'

'That's true,' said Naomi, excitedly. 'We ought to have more than one car, to cover all eventualities.'

Millie was impressed at Naomi's fearless enthusiasm for chasing around the country after Matt. She had felt quite nervous when they had been following the trailer to Hull and she was not looking forward to repeating the experience.

'Is Pete free this evening?' asked Naomi. 'Why don't you find out now? There's a phone in the drawing room.'

'I don't know the number,' argued Millie. She didn't want to have to ask him outright like that.

'I'll find it for you,' and she dashed out of the room.

'There's no stopping her when she gets her teeth into something,' remarked Neil, draining the mug and putting it down on the table.

'Well, she's right isn't she Neil?' said Andy. 'After all, if we're going to get the bastards we've got to 'ave proof, 'aven't we?'

'Too right, mate.' Neil was putting his jacket on. 'I'm going to have a look at that Lodge. I haven't been up there yet, not like everyone else.'

'I'll come, shall I Neil?' asked Andy. He obviously didn't want to miss out on any detective work that might be taking place.

'Yeah, sure, mate.'

Andy beamed and jumping up, headed for the door.

When Naomi returned with the number, they were gone, leaving Millie to explain what they were up to. Then she went and phoned the surgery.

The phone rang only twice before it was answered by the receptionist. When Millie asked to speak to Pete, she frostily asked who was calling and when Millie gave her name there was a silence. She hung on, wondering if she had been disconnected but after about a minute she heard Pete's voice saying hello. The sound made her stomach churn and she felt quite nervous.

'Pete?' she asked, unnecessarily.

'Millie?' he spoke gently and had a smile in his voice. 'Is there something wrong?'

'No, it's alright. I just wondered, well, if you were busy tonight.'

'Why? Are you asking me out?' He was laughing at her, she thought, blushing.

'No.' She paused to work out what to say and he intervened, 'That's a shame. Can I ask you then?'

'Well I want to go to Hull.' He roared with laughter at the other end.

'Pete!' She was cross with herself for not being more coherent and with him for not taking her seriously.

'What is it, Millie?' He sounded genuinely worried now. She explained what had taken place last night and how important it was to meet the ferry and see where Matt went.

'I see,' he said slowly. 'I'm supposed to be on duty but I'll do a swap, shouldn't be too difficult tonight. I can finish at three, would that be early enough?'

'That would be great.'

'It's nothing illegal is it? I mean we won't be breaking into anywhere?'

'No.' Millie laughed. 'It's alright. Neil's a policeman. We can trust him.'

'Is he coming too?'

'Yes and Andy and..' she hesitated. 'And Naomi.'

'Oh dear,' he said. 'Better get back, there's a rabbit waiting for me. Bye love.'

'Bye, Pete.' She put the receiver down, very conscious of the way he had ended the conversation. Reddening, she returned to the kitchen where Naomi looked up expectantly. 'Well?' she asked. 'Is he coming?' Millie nodded.

'Good. Now we have to get back down to the Jackson's before he goes off to work.'

'What?'

'We need to see Irene again. Find out what she knows.'

'Shouldn't we wait until Neil comes back?'

'He could be ages and Jim Jackson will be going to work, if he hasn't already gone.' She looked at her watch. 'It's half eight now. We've probably missed him.'

Millie tried to persuade her to wait but Naomi was determined and she threatened to go on her own if she wouldn't go with her. That settled it. Millie didn't dare let her go alone. They marched down the lane and up to the front door of the cottage. Millie felt nauseous at the thought of the little room and hoped that it was too early for the fire to be alight.

The door was opened by Irene. She seemed taken aback to see them standing there side by side on the doorstep. She was dressed in a flowery overall and had a scarf tied round her hair. When she saw who they were she quickly untied the scarf and began undoing her overall.

'Do come in, miss and 'er,' she muttered, turning and leading the way into the little room. Millie followed Naomi and shut the front door behind her. The fire was already alight but issued only the smoky smell of coal that hasn't really got going. The room had not yet become uncomfortable. She motioned to them to sit down and they took up their now regular spot, side by side, on the sofa. She sank into her armchair and waited.

'Mrs Jackson,' began Naomi. 'We came to see how you are and to ask you some questions.' Millie held her breath.

'Questions? What d'you mean questions?'

'About your nephew.'

'My nephew?' she looked puzzled.

'Nick.'

'Oh Nick!' She paused. 'He's not my nephew. He's Jim's cousin's lad.' The sound of footsteps came from the back of the cottage and they all looked towards the door.

'Jim! Is that you?' called Irene.

'Ay.'

'Miss Naomi wants to know about young Nick.'

Jim Jackson appeared from the back in his shirt-sleeves, drying his hands. 'Morning.' he said.

'Jim. They've got questions.'

'Have they?' He stood attentively.

'Mr Jackson,' began Naomi, 'We know that Nick is working for a man from Holland.' She paused but neither of them spoke. 'And I believe you do as well?' she asked, looking at Jim Jackson, who remained standing by the door. Still no-one said a word. Naomi continued.

'My friend is a police officer. He interrogated Nick yesterday'.

Millie cringed.

'Nick said he was working for a Dutchman and so was his uncle.' Irene looked at her husband.

'His uncle's *John* Jackson,' said Jim. 'Nothing to do with us.'

'But you know him?' asked Naomi.

'Ay.'

'Nick admitted that he was responsible for abducting my grandmother's dog. He admitted that this Dutchman was terrorising my grandmother. The Dutchman *and his own uncle.*' She waited.

'Too clever 'e was. It'll come to no good.' said Jim, shaking his head.

'Did you know he had something to do with my grandmother's death?' asked Naomi quietly.

'No, never!' shouted Irene, standing up. 'He's done nothing!' and she sat down abruptly.

'We weren't sure like,' said Jim shrugging his shoulders. 'But we thought there were summat.'

'What d'you mean?' asked Irene indignantly.

'Well, you know, about the key.'

'What key?' asked Naomi sharply.

'The key for cleaning. The key to the Manor. It 'ad gone. Yer couldn't find it, could yer?' asked Jim Jackson.

'Didn't mean he took it, does it?' replied Irene, angrily.

'No. But we 'ad our suspicions, didn't we?'

Irene starting sniffing, 'Can't be sure,' she said unconvincingly.

Millie was thinking about the Manor, how the Dutchman could have got in and maybe struck Lizzie. Had they done the same to Bert? Had he seen him coming down the garden with the uncle? 'Who is Roy?' she asked suddenly.

Irene seemed startled. 'Roy? Jims uncle was called Roy. He was a grocer in Leeds. Why?'

Millie didn't know. 'Who was Roy's Lad?' she tried.

This time Jim answered. 'John. John is Roy's lad. My father's brother was called Roy. 'E 'ad four boys altogether. Roy junior, John, Edward and James. Edward and James were killed in the war. Roy junior was in the navy. John was always the bad 'un.'

'You mean that Roy's lad is John, Nick's uncle?' shouted Naomi.

'That's right,' agreed Jim Jackson.

'Well that's it then, isn't it Millie? Where is he now, Mr Jackson?'

'In 'Olland. 'E's got my Land Rover and gone to 'Olland. That's why I've got to wait for master David to fetch me.'

As she watched the mystery unfolding it was dawning on Millie that John, this uncle of Nick's, was probably also responsible for Bert's death.

Naomi was continuing to fire questions at the Jackson's. 'Did David have anything to do with all this?'

'No, nothing, I'm sure Miss Naomi.' Irene was crying.

Millie was unsure how to express her fears but felt it was important to have the Jacksons on their side.

'Mrs Jackson,' she began, 'I think that this Dutchman, and perhaps John, might have been around when your father was taken ill.'

'Of course he was!' shouted Naomi. 'Roy's lad is the proof. He wrote it down to tell us didn't he?'

Millie glared at her. 'I think we should be very careful,' she continued calmly. 'We must do and say nothing until the police are informed. Can you do that for us please?' she was looking from Irene to Jim and back. 'When is John due back with your Land Rover, Mr Jackson?'

'Tomorrow. There's a darts match. 'E's got to get it back for that. I'll kill 'im when 'e comes 'ere.'

'No please, all you must do is wait until he returns and do nothing before then. Don't tell Nick that we've spoken to you. Just act normally.' Millie looked at Irene sobbing and her husband standing, where he had been throughout the discussion, by the door. 'Isn't that right Naomi?'

'Yes,' she agreed, solemnly. 'We'll inform the police and we need your complete co-operation until they arrest him.' This initiated a new series of sobs from Irene. Millie signalled to Naomi that they should go and they let themselves out.

As soon as they were back in the lane Millie told Naomi that they should contact the police.

'What with? We've got nothing to go on yet. We just have to wait until they're back in the country, then stop them.'

'You must be joking Naomi. They've already killed two people, we can't do this on our own. We've got to alert the police.' Millie noticed that she was also beginning to use Naomi's ridiculous jargon. It's like a game, she thought, it's just like a game. It required patience and hers was beginning to run out.

It wasn't helped when they got back to the Manor. Neil and Andy were still out and Naomi paced up and down, desperate to tell Neil what they had found out. In the end she suggested that they went up the track to meet them but Millie refused. Her grandmother would be back from Reeth soon and she would have to talk to her about the fact that she would be out that evening, possibly until late. As they parted at the end of the drive, Millie made Naomi promise to ask Neil to inform the local police about what was going on. They arranged to meet back at the Manor as soon as Pete arrived, to plan the evening's activities.

Helen was waiting for Millie when she let herself into the cottage. She seemed a little put out.

'I didn't know where you were or when you'd be back,' she exclaimed shrugging her shoulders and waving her arms in the air. Bernie came running out of the kitchen to see what was happening.

'I'm sorry, Gran. I was only at Naomi's. You could have rung.'

'Well, I didn't know if you'd gone off somewhere. Jean phoned about the dinner again and Pete was trying to get you. You're never here.' She was beginning to calm down a little. 'Pete said you were out tonight again.' It was a statement not a question.

'Yes. I'm sorry. He asked me to go somewhere… for a meal,' she lied.

'That's nice, dear. I didn't mean to sound, well, grandmotherly.' They both laughed. 'But you see I've been worrying about all the coming and going, with Naomi and the policeman with the pony-tail. It's as if, well, there's some sort of mystery you're all involved in. Even Andy is acting oddly and Matt seems to have disappeared off the face of the earth. It's nothing to do with Bert and Lizzie is it? '

Just for a second Millie was going to gloss over it and pretend to her grandmother that there was nothing to concern herself with. Then she changed her mind. She couldn't lie to her Gran; she would just have to be 'economical' with the truth. She told her that Matt was coming back on the ferry that evening and they were all going over to meet him. They would drive over to Hull to meet the ferry at five o' clock and come back with him. Probably stopping on the way for a meal.

'In that case will you please ring Jean and tell her when you can go for dinner. You go home on Thursday.'

'Friday,' corrected Millie. She had already decided to leave at the very last minute. Dad and Fiona wouldn't be back until Saturday morning and she didn't want to go until the latest time necessary. 'But I can't ring her until I've spoken to Pete and he'll be here at three.'

'In that case, why don't we have a quiet, leisurely lunch. You can tell me what you have been up to these last two weeks. I've hardly seen you!'

Millie was happy with that suggestion. She went through with her grandmother to the kitchen where they worked together preparing a lasagne from scratch. She was surprised to discover that Helen also liked Mediterranean recipes and often cooked dishes just for herself, experimenting with ingredients.

'Of course, it's not easy finding sun-dried tomatoes in the Dales, but not impossible. You'd be surprised.'

Millie remembered the supermarket she had visited with Neil. It seemed to have everything you could think of. Was it only a week since they had been down in Skipton? It was unbelievable.

'I had a chat with Pete on the phone,' said Helen casually. 'He's such a nice boy, isn't he?'

'Yes.'

'I shouldn't really ask but, well, do you like him? Jean was saying that she thinks he's quite smitten you know. I didn't say anything, well you don't like to, it's not really her business, is it?'

'No.'

'I should have told her to mind her own business, shouldn't I?'

'Probably.'

'But I think she takes a genuine interest in him. She likes to think that she'll find him someone suitable eventually.'

'Right.' Millie was spreading garlic butter into the bread. Helen was putting the finished lasagne into the oven.

'Let's sit in the garden,' suggested Helen.

She unlocked the back door and Bernie ran ahead into the small yard. The sun was shining and because the garden was sheltered from the light breeze, it was quite hot. Bernie sat sniffing the air. He looked pretty contented and Millie wondered whether he would stay at Laurel Cottage or end up with Naomi.

'I popped in to see Irene this morning,' said Helen lightly. 'She didn't seem very happy at all but that's not really surprising is it? I really wanted to know what the funeral arrangements were but she wasn't very communicative at all. I noticed that Jim was still at home and that's not like him. Perhaps she's taken it very hard. I know he was a cantankerous old man but she was devoted to him, you know. I think she'll miss him a lot.'

Pete arrived at exactly three o'clock and Millie said goodbye to her grandmother. She had enjoyed the opportunity to spend some time with her at last and Helen seemed happy to wave her off.

Naomi was in high spirits and ordered everyone about to an extent that began to irritate Millie. Even Neil was concurring with her plans. She suggested that Pete took Andy and Millie while she and Neil went together.

'So what are we supposed to do?' Millie asked rather sulkily.

'Well, I think we should all start off at Hull together. The trailer doesn't travel fast and I imagine they'll use the same route on the way back, don't you? If so, then Pete could pick them up on this side of York and we can cover them from Leyburn. It's only a matter of checking that they come back to the Lodge.'

'It's good that it'll still be light then.' Pete sounded less than optimistic about the success of the venture.

'There shouldn't be any problems,' said Andy. 'Matt said they were coming back to Mossy Bank.'

'Right,' said Neil. 'This is just to check that they do. We must make sure that we keep on their tail until the other car takes over.'

It was with many reservations that Millie climbed into the car and opened the rear passenger door for Andy. Pete climbed into the driver's seat.

'We must be careful. I must admit I'm a bit worried about all this you know.'

'I told Naomi to get Neil to contact the local police, I hope she did.'

'Have you asked her?'

'No,' she replied. 'And it's too late now!' Naomi and Neil disappeared down the drive.

'We'd better get moving!' He started the engine and set off in pursuit.

The traffic was light and they sped along in convoy, skirting York before the rush started. Millie was sure that York could not be like London but Andy assured her that it could get quite congested. Pete found it quite hard to keep up with Naomi. She was more adventurous when it came to overtaking on curving roads and once or twice she had clearly waited for them to catch up. Andy was good at spotting her car and Millie was grateful that he would be there to help keep an eye on the Land Rover when it was their turn to follow it.

It was nearly six when they reached the docks and Millie expected that they would be turning round almost immediately. However, they were actually there before the boat. The ferry had been delayed and was not due for half an hour. The waiting made it worse and if it hadn't been for Pete's calming influence Millie might easily have got angry with Naomi. She talked non-stop, going over the plans and describing exactly where they should change 'tails'. Pete was to wait in the car park on the square in Leyburn, so she would get a clear view of the trailer. He would be able to stop there and check that she'd set off.

'What do I do when they go up to the Lodge?' He asked. No-one had suggested what happened then.

'You keep an eye on them and ring through to us.' Naomi had an answer for everything.

'What with? The mobiles don't work up there.'

'I can go to the Manor and ring,' offered Andy.

'The ferry's here,' said Pete, nodding in the direction behind them. The huge ship was drawing slowly into the dock.

'Right into the cars everyone!' called Naomi, 'And good luck!'

'We'll need it,' muttered Millie under her breath. She felt Pete's strong hands on her shoulders. She smiled bravely but inside she felt rather frightened.

They sat in their respective cars and waited for the trailer to appear. First came the big lorries and then the smaller ones. Finally Andy yelled out. 'Look, it's them! It's Matt! He's on the passenger side. Looks as if he's asleep.'

The Land Rover turned smoothly out onto the road and Naomi pulled out behind the following car. Pete waited until a few more cars had gone before he followed. Millie wasn't sure that they knew the way. She kept her eyes fixed on the back of Naomi's car and Pete also stared silently at the cars ahead.

'So far so good,' he said as they took the road to York. 'It's just the bit round York that's going to be a bit tricky.'

Too right, thought Millie but she was determined that they would make it. It was still light and the traffic was less busy on the return. Millie found that Pete was slowing down to keep back from the trailer, which was travelling quite slowly along the main road. The pace suited her better and her stomach began to settle down as she felt less panicky. Soon Pete would have to take over from Naomi. They drove along in silence, waiting for Pete to change speed. Finally, as they seemed to have left York behind them, Pete indicated that he was overtaking and passed Naomi, tucking himself just one car away from the trailer.

'Don't forget we don't go into 'Arrogate. There's a right turn to Ripon in a little while.'

Cars were beginning to switch on their lights and Pete did the same. The journey seemed much longer than when they'd come and Millie asked Andy how much further before Leyburn.

'Only another twenty odd miles.' His reply depressed her. That would be another half hour or more at this rate. It would be pitch dark when they got to Leyburn. They continued in silence, all eyes on the trailer bobbing along the road ahead of them.

They left Leyburn on the moor road to Reeth and once they had left the town, Millie realised how isolated they were. Theirs was the only set of headlights in sight. In fact they could be seen so clearly that she told Pete to hang back a bit.

'Where's Naomi?' asked Millie. There was no sign of her.

'Probably thought it best to stay back,' suggested Andy. 'Over 'ere it's fairly obvious if you're following.'

Pete fell further and further back to avoid any suspicion but kept close enough that they could follow the red rear lights as they made their way over the winding moor land road.

'Maybe they've gone round the other way,' added Andy, looking round. 'Yep, they probably decided to whiz round on the Richmond road. They can do it faster and catch up in Reeth.'

Suddenly, in the distance, they could see the brake lights of the trailer ahead.

Chapter 20

'They're stopping!' shouted Andy. 'Quick, let me out and drive on. I'll see what they're up to. Wait for me further down the 'ill.' Pete stopped the car and Andy jumped out. The interior light went on for a second and the door was slammed shut. In fact it hadn't closed properly and as they drove slowly past the trailer it rattled. The lights had been turned off and Millie couldn't see anyone or anything. Pete had to manoeuvre several bends and she realised that they were nearing the path to the smelting mill. There was a turning to the left where Pete stopped the car and turned off the engine. Millie's heart was thumping loudly and her mouth felt dry.

'Now what?' said Pete

Millie sat for several minutes, waiting for her heart-rate to slow down while she desperately thought about what they should do. As she battled with the adrenaline rush that had taken over her body, she tried to concentrate and stay calm. They could drive down to Reeth and try to catch the others up to tell them what had happened. They could stay where they were, wait to see what they did and follow them if they continued the journey. But what if they didn't? What if they saw Andy get out of the car? What if he was in danger? She was very frightened and it would have been an easier decision to continue to safety in the car. Perhaps because she knew that, she decided to go back and find out what had happened to Andy.

'I'll stay here,' she heard herself saying. 'You go and tell the others what's happening.'

'No!' Pete sounded firm. 'I can't leave you here.'

'Yes. I won't do anything. I'll just wait here so Andy knows where you are.'

'Promise me that you won't go anywhere?' Pete leant across and held her shoulders.

'I promise'

Without another word he kissed her, on the mouth, and pulled away. 'Be careful. I'll be back as soon as I can'.

Her hands were still shaking as she let herself out. The interior light went on again and she quickly closed the door. Now it seemed even darker outside. The air was cold and she wanted to get her jacket from the car but she daren't open the door again in case it attracted attention. Her sweater was thick and it would have to do. Shivering with cold and fear she watched the car pull slowly away and then gather speed.

It was pointless standing there waiting so she started back up the road, hoping to find Andy where he had jumped from the car. Although it was a dark night Millie thought she could see the light of the moon hidden behind the clouds. It meant that if she concentrated she could keep to the edge of the tarmac. She made her way gingerly, keeping her eyes on the way ahead, even though she was feeling rather than looking where she was going. She tripped on an occasional rock and stopped each time as she listened to it rolling along the road. As her eyes became used to the darkness she could make out the junction ahead and she turned up the hill carefully. She had no idea how far they had travelled after Andy jumped out of the car but she was sure that they had come round at least two bends. It seemed to take ages to reach even the first of these and then she saw lights coming round the corner. She threw herself into the bracken at the side of the road and looked up in time to see a small family car go past. She found herself crying but whether it was the pain in her leg, or relief that it was not the trailer, she didn't know. Whatever it was it did her good. Now she felt more angry than nervous and almost ran up the road determined to find out what was going on.

She was travelling faster now and counted three bends before she began to wonder whether she had passed the spot where the Land Rover has stopped. She decided that she would walk another hundred, no two hundred, paces before turning round. The cloud must have thickened as she walked because by the time she reached a hundred and ninety nine she was in total blackness. She stopped and listened but it was silent. She was standing, staring ahead when she saw a set of headlights, a long way off, coming across the moorland road. She would wait for this car to arrive and hope that its lights might show her where the trailer had gone. Feeling her way to the edge of the road she stepped into the thick bracken and ducked down, prepared to jump up as soon as the car had gone passed, to catch the road in the sweep of the headlights. She could hear the engine now and suddenly she was bathed in light. The car was travelling fast and she was only standing as the car began to take the bend, but it was enough to see a track going off to the left, just as the road curved. The only logical explanation of the disappearance of the Land Rover and trailer must be that they took this track onto the moor. Perhaps there was a farm down there. Millie resolved to find out.

Please let Andy be alright, she thought as she struggled in the darkness. The bracken was thick at the side of the road, so the break where the track started was not hard to locate but once she was on the moor it became very difficult to follow. Again she stopped and waited. She stared up at the sky searching for the moon that had at least been glimmering before. The clouds seemed to be moving fast and after a minute or two the weak moonlight did break through and make progress a little easier. She moved so slowly sometimes it seemed as though she travelled only two or three paces a minute. She wondered how long it was since they had stopped the car and what had happened when they did. Was Andy with the trailer or was he wandering over the moor looking for them too? Had the trailer gone and was this a complete waste of time? 'I'll go another hundred paces and then I'll stop,' she said to herself. Her steps were slow but she was getting into a rhythm and felt more secure on the track. It was the sort of stony track where the wheels had worn ruts on either side. If she kept to the middle she could feel the tufty grass and knew when she stepped out of line.

A hundred and fifty four, a hundred and fifty five. She had reached the one hundred and decided to go to two hundred. The track was turning downhill and there in the distance was the trailer. She could see it easily because there was a flashlight trained on the back. It was parked next to what looked like a barn or small house. Perhaps another shooting Lodge? She stood watching, trying to focus on the picture, Where was Andy? Where was Matt? And what was the uncle doing? She edged closer, until she was only about a hundred metres away. The scene was played out in front of her as she stood unable to move or react in any way. First she saw a figure carrying a torch and a spade, emerge from the barn but immediately her attention was diverted to a movement by the Land Rover. A figure was opening the door on the passenger side illuminating the inside. Millie could see that it was Andy trying to drag Matt out of the cab. Matt wasn't responding and she watched in horror as the other figure disappeared behind the trailer and then stood poised with the spade, bringing it down on Andy's head. Millie expected Matt to respond but he remained slumped in his seat. She stood transfixed, unsure what to do next. She didn't think she could deal single-handed with the man, she would have to go for help now. As she watched, he dragged Andy's body along the ground behind the trailer and reappeared to pull Matt from the Land Rover and deal with him in the same way. Matt was obviously unconscious. The man came back for his spade and then went into the barn. Millie panicked. She turned and ran down the track, determined to fetch help as soon as possible. Tears were streaming down her face as she ran, stumbling over rocks and tufts of grass, sometimes plunging into the bracken. She was crying audibly and she didn't care who heard her. Maybe there would be a car passing out on the road.

She stood panting on the tarmac. The night was still and there was no-one about. Please, please let someone come now, she begged out loud. No blue flashing lights, no sirens, nothing. She carried on down the middle of the road, not caring if anyone heard her or saw her. She was running fast down the hill, blinded more by her tears than the darkness. The headlights of a car were moving slowly up the road towards her. By now she didn't care who it was, she just needed help. Jumping into the middle of the road she waved frantically. The headlights were getting nearer and she jumped to avoid the car as it approached and seemed to come straight at her. The driver jumped out and ran up to her, grabbing her by the arms.

'Millie, are you alright?' It was Pete. She couldn't answer but stood hugging him and crying.

'What happened?' He was gripping her arms too tightly and shaking her gently.

'Where's Andy? Where's the Land Rover?' Millie pointed back up the hill.

'In the barn, up there. Please get the police.'

'What's happened?' Pete released his grip slightly and sounded calmer.

'Andy went to help Matt and now they're both... I don't know.'

'Get in the car, we'll drive down to Reeth and get help.' He pushed her towards his car and opened the door.

'There's a road up there to the right where you can turn round,' said Millie, feeling calmer already now that Pete had taken over. 'The trailer turned off to a barn further up.'

'On the left or right?'

'Right going this way.'

'I don't know it, I...' He hesitated as a pair of headlights appeared ahead of them, slowing the car as the Land Rover and trailer sped past them.

'It's him,' cried Millie. 'Quick, where's Andy?'

'I couldn't see,' said Pete, slowly.

'We'll have to go and look for them,' shouted Millie. 'It'll be safe now the Land Rover's gone. I know where they are.' She was quite happy to brave the moor now that she knew that Nick's uncle had left and she had Pete with her. They could go straight to the barn and see what had happened to them, safe in the knowledge that there was now no danger. If Pete had any doubts he didn't say so as he turned the car onto the rough moorland and they made their way steadily towards the barn, illuminated in their headlights.

There was no sign of anyone outside the barn as they climbed out of the car. Pete left the headlights on the entrance and Millie could see quite well as she went cautiously inside. Unsure what to expect, she was surprised to hear the sound of crying. She searched across the rough stone walls and timbers and found herself looking at the frightened white face of a young woman, crouching down next to a figure lying limp on the ground. She held a bundle of clothes in her arms, a baby that was whimpering quietly now.

Startled, the woman jumped up and started shouting at her. Millie couldn't understand what she was saying and realised that she was speaking in a foreign language.

'Don't be frightened,' Millie said.

Pete went over to examine the figure lying on the floor. There was a makeshift bandage stained with blood on his head. The woman was pointing and waving the wailing bundle of clothes at him. The pathetic family were the only people in the barn. There was no sign of Matt or Andy.

'Wait here!' she called to the woman. 'We'll get help!'

There was no point staying there, the boys must have been in the Land Rover all the time. These people must have come over from Holland in the trailer. They needed help. She would have to go where she felt instinctively they would be heading, to the Lodge. She was in full control now, no panic, no tears. The boys were probably lying unconscious in the trailer and she needed to reach the Lodge, where they would find the others, and then the police.

'Quick, in the car,' said Millie. 'We must find the others.'

'What about the man? He's hurt.' Pete stood still.

'No, we've got to get help,' Millie insisted.

It seemed a long drive down the narrow lanes after the wide roads from Hull. She didn't know what time it was but the pubs in Reeth were still open and there were a few cars on the road near Healaugh. The pub in Gunnerside had its lights on and there were a few people walking across the bridge as they swung round the corner. Finally they were over the Ivelet Bridge and heading for Mossy Bank. Millie was unsure what to expect when they entered the village. They carried on past Laurel Cottage and stopped at the end of the drive to the Manor, no lights. As the car joined the track she looked up at the Lodge, it was dark and she could see nothing but as they got nearer she thought she spotted the cars. Before Millie could be sure, there was a flare of light that lit up the entire scene. She could see the Land Rover and trailer and cars. She could even see some figures running around outside the Lodge. It was on fire.

Pete stopped the car halfway up the rough track and jumped out. Millie followed. Flames were visible at one of the windows of the Lodge. Coming down the track towards them at high speed was the Land Rover. It slowed, swerved and ploughed into the bracken travelling for some yards before there was a loud crash and it suddenly stopped. Another vehicle followed and she recognised Neil jumping from Naomi's car in front of her.

'Are you alright, Millie?' he shouted as he ran into the bracken.

'Yes!' she shouted after him, 'but where are Matt and Andy?'

Neil stopped and turned. 'I thought you were with them,' he shouted waving his arms. They both looked at the burning building. As he spoke a figure was emerging from the Land Rover and Neil sprinted after him.

'Oh God! I'll go,' shouted Pete. 'You get that bastard.' They leapt up the track with plenty of energy now and as soon as Millie was within earshot of Naomi she shouted at her.

'Matt and Andy. They're not there!' She turned round at her voice. 'I couldn't find them,' she continued. 'Have you seen them?'

'Oh no!' shouted Naomi. 'Where are they?' and before Millie could stop him, Pete ran towards the door.

Naomi dashed after him and Millie stood wondering what to do. She could still see flames through the far window but mainly the Lodge was full of smoke. It might be possible to locate the boys if they were there but Millie was concerned that Naomi and Pete would be overcome by fumes. She looked down the valley and saw a blue flashing light. Please hurry, she thought. It didn't seem to be moving. She heard a crash and looked back at the Lodge. Someone had smashed the window; smoke bellowed out but there were no flames. She heard coughing and saw Pete's face by the window.

'They're in here!' he shouted and disappeared. Millie stood by the door and watched as Pete dragged a body down the smoke-filled hall.

'What do I do?' she asked but Naomi pushed her out of the way and bumped the body down the step. Millie recognised Matt's dark hair. Naomi was pulling at his collar and bent over him, reaching into his mouth and then, grabbing his nose, began mouth to mouth resuscitation. Looking back into the house, searching for a sign of Pete, all Millie could see was a dense pall of smoke. She felt her way down the hall but soon retreated unable to breath. She ran outside and looked in through the broken window. She could just make out Pete bending over Andy, who was half sitting up and coughing.

'Bring him out into the fresh air!' ordered Millie from outside and Pete looked up. 'I think he's OK,' he said and began to pull him to his feet. Millie ran round to the door again and waited to help Andy as Pete brought him down the hallway. It was still hot inside but the smoke was beginning to clear. When Andy saw Matt he tried to move towards him but stumbled coughing and fell clumsily into a sitting position.

'It's OK, Andy,' said Millie, trying to sound calm. 'I'm sure he'll be alright.'

'Can someone take over?' called Naomi and Millie went over to kneel down beside her. 'What do I do?' she asked.

'Just keep up the breathing,' said Naomi. 'Hold his nose and keep breathing gently into his mouth. Like this.' She demonstrated and Millie took over rather nervously. She was conscious of activity behind her but daren't look round. Naomi was telling Pete that Matt would be alright but they needed to get him to hospital fast. Pete said he could put the seats down in his estate car and put him in the back. Millie kept going, she had a rhythm now and although she didn't try a pulse she was sure that he was alive, he had to be.

'OK, now let me take over for a second.' Millie was relieved to pass him into Naomi's expert hands again. Andy looked exhausted and sat holding his head. She looked down the hill. A blue light was making its way up the track.

'The police are here,' she shouted.

'About bloody time!' shouted Pete and started down the track to meet them. Millie went and sat beside Andy. He looked so desolate. She put her arm round him and realised how cold he was. Taking off her jacket, she put it on his shoulders and sat watching Pete talking to the policeman. They came back to where Naomi was still trying to resuscitate Matt. There was more talk and they began to carry him down the track to Pete's car. Naomi followed, climbing into the back with Matt, while Pete went round to the driver's door.

'Would you and the boy like to come with me, Miss?' asked the policeman. 'I'm going to follow them to the hospital.' She helped Andy up and they took him to the police car. He was like a zombie, obeying their orders without expression. Once they were moving he seemed to fall asleep.

'Might be shock, Miss. Best take 'im to the hospital with the other lad.'

'How is he?'

'What the other youngster? Difficult to tell. Don't look good.'

The two vehicles turned round gently and Millie took a last look at the Lodge. You wouldn't know there had been a fire, hardly. Just some smoke hanging around the door and windows. Lucky there wasn't much in it to burn, no curtains, very little furniture. She supposed the fire was deliberate. They had been lucky, especially since there was no fire engine.

'What happened to the fire brigade?' she asked.

The policeman laughed. 'And how would you get a fire engine up here? No point in sending it up here, it wouldn't make it up the track.' She realised that no-one would have come.

They were almost at the bottom of the track and Millie could see the crowds collecting in the village. The policeman started the siren and a way was made through. He waved Pete past and stopped where Neil was standing beside a group of people including Irene and Jim Jackson, Nick and, in the middle, the man they knew as Nick's uncle or John Jackson. It was clear that he was being kept under control by the crowd. Neil was talking to two policemen who were holding another man firmly by the arm. She recognised him as the Dutchman. Millie's policeman jumped out and talked to his colleagues before returning and setting off down the road. He started the siren again and they sped off in the direction of Darlington. Millie expected to catch Pete up but they were nearly in the town before they saw his tail-lights.

'He'll be alright,' said the policeman, as if to convince himself. 'He's in good hands with that young doctor.'

They reached the entrance to the accident and emergency unit and gently coaxed Andy to climb down and be escorted inside. Matt was already being rushed on a stretcher into a side room and Naomi was with him. Pete put his arm round Millie as nurses fussed round Andy and ushered him away.

'Well,' said the policeman, taking a notebook from his pocket, 'perhaps you would like to tell me what's been going on?'

Chapter 21

They drove back slowly as the sun rose in the distance behind the fells. A light mist shrouded the tops and its sombreness matched their mood. Millie frequently looked over her shoulder to check that Naomi's car was still close behind them. She needed to be sure that they kept together, it was bad enough leaving Matt and Andy in hospital, and she wanted to get back to Mossy Bank to see Neil and make certain that he was safe. They had all become important to her, especially Pete. She couldn't have coped without him, she told herself, or could she? She had managed pretty well on her own until he had arrived hadn't she?

'Slow down,' she told him, 'I can't see Naomi.'

'It's OK she's just behind us,' he answered, checking his mirror as she appeared from the bend behind them. 'It's OK.' He patted her knee and smiled at her. She sat in silence as they passed through the deserted villages and waited for the first sign of Mossy Bank. They sped over Ivelet Bridge, past the entrance to David's farm and soon they were turning up the lane to Laurel Cottage. The village was silent and they instinctively shut the car doors quietly and stepped slowly up the path to the cottage. Millie opened the front door and the others followed. Neil was lying slumped on the sofa with one arm across his face, the other dangling on the floor. Bernie came out of the kitchen stretching and Neil lifted his arm.

'Hi! Is everyone alright?' he asked jumping off the sofa suddenly and clutching his back as he tried to straighten up. 'God, my back's killing me!'

'Everyone's fine - except Matt,' answered Naomi. 'He's suffering from an overdose of drugs of some sort. They're doing more tests tomorrow, no - today.'

'Where's Andy then?' asked Neil.

'They're keeping him in for observation. He's OK but a bit stressed out over Matt.'

'How's Gran?' Millie wondered how her grandmother had coped with the excitement.

'Oh she's fine. I told her to get some rest. She was waiting up but when Naomi rang she seemed happier and agreed to go up. That was about two.'

'Did you fill her in with what was happening?' Naomi asked.

'Yes. As you suggested, it helped calm her and to pass the time. She's up to date as far as I know it. What I want to know is what went on after you took over tailing the trailer,' he said, looking at Millie.

Pete put a hand on her shoulder. 'Why don't you go and show Helen that you're OK and have a hot bath. I'll tell Neil what happened.' She was grateful.

'Shall I put the kettle on?' asked Naomi and went off into the kitchen.

Helen was awake when Millie went in. She was lying on the bed and was still dressed. She sat up when Millie opened the door and her face changed to an expression of relief.

'Millie, thank goodness you're safe. I was so worried. Even when Naomi told me you were alright, I was still not entirely sure. Silly, really. Neil said that Pete would look after you.'

'I'm fine. It's just Matt who's bad. Did Neil tell you what happened?' she asked unnecessarily.

'Well, yes but it seems incredible, really. It hasn't sunk in.'

'There's tea down here if anyone wants some!' Naomi called from the bottom of the stairs.

'Is she here?' asked Helen.

'Yes and Pete.'

'I bet they're hungry. I'll go and get some breakfast for them.'

Millie was about to stop her but decided that it was probably the best thing for her to do. She would have a quick bath and change.

By the time Millie went back downstairs there was a strong smell of bacon and toast. Everyone was in the best of spirits, sitting round the table exchanging pieces of the story that the others had not seen or heard. Neil had quite a bad bruise on the side of his face which he explained had happened when he had tackled the driver of the Land Rover.

'Where are they now?' asked Naomi. 'What's happened to the Dutchman?'

'Off to the station,' answered Neil, through a mouthful of toast. 'I got the Dutchman and handed him over but the Jacksons had the other one and wouldn't let him go until he had handcuffs on. They caught him as he made a dash through the village.'

'What about Nick?' Millie remembered the promise that Neil had made to him.

'No problem. They want to question him but they'll let him go. They wanted to get statements from everyone, by the way. They're coming over at eleven. I said we'd be at the Manor. Oh, and Millie, they want you to go with them to Grinton Moor.'

'Why's that?' asked Naomi.

Millie had assumed that Pete had told them.

'It was when we went back to the barn to look for Matt and Andy. I thought he'd left them there. But there was this family, from abroad. A woman and a man and a baby.'

'They were illegal immigrants,' Neil said. 'Must have paid thousands. Smuggled from Holland in the trailer.'

'So that's what it was all about,' said Naomi, 'People smuggling. They must have been doing it for years. Using the Lodge as a base. I wonder why they went to the barn?'

'Probably getting nervous of the interest we were taking in the Lodge.' remarked Neil.

'So what has happened to them?' asked Millie, thinking of the poor woman and her crying baby, and the injured man.

'They're all safe,' replied Neil, 'although they will probably have to go back to wherever they came from.'

Pete got up without a word and started putting his jacket on.

'Are you going?' asked Helen.

'I'd better get back and check the dogs. They've been left all night.'

'Will you come back for eleven?' asked Naomi.

'Will they need me, d'you think?'

'Definitely,' said Neil. 'You're a key witness.'

'Righto. I'll be back.'

Millie walked to the door with him and followed him to the car. 'See you later then.'

'Yes, of course. You should get some rest before then, Millie.' He looked down at her and smiled, moving a piece of hair that was falling in her eyes. 'Bye for now.'

'Thanks,' she called after him, but it didn't sound right.

The others came out and climbed into Naomi's car. She leant out of the driver's side and reminded Millie to be at the Manor for eleven o'clock sharp. 'We don't want to keep the boys in blue waiting,' she called gaily as she sped up the lane. There she goes again, thought Millie. She enjoys this, it's a game to her.

Back inside, Helen wanted to know why she hadn't been told what was going on.

'I could have helped, if you'd said. I thought you were having fun with your new friend and all the time you were involved in this dreadful business. It could have ended in disaster. What about poor Matt, he may never recover from it!'

'I know, Gran, and I'm sorry but at the time it didn't seem like anything particularly serious. It was more like a game, not fun but something to unravel. We thought it was the sheep, something illegal about the exporting. We didn't know they were dangerous.'

'Well, Naomi knew. She knew they were involved in poor Lizzie's death and then Bert. It could have been one of you next. It may even be Matt anyway.' She pulled a handkerchief from her pocket and dabbed her eyes. 'Naomi said that Matt has been given an overdose of drugs. We know he isn't a drug addict. Imagine how his family must feel. She asked me if I would go with her to the hospital this afternoon. It might help if I talk to his poor mother. I know how I would have felt if this had happened to you. Goodness knows what she must think of the university letting this happen.'

'What about Irene?' Millie asked. 'How is she, have you seen her?'

'Only last night but she was bearing up well. It has helped her knowing that the criminals have been caught and will pay for their sins. Of course it's Bert's funeral tomorrow and I hope that will help draw a line under the business. It's a small village and it's affected everyone in it. Oh, and before I forget – Jean says that you must all go down for a meal tonight, she won't take no for answer.'

'All?' asked Millie.

'Well, you and Pete, Naomi and Neil. Perhaps not Andy, he should take it easy I think.'

As soon as Millie arrived at the Manor she was taken in a police car to the barn up on Grinton Moor. It looked different in the sunshine and she felt sure that she wouldn't have recognised it if she had come across it walking on the fells. There was already a police vehicle parked and a man was wandering round the building with a dog on a lead.

'We just want you to identify the barn and tell us what you saw, Miss,' the policeman said.

She explained what had happened as they walked to the entrance.

'Were they illegal immigrants?' Millie asked the policeman.

'We're pretty sure, Miss. Our colleagues in Holland are verifying it now.'

Millie couldn't believe it. 'No wonder they wanted to keep it a secret,' she said feebly.

They completed her statement when she got back to the Manor and by one-thirty they were all finished. Naomi took Helen to Darlington to see Matt's parents and to bring Andy back. Neil went off with one of the policemen to identify the men and provide any further details that were required, leaving Millie and Pete alone.

'So what do you want to do?' he asked.

'I'd like to go for a walk,' she said, 'but I can't face the Lodge or the gill today.'

'Well why don't we just walk along the river?'

So they wandered down the lane towards Ivelet Bridge and Pete explained about the coffin stone and how the mourners rested their grim burden on it during their march along Corpse Way to Grinton church.

'I do hope that Matt is going to be alright,' said Millie aloud.

'I'm sure it will be OK. They have a lot of practise treating overdoses these days, after all.'

They turned back along the river, following the Corpse Way. Millie, thinking of Matt, prayed that there wouldn't be a third corpse as they walked back up to Mossy Bank. Inside Laurel Cottage, Helen was plying Naomi and Andy with sandwiches and they looked happier than Millie could have hoped.

'What's the news?' she asked.

'Getting better,' said Naomi. 'Over the worst, poor lad. And this one,' she said, pointing at Andy, 'is absolutely fine now.'

'Apart from the bruise on my 'ead,' he said rubbing it gently.

'Sorry, I must dash,' said Pete. 'but I've got surgery in five minutes.'

'You should have said.' Millie was embarrassed.

''It's OK, honest. I'll be there at eight,' called Pete making for the door.

'Where are you two off to tonight?' asked Naomi.

'You and Neil are coming too. Jean rang to invite us.'

'Well, Andy isn't going anywhere,' Helen broke in. 'I promised Matt's mother that I would keep an eye on him.'

'I'm glad she asked us. We owe them an apology and,' Naomi winked, 'we can return that file that we borrowed.'

Naomi picked them up just after eight. Neil was with her and there was quite a party atmosphere in the car as they rumbled down the lane to the farm. None of them had dressed up and this time it was Jean who looked out of place. She had tied her hair up and wore a black dress that fitted her closely at the waist. She welcomed them excitedly and ushered them through to the comfortable lounge where David was putting a log on the fire.

'Oh, ay, the Famous Five' he said, straightening up, and added, as he turned round, 'Oh it's just four today!' He was grinning cheerfully and Millie smiled at him. He seemed more relaxed and pleasant than he had been when they had met before.

'David,' began Naomi, 'I owe you an apology.'

'Why's that?'

'Well, it's this really.' She produced the folder. 'This is yours.'

'Is it?' He looked surprised and taking it he opened it and studied the pages. 'Good Lord! It is! Where did you find it?'

'In your study,' admitted Naomi, and before he could say anything, she added, 'I took it, I'm sorry.'

David, still looking bemused, sat down and the others followed suit. Naomi explained why she had taken it and he asked her a lot of questions about what the Dutchman had been up to. Soon, with help from the others, Naomi had given him the full story.

Jean had come in and stood silently by the door as the story unfolded and then she perched on the arm of David's chair. Eventually she said, 'You know that he's been blackmailing us?'

They all looked at her. 'Oh yes,' she said bitterly, 'for over a year now, Since before I became pregnant with Lucy.'

'It was after he asked me to get Lizzie to sell up,' said David. 'When I wouldn't he got nasty and I said I'd to go to the police. Then he threatened me.'

'What did he do?' asked Naomi.

'Nowt, he didn't do anything,' said David.

'He stopped giving you work,' said Jean, angrily, 'That was bad enough!'

'Yes and he suggested that the family might not be safe if I went t'police. That's why I was so cagey when thee started asking me about him, Millie.'

'It must have been awful,' was all Millie could think to say.

'Well, you must tell the police now,' said Naomi, 'We've got to make sure that they are put away for as long as possible.

'What is going to happen to them now?' asked Jean, nervously.

'I can answer that,' said Neil, 'They've been charged with smuggling of illegal immigrants into the country and with attempted murder of Matt and Andy. The police need more evidence of their connection with Lizzie and Bert's deaths but with luck John Jackson will spill the beans. After all, he was only a small fish in the Dutchman's pond.'

'I think we all need a drink, David,' said Jean, getting up and heading for the kitchen.

By the time they sat down to eat, Millie was feeling very tired. Naomi's voice sounded a long way away as she described to Jean what had happened the night before. Was it really all finally over? Bert's funeral was the next morning and she began to visualise the events. Somehow Bert's coffin was being carried down to Ivelet bridge. Irene and Jim Jackson were walking beside it, and there was Dr Mellor...

'Is that right, Millie?' Jean was asking her.

'Sorry, I was miles away.'

'We could see that! You must all be tired after what you've been through.'

Pete took her arm gently, 'Naomi said that you go back tomorrow. That isn't right, is it?'

'Well tomorrow or Friday. It's the funeral tomorrow so I thought I'd leave Friday.' As she spoke the words they became real to her and she couldn't hide her disappointment at having to leave so soon.

'I suppose *I'll* have to go back at the weekend,' said Naomi to break the silence. 'Can you stay 'til Sunday, Neil?'

'No. I'm back tomorrow. I said I'd help with the trace on the rest of the Dutchman's friends in Holland. We know that there's a second man involved. We've got some information on him already.'

'So, Neil goes back tomorrow, Millie on Friday and you on Sunday. It's going to be quiet here next week, isn't it David?'

'Well, Pete's here until September, aren't you,' said Naomi, with a grin, 'and we're bound to drop in from time to time, aren't we Millie?'

Naomi was right of course, there would be times when they would meet up again.

'You're very quiet Pete,' said Jean, with that special voice she seemed to reserve for him. Millie wished that it didn't irritate her so much.

'I was just thinking how much I would miss you all,' he said, looking straight at Millie.

'Will you be at the funeral?' asked Jean.

'No, I'm on duty tomorrow.'

Millie was trying hard to stay awake but she was fading fast and she was grateful when Naomi suggested that they should leave.

They travelled back to the village in silence but as Pete climbed into his own car, he asked Millie if she would like him to drive her home on Friday.

'You mean to London?' she asked, surprised. He nodded. 'I'll think about it,' she said but she already knew what the answer would be.

The morning of the funeral was wet and grey. Once more Millie, Helen and Andy left for the church and once more Matt was not with them.

There were fewer mourners than there had been for Lizzie's funeral and Millie idly wondered if his farming friends were too busy. Those who had come looked awkward in their best clothes. Irene wore a large black hat and Jim Jackson's suit looked a size too small.

It was hard to retrace the steps of the previous week and sing a hymn for another villager who had probably been deliberately killed because of the greed of one man. Millie didn't enjoy the service and was glad to get out into the wet churchyard. Naomi found them and they stood together waiting for Irene and her family to leave.

'I think I should go back to the Jackson's,' said her grandmother as they pulled up outside Laurel Cottage. 'Otherwise they'll think we bear a grudge because of John Jackson's involvement but I'm sure they won't mind if you don't want to come.'

'It's OK, Gran, I'll come in for a few minutes.'

As she and Naomi stood in the tiny room, Millie was struck by the difference to Lizzie's funeral. That had been so pleasant and relaxed, so peaceful. Perhaps that was because they were ignorant of the nature of her death at that stage. Perhaps because she was so well loved by everyone. Poor Bert, he had been a difficult character and now he was dead they were awkward about mourning him. Irene, however, didn't seem to notice but rushed about with sausage rolls and meat pies. Helen was helping her.

'Well, Neil's gone to Halifax and you're off to London tomorrow. How are you travelling?' Naomi asked.

'By train, from Darlington,' replied Millie

'D'you want a lift?'

'What, to the station?'

Yes, I'm not doing anything until Dan comes down on Saturday, to discuss the Manor. I think this business has frightened him. He realises that he could have sold the house to a man who makes money out of illegal immigrants, so he's less sure about selling at all.'

'That would be nice. Pete offered, but I'd rather not.'

'Why ever not?'

'I don't know really. I'd rather say goodbye here, in the Dales.'

They both laughed.

That afternoon Millie went to Reeth and waited for Pete to finish surgery. At one o'clock he appeared and was obviously surprised to see her. Millie took a deep breath and told him that she would go to Darlington with Naomi but she wanted to go for a walk on the fells with him that afternoon.

He looked disappointed, 'I arranged to go on the rounds today so that I'd be free this evening,' he said, 'but if you've got half an hour now, I've got a surprise.'

'What?'

'We have to go up to the smelt mill,' he said mysteriously.

Millie was puzzled but didn't ask, preferring to let him lead the way. They took his car and climbed the road onto the moor that had been so terrifying in the dark. She began to feel uneasy and wanted him to stop the car but she felt so foolish she kept quiet. He pulled the car off the road where they had parked once before and he let the dogs out of the back. They raced off into the heather. Taking her hand, he led her down the track towards the old buildings. She stopped when she saw a Land Rover parked beside the mill.

'In here,' he indicated the entrance to the largest building. Millie hesitated and then followed him in. Inside, in the half light, she could discern the figure of a man with a spade. She let out a cry and turned to run.

'Millie,' said Pete, taking her hand, 'this is Tom Freeman. He's an archaeologist, I thought you should talk to him.'

'Hello, Millie,' said the man, putting down his spade and coming forward. 'Pete's told me a lot about your interests. We welcome help from enthusiasts like you, you know.'

'Well, I don't know about that,' she mumbled, still embarrassed at her reaction.

'Of course you are, Millie, don't be so modest. You're really keen on the industrial archaeology!'

'Yes but...'

'No buts. Tom's starting some work on the mill.'

'How interesting.' Millie wasn't sure what they had planned for her.

'Well, if you're up here next year, we'd welcome a hand.'

'Honestly?'

'Of course.' Tom smiled, he seemed amused by her lack of confidence.

'Well, I was thinking that I might come up in the Autumn break.'

'Excellent,' said Pete, looking at his watch. 'I knew you'd be interested.'

'You go back, I'll stay for a little while and find out more,' said Millie, 'if I may?' She looked at Tom.

'Are you sure?' he asked, edging backwards. 'How will you get back?'

'It's OK, I'll walk back into Reeth. See you tonight.'

'Right,' he turned at the door and left.

Millie felt rather awkward now that Pete had gone.

'What are you studying at the moment?' asked Tom.

Millie described her courses and he nodded. He talked about the opportunities for students to study archaeology at university and what qualifications they needed. Millie gained confidence as he chatted about his work as if she were a student of his. He explained that he needed help with quite mundane things like measuring, drawing plans, digging and cleaning away debris. She knew that she could cope with that.

'Would it be useful if I came up in the Autumn break?' she asked.

'When's that?'

'Mid-October.'

'Sounds ideal. We'll be getting into some of the more interesting stuff by then. It should be fun. Not too cold by then either.'

They exchanged phone numbers.

'I'll give you a call nearer the time,' he said cheerfully.

'Thanks so much.' Millie was delighted.

'Don't thank me. When Pete rang me and said you were interested, it made sense. I need all the help I can get.'

She left feeling quite elated and walked lightly back down the track to the road. The sun had broken through the clouds and the view was clear across the moor to the other side of Reeth and up Arkengarthdale. She followed the bends of the road down past the youth hostel and came in view of Grinton Church. As she wandered through the graveyard she read the headstones and thought of the bodies in their linen shrouds and wicker coffins. The final resting place of the dead that came from the Swaledale villages down the Corpse Way. Inside the church it was quiet and still. No ghosts just dust in the rays of sun that shone through the stained glass window. She sat for a few minutes before opening the big oak door and making her way down to the river.

As she walked purposefully towards Reeth she made up her mind. She would come back in October and spend more time with her grandmother. She would think seriously about university and discuss it with Dad. When she reached Reeth she rang Helen for a lift back to Mossy Bank. She wanted to get back as soon as possible to explain her plans to her grandmother and make arrangements for her trip back to the Dales in exactly eight weeks time.